Contested Spatialities, Lifestyle Migration and Residential Tourism

Lifestyle Migration and Residential Tourism represent a major trend in individualised societies worldwide, which is attracting a rapidly growing interest from the academic community. This volume for the first time critically analyses the spatial, social and political consequences of such leisure-oriented mobilities and migrations. The book approaches the topic from a multidisciplinary and international perspective, unifying different branches of research, such as lifestyle migration, amenity migration, retirement migration and second home tourism. By covering a variety of regions and landscapes such as mountain and coastal areas, rural and inland communities, this volume productively engages with the formal and analytical variations of the phenomenon, resulting in an enriching debate at the intersection of different areas of research. Among others, topics like political contest and civic participation of lifestyle migrants, their impacts on local communities, social tensions and inequalities induced by the phenomenon, as well as modes of transnational living, home and belonging will be thoroughly explored.

This thought-provoking volume will provide deep analytical and conceptual insights into the contested geographies of lifestyle migration and further knowledge into the spatial, social and political consequences of leisure-oriented mobilities. It will be valuable reading for students, researchers and academics from a plethora of academic disciplines.

Michael Janoschka is Ramón y Cajal Research Professor at the Department of Political Science and International Relations of the Universidad Autónoma de Madrid. His current research interests concentrate on urban transformation and gentrification in Spain and Latin America, new forms of protest, visual methodologies and the contested spatialities of lifestyle migration. He is executive director of the EU-financed research network CONTESTED_CITIES (2012–2016).

Heiko Haas graduated as a Cultural Anthropologist from the University of Frankfurt/Main. He currently works as a research fellow at the Centre of Human and Social Sciences (CCHS) of the Spanish National Research Council (CSIC) in Madrid, Spain. His main research interests are retirement migration, transnational families, mobility, and aspects of ageing in the context of individualised modernity

Contemporary Geographies of Leisure, Tourism and Mobility

Series Editor: C. Michael Hall, Professor at the Department of Management, College of Business and Economics, University of Canterbury, Christchurch, New Zealand

The aim of this series is to explore and communicate the intersections and relationships between leisure, tourism and human mobility within the social sciences.

It will incorporate both traditional and new perspectives on leisure and tourism from contemporary geography, e.g. notions of identity, representation and culture, while also providing for perspectives from cognate areas such as anthropology, cultural studies, gastronomy and food studies, marketing, policy studies and political economy, regional and urban planning, and sociology, within the development of an integrated field of leisure and tourism studies.

Also, increasingly, tourism and leisure are regarded as steps in a continuum of human mobility. Inclusion of mobility in the series offers the prospect to examine the relationship between tourism and migration, the sojourner, educational travel, and second home and retirement travel phenomena.

The series comprises two strands:

Contemporary Geographies of Leisure, Tourism and Mobility aims to address the needs of students and academics, and the titles will be published in hardback and paperback. Titles include:

1 The Moralisation of Tourism
Sun, sand....and saving the world?
Jim Butcher

2 The Ethics of Tourism Development
Mick Smith and Rosaleen Duffy

3 Tourism in the Caribbean
Trends, development, prospects
Edited by David Timothy Duval

4 Qualitative Research in Tourism
Ontologies, epistemologies and methodologies
Edited by Jenny Phillimore and Lisa Goodson

5 The Media and the Tourist Imagination
Converging cultures
Edited by Stefan Gössling and C. Michael Hall

7 Cultural Heritage of Tourism in the Developing World
Edited by Dallen J. Timothy and Gyan Nyaupane

8 Understanding and Managing Tourism Impacts
An integrated approach
C. Michael Hall and Alan Lew

9 An Introduction to Visual Research Methods in Tourism
Edited by Tijana Rakic and Donna Chambers

10 Tourism and Climate Change
Impacts, adaptation and mitigation
C. Michael Hall, Stefan Gössling and Daniel Scott

11 Tourism and Citizenship
Raoul V. Bianchi and Marcus L. Stephenson

Routledge Studies in Contemporary Geographies of Leisure, Tourism and Mobility is a forum for innovative new research intended for research students and academics, and the titles will be available in hardback only. Titles include:

1 Living with Tourism
Negotiating identities in a Turkish village
Hazel Tucker

2 Tourism, Diasporas and Space
Edited by Tim Coles and Dallen J. Timothy

3 Tourism and Postcolonialism
Contested discourses, identities and representations
Edited by C. Michael Hall and Hazel Tucker

4 Tourism, Religion and Spiritual Journeys
Edited by Dallen J. Timothy and Daniel H. Olsen

5 China's Outbound Tourism
Wolfgang Georg Arlt

6 Tourism, Power and Space
Edited by Andrew Church and Tim Coles

7 Tourism, Ethnic Diversity and the City
Edited by Jan Rath

8 Ecotourism, NGOs and Development
A critical analysis
Jim Butcher

9 Tourism and the Consumption of Wildlife
Hunting, shooting and sport fishing
Edited by Brent Lovelock

10 Tourism, Creativity and Development
Edited by Greg Richards and Julie Wilson

11 Tourism at the Grassroots
Villagers and visitors in the Asia-Pacific
Edited by John Connell and Barbara Rugendyke

12 Tourism and Innovation
Michael Hall and Allan Williams

13 World Tourism Cities
Developing tourism off the beaten track
Edited by Robert Maitland and Peter Newman

14 Tourism and National Parks
International perspectives on development, histories and change
Edited by Warwick Frost and C. Michael Hall

15 Tourism, Performance and the Everyday
Consuming the Orient
Michael Haldrup and Jonas Larsen

16 Tourism and Change in Polar Regions
Climate, environments and experiences
Edited by C. Michael Hall and Jarkko Saarinen

17 Fieldwork in Tourism
Methods, issues and reflections
Edited by C. Michael Hall

18 Tourism and India
A critical introduction
Kevin Hannam and Anya Diekmann

19 Political Economy of Tourism
A critical perspective
Edited by Jan Mosedale

20 Volunteer Tourism
Theoretical frameworks and practical applications
Edited by Angela Benson

21 The Study of Tourism
Past trends and future directions
Richard Sharpley

22 Children's and Families' Holiday Experience
Neil Carr

23 Tourism and National Identity
An international perspective
Edited by Elspeth Frew and Leanne White

24 Tourism and Agriculture
New geographies of consumption, production and rural restructuring
Edited by Rebecca Torres and Janet Momsen

25 Tourism in China
Policy and development since 1949
David Airey and King Chong

26 Real Tourism
Practice, care, and politics in contemporary travel culture
Edited by Claudio Minca and Tim Oakes

27 Last Chance Tourism
Adapting tourism opportunities in a changing world
Edited by Raynald Harvey Lemelin, Jackie Dawson and Emma Stewart

28 Tourism and Animal Ethics
David A. Fennell

29 Actor Network Theory and Tourism
Ontologies, methodologies and performances
Edited by René van der Duim, Gunnar Thór Jóhannesson and Carina Ren

30 Liminal Landscapes
Travel, experience and spaces in-between
Edited by Hazel Andrews and Les Roberts

31 Tourism in Brazil
Environment, management and segments
Edited by Gui Lohmann and Dianne Dredge

32 Slum Tourism
Edited by Fabian Frenzel, Malte Steinbrink and Ko Koens

33 Medical Tourism
Edited by C. Michael Hall

34 Tourism and War
Edited by Richard Butler and Wantanee Suntikul

36 Adventure Tourism
Steve Taylor, Peter Varley and Tony Johnson

37 Dark Tourism and Place Identity
Elspeth Frew and Leanne White

38 Backpacker Tourism and Economic Development
Perspectives from the less developed world
Mark P. Hampton

39 Peace Through Tourism
Promoting human security through International citizenship
Edited by Lynda-ann Blanchard and Freya Higgins-Desbiolles

40 Scuba Diving Tourism
Edited by Kay Dimmcock and Ghazali Musa

41 Contested Spatialities Lifestyle Migration and Residential Tourism
Michael Janoschka and Heiko Haas

42 Contemporary Issues in Cultural Heritage Tourism
Edited by Jamie Kaminski, Angela M Benson and David Arnold

Forthcoming:

Research Volunteer Tourism
Angela M. Benson

Travel, Tourism and Green Growth
Edited by Min Jiang, Terry DeLacy and Geoffrey Lipman

Gender and Tourism
Cara Carmichael Aitchison

Mega Tourist Metropolises
Mark Gottiener, Tim Simpson and Heiko Schmid

Understanding and Governing Sustainable Tourism Mobility
Edited by Scott Cohen, James Higham, Paul Peeters and Stefan Gossling

Trust, Tourism Development and Planning
Edited by Robin Nunkoo and Stephen Smith

Tourism and Development in Sub-Sahara Africa
Marina Novelli

Contested Spatialities, Lifestyle Migration and Residential Tourism

Edited by
Michael Janoschka and Heiko Haas

Routledge
Taylor & Francis Group
LONDON AND NEW YORK

First published 2014
by Routledge
2 Park Square, Milton Park, Abingdon, Oxon OX14 4RN

and by Routledge
711 Third Avenue, New York, NY 10017

Routledge is an imprint of the Taylor & Francis Group, an informa business

British Library Cataloguing in Publication Data
A catalogue record for this book is available from the British Library

Library of Congress Cataloging in Publication Data
Contested spatialities, lifestyle migration and residential tourism / edited by Michael Janoschka and Heiko Haas.
pages cm. – (Routledge studies in contemporary geographies of leisure, tourism, and mobility)
1. Emigration and immigration–Social aspects. 2. Retirement, Places of. 3. Tourism. 4. Lifestyles. 5. Space in economics. 6. Regional economics. I. Janoschka, Michael, 1975- editor of compilation. II. Haas, Heiko.
JV6225.C658 2013
304.8–dc23
2013008201

ISBN: 978-0-415-62875-4 (hbk)
ISBN: 978-0-203-10081-3 (ebk)

Typeset in Times New Roman
by Taylor & Francis Books

Printed and bound in Great Britain by
CPI Group (UK) Ltd, Croydon, CR0 4YY

Contents

Illustrations

Figures

Tables

Map

Contributors

Santiago Bastos is Professor-Researcher at the Centre of Research and Higher Teaching in Social Anthropology (CIESAS) in Guadalajara, Mexico. He studies transformations of indigenous communities produced by global forces and political struggles over identity, rights and territory.

Luís Costa is a researcher at TERCUD – Territory, Culture and Development Research Centre, Universidade Lusófona de Humanidades e Tecnologias, Lisbon. Main research interests: participatory development planning; local governance.

Ine Cottyn holds a Bachelor degree in Cultural Anthropology and graduated from the Master International Development Studies at the University of Utrecht in 2011 on the topic of residential tourism. Since January 2013 she has been enrolled as a PhD student at the same University, working on rural–urban mobility and the transformation of rural livelihoods in sub-Saharan Africa.

Sheila Croucher is a Distinguished Professor of American Studies at Miami University, Ohio. Her research interests include privileged mobility, globalisation and belonging, and the transnationalism of native-born US citizens. She is the author of *The Other Side of the Fence: American Migrants in Mexico* (University of Texas Press, 2009).

Ronnie Donaldson is Associate Professor in the Department Geography and Environmental Studies at the University of Stellenbosch, South Africa. He specialises in urban and tourism studies. His main research interests are urban social geographies of small towns and tourism developmental issues within a South African context. With over 20 years' experience as a researcher, he has published more than 60 academic journal and book chapter articles.

Rafael Durán is Associate Professor of Politics at Malaga University, Spain. He completed his MA in Social Sciences at the Centre for Advanced Study in the Social Sciences (Juan March Institute, Madrid) and gained a PhD in Political Science at Universidad Autónoma de Madrid. He has been a research fellow at the Instituto de Ciencias Sociais, University of Lisbon, and a visiting fellow at the Hellen Kellogg Institute for International Studies, University of Notre Dame. He is co-author of the Spanish-written *The political integration of immigrants. The suffrage as a pathway* (Comares, Granada, 2011).

Anton J. Escher has been Full Professor of Human Geography at the Johannes Gutenberg Universität Mainz (Germany) since 1995. His main research interests are historic cities of the Mediterranean; perception and construction of space(s) through feature films and documentaries; transformation of cultural phenomena in the context of nature, migration and tourism through media.

Sanette L.A. Ferreira is Associate Professor at the Department of Geography at Stellenbosch University in South Africa. She holds a PhD from the University of South Africa. Currently, she is responsible for a third year module in geography of tourism, tourism analysis and synthesis at honours level and supervises masters and doctoral students in the following fields: tourism and regional development, tourism and waterfront developments, tourism and crime, and tourism in transfrontier parks.

Paul Green is Lecturer in Social Anthropology at the University of Melbourne. His research on kinship, migration and nationalism amongst Brazilian migrants in Japan has appeared in several journals, including *Ethnography*, *Global Networks*, *Journal of Ethnic and Migration Studies* and *Ethnography and Education*.

Heiko Haas graduated as a Cultural Anthropologist from the University of Frankfurt/Main. He currently works as a research fellow at the Centre of Human and Social Sciences (CCHS) of the Spanish National Research Council (CSIC) in Madrid, Spain. His main research interests are retirement migration, transnational families, mobility, and aspects of ageing in the context of individualised modernity.

Colin Michael Hall, Department of Management, College of Business and Economics, University of Canterbury, Christchurch, New Zealand; Centre for Tourism Studies, University of Eastern Finland, Savonlinna, Finland; Linneaus University, Kalmar, Sweden; and Freiburg Institute of Advanced Studies, Freiburg, Germany.

Rodrigo Hidalgo is Professor at the Department of Geography of the Pontíficia Universidad Católica de Chile. After receiving his PhD from the University of Barcelona, he focused his research on the changes in the residential districts of large Latin American cities, with a special focus on social housing and gated communities. He published various books and articles in Latin American, North American and European journals, and he acts as the publisher of the *Revista de Geografía Norte Grande* and the

GEOlibros book series. He is co-editor of prestigious journals, such as *EURE*, *Scripta Nova* and the *Boletín de la Asociación de Geógrafos Españoles*.

Michael Janoschka is Ramón y Cajal Research Professor at the Department of Political Science and International Relations of the Universidad Autónoma de Madrid. His current research interests concentrate on urban transformation and gentrification in Spain and Latin America, new forms of protest, visual methodologies and the contested spatialities of lifestyle migration. He is executive director of the EU-financed research network CONTESTED_CITIES (2012–2016).

Olga Lipkina, Centre for Tourism Studies and Department of Geographical and Historical Studies, University of Eastern Finland, Savonlinna and Joensuu, Finland.

José António Oliveira is a professor at the Geography Department and a researcher at TERCUD – Territory, Culture and Development Research Centre, Universidade Lusófona de Humanidades e Tecnologias, Lisbon. Main research interests: spatial planning and development; housing policies.

Sandra Petermann is Assistant Professor of Human Geography at the Johannes Gutenberg Universität Mainz (Germany). Her general research topics are urban and social geography with a regional focus on Morocco and France. She specialises in transformation processes of old cities, theories on rituals and places, and has now started a new project on rural geographies and protest movements.

Maria de Nazaré Oliveira Roca is a professor at the Geography and Regional Planning Department and director of e-GEO Research Centre for Geography and Regional Planning, Faculdade de Ciências Sociais e Humanas, Universidade Nova de Lisboa, Lisbon. Main research interests: spatial mobility and development; demographic sustainability.

Zoran Roca is the director of the Geography Department and of TERCUD – Territory, Culture and Development Research Centre, Universidade Lusófona de Humanidades e Tecnologias, Lisbon. Main research interests: territorial identity and local and regional development.

Vicente Rodríguez is a geographer and research professor at the Centre for Social and Human Sciences (CCHS) of the Spanish National Research Council (CSIC). He was the main researcher in the Project MIRES (International Retirement Migration in Spain) and published extensively on retirement migration and residential tourism in Spain.

João Sardinha is an Associate Researcher and Coordinator of the Migration Research Group at the Centre for the Study of Migrations and Intercultural Relations (CEMRI), Open University (UAb) in Lisbon, Portugal.

His current research focuses on return migrations, youth mobilities, lifestyle migrations and the Portuguese diaspora and transnationalism.

Catherine Therrien defended her PhD thesis at the University of Montreal, Canada, exploring the trajectories of mixed couples in Morocco. She is a Professor with International Studies Abroad (ISA) in Morocco, where she has been living since 2001. Her fields of research include questions of identity, mixedness, lifestyle migration and intercultural issues.

Kate Torkington is Senior Lecturer at the School of Management, Hospitality and Tourism, University of the Algarve (Portugal). She has a PhD in Applied Linguistics from Lancaster University and her research interests include language practices in migration contexts.

Sanne van Laar holds a Bachelor degree in International Tourism Management and Consultancy at the University of Applied Sciences NHTV, Breda. In 2011 she graduated from the Master of International Development Studies at Utrecht University, on the topic of residential tourism. Currently she is collaborating on different projects with the Faculty of Geosciences as external advisor.

Ieva Zebryte is an International Lawyer at the University of Vilnius (Lithuania), and has worked in different international organisations and law firms. She is currently based in the City of Pucón (Chile), where she is the Coordinator of the International Centre for Studies on Patagonia (CIEPatagonia) of the Universidad de La Frontera (Chile). Current areas of research include lifestyle migration, socio-cultural transformations and sustainability.

Annelies Zoomers is Professor of International Development Studies (IDS) at Utrecht University and the Chair of the Dutch Academy on Land Governance for Equitable and Sustainable Development (LANDac, see: www.landgovernance.org). She has published extensively about various themes, focusing on rural development and changing land policies, sustainable livelihood, tourism and international migration. IDS is currently involved in various research projects related to large-scale land acquisition and land 'grabbing' in Latin America, Asia and Africa.

Hugo Marcelo Zunino is Associate Professor at the Universidad de La Frontera (Chile) and Founding Director of the International Centre for Studies on Patagonia. He earned his PhD from the University of Arizona in 2004. Currently, he is the leading researcher of a far-reaching project that aims at exploring the capacity of lifestyle migrants to bring about socio-cultural and political transformations in the Patagonia region.

1 Contested spatialities of lifestyle migration

Approaches and research questions

Michael Janoschka and Heiko Haas

Within contemporary scientific discourses, lifestyle migration and other lifestyle-oriented mobilities, such as second home or residential tourism, are usually conceived as a temporary or permanent spatial movement of relatively affluent persons of all ages that travel and move between meaningful places with an individually imagined and collectively perceived potential to provide a better quality of life (Benson and O'Reilly 2009). There is qualitative and quantitative evidence that such privileged forms of mobility and migration have recently experienced a significant increase in terms of scale, scope and intensity worldwide. Similar to the conversion of tourism from an exotic experience and individual adventure into a mass phenomenon that took place earlier in the twentieth century, lifestyle migration, second home tourism and residential tourism have also experienced a general popularisation. In other words, such mobility strategies, which had for a long time been the privilege of aristocratic and upper classes, have now diffused to broader parts of the population. Additionally, with more people from various cultural and national backgrounds and diverging personal motivations involved, a growing variety of lifestyle mobilities can be observed with examples ranging from 'counter-cultural dropouts' or 'downshifters' searching for a more meaningful way of life away from global capitalism to sun-worshipping retirement migrants in tropical climates. The expanding debates about lifestyle migration and other forms of mobility related to long-term tourism prove this, and they have disembogued in a multi-layered research field which is inspired by and rooted in different approaches from Social Anthropology, Sociology, Political Science, Tourism Studies, Urban Planning, and Human Geography – an interdisciplinary character which is mirrored in this volume.

In order to approach the subject of this book about *Contested Spatialities, Lifestyle Migration and Residential Tourism* more precisely, three preliminary remarks are required. First, we propose to consider lifestyle-oriented migration as a privileged form of mobility taking place in a contingent relation between the two poles of tourism and migration. Lifestyle migration is privileged, because it usually does not occur primarily for economic reasons. Lifestyle migrants predominantly belong to wealthy societies in the Western hemisphere, and they choose to relocate themselves partially or permanently in places with lower costs of living (often, but not necessarily located in lower-income countries), thus capitalising the multiple opportunities that the existing differences of purchase power and social and symbolical power relations facilitate in a globalised world. This implies also that lifestyle migrants possess a privileged citizenship status and express privileged ways of approaching local inhabitants, especially if they are compared with other migrant groups (Croucher 2009). Although often not a part of the economic and social elite of their home country (and sometimes even disfavoured parts of their society of origin), they usually live far above minimum and medium standards in the country they have decided to relocate to.

Second, we consider it crucial that, given their economic and social characteristics, lifestyle migrants have recently been targeted strategically to boost economic development in many countries around the world, particularly in Central America, Southeast Asia, South Africa and the Mediterranean. Especially if related to other politically desired mobile groups such as highly skilled migrants, 'first-class' tourists and transnational entrepreneurs, their relocation is likewise expected to produce a positive economic impact on the host society. Differently from most economic migrants, they are usually addressed within political discourses as highly welcome and respected newcomers which provide substantial returns for society.

Finally, it is also important to consider that leisure and lifestyle-oriented migrations and movements as rather new forms of global mobilities do not only include people, but also involve capital, objects, information, knowledge and cultures associated with this voluntary relocation (Janoschka 2009; McIntyre 2009).

This complexity has not been fully addressed in many of the studies which often primarily focus on the subjective dimensions and the individual self-fulfilment strategies of lifestyle migrants and their personal ideas and projections. In other words, much of the conducted research, financed by research societies located in the 'Global North' has explicitly focused on the manifold consequences lifestyle migration has for the people who are mobile. However, the voices of those who suffer the social and economic consequences of this mobility have been dramatically underrepresented so far. This absence of critical perspectives 'from below' is, on the one hand, a consequence of the post-colonial relations within the scientific community and the construction of the research field in terms of Bourdieu in which, as a hegemonic feature for excludes and silences systematically the perspectives enunciated from the margins of this field. On the other hand, most researchers from the Global North share with their research subjects the absence of necessary language skills to investigate the effects of lifestyle migration on local communities. Yet, it is more than interesting that they also widely lack a commitment to participative research methods which include the absent 'others' into their research design. As a consequence, the complex relation between individualisation, consumption and the transnational mobility of people and capital lying behind the phenomenon of lifestyle migration still offers important research gaps. For example, only a couple of critical studies have picked out the manifold conflictive dimensions of lifestyle mobilities and residential tourism as a key dimension for their analytical approach (Jackiewicz and Craine 2010; Janoschka 2010) – an important aspect that will be addressed in this volume.

For such a purpose, this introductory consideration will reflect critically upon some of the central sociological questions raised since the early days of the discipline, especially with regard to the structural forces of domination taking place in capitalist societies, as a part of how lifestyle migration has been constructed in scientific discourses so far. With regard to this, it is important to reconsider that approximately a century ago, Max Weber, one of the founding masters of sociology as a scientific discipline, illustrated that capitalism does not only imply a specific way of economic activity and social structuring, but also contributes decisively to the type, form and focus of modern life. In this reference to modern life he indubitably meant the ways and modalities of individual and collective conduct of life, or *lifestyle* as we would say today (Weber 2010). He further analysed that contemporary capitalism educates and produces economic subjects with an 'appropriate' conduct of life, professional ethics and, as one could add, consumer behaviour (Rosa 2012: 151). 'Appropriate' indicates here primarily the incorporated dispositions of habitus that stabilise, naturalise and legitimise the economic system itself. Stimulated by (neo-)liberal political and philosophical doctrines championing individual autonomy as the key ethical dimension of the 'good life', capitalism has since then produced a dense grid of discourses and practices that enhance individual freedoms and structure the public sphere in detriment of collective demands. However, it is commonly justified and authorised that the negotiations and definitions of the form and content of the 'good life' will intrinsically take place on the level of the individual subject. This statement is yet another expression of general trends towards individualisation and the desire for self-realisation which are consistently proclaimed and empirically observed in late-modern societies (Baumann 2000; Beck 2006). But within growth-orientated capitalist societies it is important to reckon that individualisation and self-realisation are not only a part of the freedoms granted to individuals, but also necessarily guaranteeing increased consumption of commodities and services, thus providing the internal stability of capitalism. Bringing together both observations, one can state that the individual construction of identity is commonly related to consumption habits which embody and express the individualisation of lifestyles. But within late capitalism, consumption does not exclusively mean the purchase of manufactured goods. It is also related to rather intangible services and, particularly in our case, to the consumption of produced places and natural landscapes. For instance, the popularity which mass tourism had reached, especially during the second half of the twentieth century, can be interpreted as an unequivocal sign of consumerism and individualisation, additionally paired with an increasing mobility of people and capital. In general terms, such paradigmatic shifts have recently been addressed in debates regarding the performativity of everyday mobility practices (Büscher and Urry 2009; Cresswell 2006). Embraced by what has been defined as the 'mobility turn' in Social Sciences (Sheller and Urry 2006; Urry 2007), these discussions claim that consumption, mobility and movement bring together powerful Western cultural narratives, communicating and appraising the multiple benefits of individualism. However, we shall not forget that tourism as well as residential tourism and lifestyle migration is often promoted by highly internationalised real estate business regularly exploiting the assets which such tropical paradises and other symbolically charged places and landscapes have, both for the ruling and subaltern classes of the countries dominating the contemporary world order. In many cases, this means that mobilities which are supposed to be an expression of individual desires are at the same time a central piece of capitalist strategies of asset exploitation, producing an extensive 'accumulation by dispossession' (Harvey 2005), especially among the 'original' inhabitants, occupants and users of the corresponding spaces and places. Such dispossession is usually widely assisted by liberal governments of the corresponding areas, not surprisingly and quite regularly resulting in the production of more or less virulent conflicts and processes of contention.

Within this introductory chapter, we will return shortly to this conflictive dimension of lifestyle migration and residential tourism – a facet that has been successfully omitted in many of the dominant debates within the research field. But before that, our aim is to better identify and shape the terminology applied in this volume. Hence, it seems important to address the notions of terms such as lifestyle migrations, amenity migration, residential tourism and second home development, which are being applied within rather disconnected fields and areas of research, while addressing a common phenomenon of social and spatial transformations that is taking place. In order to approach a common perspective, we can first state that lifestyle migration literally embodies important transformations related to scientific debates in fields like mobility, flexibility and individualisation. Among others, and as already sketched above, such changes respond to broader globalisation processes and simultaneously challenge conceptions of migration, tourism, culture, home, community and identity. In this regard, lifestyle migrants and leisure-oriented movers can be considered prototypes of how people organise their life in a postmodern or liquid world, thus challenging some, or even most of the common assumptions used in migration studies (Favell 2008), namely those based on the assumption that people only have one (or, exceptionally two) residential places (Borsdorf 2009). Possible reconsiderations include the critical engagement with certain terminological confusion which responds to the existing continuum between varying but interconnected forms of (spatial) mobility within the fields of tourism and migration (Williams and Hall 2002). For example, it has been addressed that concepts referring to 'privilege' and 'elite' somehow contribute to the conceptual marginalisation of the phenomenon (O'Reilly 2007). With regard to this, we acknowledge that a significant number of migrants are neither elite nor of a professional background but persons who may even move themselves in order to leave behind the constraints of social class (Oliver and O'Reilly 2010). Even though it is true that in the case of European destinations, the reference to 'privilege' and especially to 'elite' may be erroneous, the situation is different in many other parts of the world where declaring lifestyle migrants as rather privileged individuals in comparison to local standards may be adequate, as was mentioned earlier. Moreover, different concepts relating to the mobility–migration nexus from a perspective reinforcing tourism behaviour might also fall into a trap. Following Hall and Müller (2004), local population and local politicians may consider second home owners and residential tourists as outsiders and even invaders, with the consequence of them being systematically denied the rights of participation in political questions. Although they bring important investment to an area, and their lifestyle choice includes a long-term commitment to the place (Hall *et al.* 2009), they may even cause substantial resentment among the 'native' population, as has been reported repeatedly (McWatters 2009). Furthermore, the once prominent term 'retirement migration' does not resolve the stated problems either, as the concept itself fails at least in recognising two aspects: first, there are rising numbers of individuals and families of working age participating in the search for a better life (O'Reilly 2007). Second, many supposed migrants do not migrate permanently but can be considered rather as seasonal or temporary movers. And as such mobility patterns do not respond to the binary opposition between 'migration' and 'residential stability', it was recently proposed that they should better not be considered migrants at all (Janoschka 2009). Moreover, and although this does not necessarily mean mobility as a spatial attitude, many individuals conduct their own life somehow in between different but mutually entangled 'worlds' that represent meaningful cultural narratives (O'Reilly 2000). If we integrate in our analytical frame the transnational movements of 'people, capital, information and objects associated with the process of voluntary relocation to places perceived as providing an enhanced or, at least, different lifestyle' (McIntyre 2009), the widespread consequences of tourism- and lifestyle-oriented mobility, like questions of political participation and mobilisation in specific place-oriented struggles about local development, for example, can be analysed more holistically and within their specific socio-cultural contexts (Janoschka 2013).

The reference to lifestyle mobility and migration may offer an analytical strength in circumstances as given in many of the scenarios presented throughout this volume. In this regard, it aims at connecting some of the separate debates existing about the mentioned phenomenon, recognising the strengths of each of them: for instance, the debates in the heart of the discourse about amenity migration, especially prominent in the Americas, have produced a specific sensibility from a geographic and planning perspective that is committed with the sustainable development of local communities. On the other hand, discussions embedded in the field of residential tourism and second home developments raise questions towards the consequences that cities, villages, landscapes and places suffer if an important part of their constructed environment is empty during broader parts of the year. This relates directly to questions in the heart of tourism geographies which prominently discuss the seasonal uses of touristic infrastructure and the constraints that second home tourism development produces. Among others, the aim of this volume is to bring together and to foster a constructive dialogue between these dimensions. It departs from the conviction that such dialogue, as well as the inclusion of different authors and actors who are not related to the mentioned discourses at all, will produce important synergies and enable us to sharpen the key perspective of this volume, namely the question of how conflicts and contested spatialities are negotiated within destinations of lifestyle mobility.

This relates to the main research questions guiding this volume. Its main idea was based on a series of conference papers presented at the Second International Workshop on Lifestyle Migration and Residential Tourism, which was titled 'The Contested Spatialities of Lifestyle Migration: Public policies, local democracy and global market forces' and which was held during March 2011 in Madrid by the editors of this book. This international and at the same time transdisciplinary gathering focused mainly on the conflictive consequences and transformations that take place in destinations of lifestyle migration and residential tourism worldwide. Taking into consideration the previously mentioned research gaps within the contemporary scientific discourses, the aims of this volume as an output derived from debates that took place in the mentioned meeting can be subsumed as follows.

First, we aim at producing a nuanced vision that critically reflects upon the key transformations taking place in destinations of lifestyle migration and residential tourism around the world. In this regard, we feel that it is of major importance to include especially novel destinations in Latin America, Africa and Southeast Asia, in order to de-centre a debate that is dominated by interpretations produced by scholars from and in the United States and Britain and rooted in their scientific perspectives.

This leads us to the second aim, which is intrinsically related to the hegemonic production of knowledge within the field of lifestyle migration. Here, our interest lies in providing alternative ways of how the field can be approached, especially if key perspectives of the Anglophone 'Global North' are considered and challenged. This is why we decisively attempted to introduce visions from Latin America, Southern Europe, Morocco and from other countries that are placed outside the hegemonic Anglophone-centred linguistic sphere. This proposition has not always been an easy undertaking, but it has permitted us to approach an extremely rich variety of perspectives providing novel insights into the contested spatialities of lifestyle migration and residential tourism – perspectives which are usually absent in most of the mainstream debates.

This relates to a third relevant issue, namely the critical approach that guides many of the texts presented here. In contrast to the hegemonic glorification of lifestyle migration inherent in broader parts of Anglophone world, much research undertaken for this volume has explicitly focused on developing a critical point of view in order to enrich the mainstream debates and to shed a different light on the discussed phenomenon. All this has been enabled by internalising the perspective of critically addressing conflicts that might be open, or of a more hidden nature.

Finally, this volume further develops a perspective addressing both the structural and intercultural clashes which occur when people belonging to different social positions share a common space and struggle about its possible symbolic appropriations. In summary, this volume claims to give critical research on the contested spatialities of lifestyle migration and residential tourism a more prominent place within the disciplinary debates. Discussions about the local conflicts, disagreement and the structural forces behind the dispossession that many local inhabitants may suffer from, due to the fulfilment of individual dreams of lifestyle migrants – especially if happening in countries of the so-called 'Global South' – can inspire an understanding of the Social Sciences as a discipline that critically engages with the contested realities of contemporary capitalism.

The mentioned attempts to provide a critical observation of the contested spatialities of lifestyle mobilities will be structured around three interdependent parts of the book. The first part we have titled 'Conflicts and Frictions in Paradise'. The selection of texts presented in this first part revolve around variations of one of the main aspects of our book, namely the conflictive nature and potentially contested spatialities of lifestyle migration caused by social imbalances and economic and cultural gaps between local residents and newcomers. Concretely, the following contributions shed a new light on such different aspects as the gendered reality of lifestyle migration in Mexico, the consequences and excrescences of gentrification processes induced by lifestyle migrants in Marrakesh/Morocco, the strategies and implications of civic participation of European lifestyle migrants in formal politics in Spain, and the example of local resistance and protests of indigenous people in Mexico revitalising and mobilising their ethnic identity and community. The first text is provided by Sheila Croucher, a sociologist from Miami University, USA. She has worked and published intensively on the topic of US migration to Mexico. Focusing on the yet largely neglected aspect of gender in lifestyle migration studies, her chapter 'The gendered spatialities of lifestyle migration' addresses that void by examining the role of gender, in intersection with other sociocultural and political identities, in the context of US lifestyle migration to Mexico. Drawing on insights from studies of transnational migration, travel and tourism that have adopted a gendered lens, the contribution examines the gender-specific opportunities and challenges lifestyle migrants encounter, and how sex and gender intersect with other identities and social hierarchies, such as race, nation and class, and the implications of this intersection for the migrants and the communities where they settle. The following chapter is provided by Anton Escher and Sandra Petermann, human geographers working at the University of Mainz, Germany with a strong expertise in North Africa and the Arab World. Their chapter titled 'Marrakesh Medina:

neocolonial paradise of lifestyle migrants?' analyses the social and economic repercussions that a massive influx of foreign residents has on the old city of Marrakesh. Social displacement, gentrification and sexual exploitation are a few of the aspects that are scrutinised in their empirically funded investigation. They critically question the dimensions of how 'paradise' is discursively constructed among lifestyle migrants, portraying a perspective that brings together neocolonialism with lifestyle migration. Additionally, by providing a typology of potential lifestyles, the authors pose relevant questions about power, neocolonial appropriations of urban spaces and the consequences of unbridled tendencies of self-actualisation and expressive lifestyles of the new residents in Marrakesh. A similar approach guides the following chapter by Santiago Bastos, working at the Centre of Investigation and Superior Studies for Social Anthropology (CIESAS) in Guadalajara (Mexico). His ethnographic study with the title 'Territorial dispossession and indigenous rearticulation in the Chapala Lakeshore' provides a series of interesting insights into a multiplicity of conflicts about the appropriation and defence of territory against transnational newcomers and the real estate industry that acts behind these movements. The text deals with the variegated forms of dispossession suffered by indigenous population at the Chapala lakeshore, one of the most important destinations for North American lifestyle migrants in Latin America. By utilising Harvey's concept of 'accumulation by dispossession' Bastos is able to show how social frictions and contest are leading to a strategic revitalisation of ethnic identity and community as a conscious means of the local population to claim their rights. The last contribution of this section, 'Lifestyle Migrants in Spain: contested realities of political participation' by Michael Janoschka (Madrid) and Rafael Durán, a political scientist from the University of Málaga in Spain, leads us to an interpretation of the manifold strategies employed by European lifestyle migrants in Spain to gain legitimation for the legal political participation they develop at their destinations. Although such political participation of foreigners belongs to the practices that were fostered by European citizenship, the considerable level of representation reached in many municipalities responds to a still unique situation in the European Union, which at the same time is full of often conflictive contradictions. In summary, the four case studies have in common that they critically reflect upon questions usually marginalised in the mainstream lifestyle migration debates, and they are all related to the symbolical and/or spatial appropriation of the environment and social sphere in specific destinations, which is in all cases rather conflictive.

In the second part, we will focus on a series of novel conceptual perspectives on lifestyle migration and residential tourism. It begins with the chapter by Kate Torkington from the Algarve University in Portugal, named 'Lifestyle migrants, the linguistic landscape and the politics of place'. She critically questions the discursive construction of place-identities in a Portuguese destination and shows how spatial power relations are expressed by the discretional use of language in the public sphere. The chapter focuses on how real estate advertising practices in a particular lifestyle migration destination impact on the politics of place. It refers in particular to the way in which 'legitimate' (and, conversely, marginalised/excluded) collective identities are shaped within places, and thus has a strong impact on notions of belonging. By extension, the ways in which identities for places are constructed has material implications for the ways in which these places develop and change. Such language use shows the existence of a whole series of hidden conflicts, demonstrating additionally that the contested spatialities of lifestyle migration not necessarily pass through easily visible contestation. In the next chapter, developed by Hugo Zunino, Ieva Zebryte (Universidad de la Frontera in Pucón, Chile) and Rodrigo Hidalgo (Catholic University of Santiago de Chile), we approach another hidden dimension of lifestyle migration, namely that of so-called 'utopian' migrants in the South of Chile. As the authors show in their chapter, utopian lifestyle migrants challenge in rather silent ways the values and customs of late capitalist societies, aiming at a long-lasting social transformation that begins from the redevelopment of the individual as an autonomous subject. This perspective gets into a semantic tension in the subsequent chapter by Catherine Therrien from the University Moulay Ismaël, in Meknes, Morocco. Her chapter titled 'Quest migrants: French people in Morocco searching for "elsewhereness"' offers a conceptual approach to a specific group of lifestyle migrants in Morocco which have quite distinct aims and perspectives in their respective destinations. Finally, the Portuguese research team of José Antonio Oliveira, Zoran Roca, Luis Miguel Costa and María de Nazaré Roca, based at the New University of Lisbon, complete the function of different conceptual approaches with a perspective on 'Second home expansion in Portugal: spatial features and impacts'. Their chapter brings forward a spatial typology of second homes expansion in Portugal. Considering that the growth rates of second homes expansion have been higher in Portugal than in other countries, the impacts are actually more intense, as the authors will explain.

Finally, the third part is dedicated to what we have labelled 'Emerging geographies of lifestyle migration and residential tourism' referring to upcoming and hitherto under-researched geographic areas of lifestyle migration and residential tourism. Although the rather novel appearance of these destinations on the research map is the common ground of all of the chapters at first sight, the actual thematic scope and foci of the following chapters go far beyond the fact of mere academic novelty in terms of place. Rather, these contributions provide fascinating insights into distinct local conditions and situations which remind us that research on such diverse and complex sociocultural fields like lifestyle migration and residential tourism will never be practised from a generalising viewpoint. Instead, the specific local situation, historic and cultural peculiarities and the variegated and often diverging social actors involved in the process have to be taken into consideration. Only by this, existing and potential conflicts, specifications of social imbalances and frictions, as well as forms of social contacts and cultural exchange can be fathomed, all of which are recurrent themes in the chapters of this part. Paul Green is a socialanthropologist working at the University of Melbourne. His chapter 'Contested realities and economic circumstances: British later-life migrants in Malaysia' provides us with a new and insightful perspective on lifestyle migration in Southeast Asia. Based on ethnographic fieldwork, his contribution not only introduces a rather unexplored geographic area in terms of lifestyle migration, but it also investigates the important aspect of the personal economic conditions of the migrants. By this, Paul Green is able to recognise the existing socio-economic differences and general heterogeneity within this group, which results as a powerful tool to explain how diverging lifestyle choices, strategies of settlement and aspects of social distinction, as well as national immigration frameworks and policies are based and governed by economic circumstances. Olga Lipkina from the Centre for Tourism Studies and Department of Geographical and Historical Studies at University of Eastern Finland, and Colin Michael Hall, Department of Management, College of Business and Economics at the University of Canterbury, New Zealand, have provided a chapter dealing with transnational second home migration titled 'Russian second home owners in Eastern Finland: involvement in the local community'. It represents results from a survey among Russian second home owners and local Finnish inhabitants and investigates aspects such as community involvement, local participation and use of services, as well as social relations between hosts and newcomers and the general impact of the phenomenon in this emerging area of lifestyle migration. João Sardinha is currently working at the Universidade Aberta, Portugal. His chapter titled 'Lifestyle migrants in Central Portugal: strategies of settlement and socialisation' shows that new destinations do not necessarily have to be situated in another country, but can also refer to new areas within a country which are becoming residential areas of lifestyle migrants, as his vivid example of inland Portugal illustrates. Based on the concept of intra-community connectedness, community involvement, network building and lifestyle variations are explained for the particular group of lifestyle migrants who consciously decided for a new location 'off the beaten track'. The Dutch and South African research team of Saan van Laar, Ine Cottyn (Utrecht University), Ronnie Donaldson (Stellenbosch University), Annelies Zoomers (Utrecht University) and Sanette Ferreira (Stellenbosch University) contributes a chapter about '"Living apart together" in Franschhoek, South Africa: the implications of second home development for equitable and sustainable development'. Based on empiric fieldwork and revolving around the topics of gentrification and economic implications, this illuminative contribution discusses the socio-spatial impacts of second home tourism within South Africa's specific social and historic context of Apartheid.

Despite the different geographies, all text have in common that they place again a rather conflictive perspective about the nexus between lifestyle migration and second home development, an aspect that will be additionally addressed in the concluding epilogue of this volume.

References

Baumann, Z. (2000) *Liquid Modernity*. Cambridge: Cambridge University Press.

Beck, U. (2006) *Cosmopolitan Vision*. Cambridge: Cambridge University Press.

Benson, M. and K. O'Reilly (2009) 'Migration and the search for a better way of life: A critical exploration of lifestyle migration' *The Sociological Review* 57: 608–25.

Borsdorf, A. (2009) 'Amenity migration in rural mountain areas' *Die Erde* 140(3): 225–28.

Büscher, M. and J. Urry (2009) 'Mobile methods and the empirical' *European Journal of Social Theory* 12(1): 99–116.

Cresswell, T. (2006) *On the Move: Mobility in the Modern World*. London: Routledge.

Croucher, S. (2009) *The Other Side of the Fence: American Migrants in Mexico*. Austin: University of Texas Press.

Favell, A. (2008) *Eurostars and Eurocities: Free Movement and Mobility in an Integrating Europe*. Oxford: Oxford University Press.

Hall, C.M. and D. Müller (2004) 'Introduction: Second homes, curse or blessing? Revisited' in C.M. Hall and D. Müller (eds) *Tourism, Mobility and Second Homes: Between Elite Landscape and Common Grounds*. Clevedon: Channel View Publications, 3–14.

Hall, C.M., Müller, D. and J. Saarinen (2009) *Nordic Tourism. Issues and Cases*. Bristol: Channel View Publications.

Harvey, D. (2005) *A Brief History of Neo-Liberalism*. Oxford: Oxford University Press.

Jackiewicz, E. and J. Craine (2010) 'Destination Panama: An examination of the migration-tourism-foreign investment nexus' *Recreation, Society in Africa, Asia and Latin America* 1(2): 5–29.

Janoschka, M. (2009) 'The contested spaces of lifestyle mobilities: Regime analysis as a tool to study political claims in Latin American retirement destinations' *Die Erde* 140(3) 251–74.

——(2010) 'Between mobility and mobilisation – Lifestyle migration and the practice of European identity in political struggles' *The Sociological Review* 58 (Issue Supplement 2): 270–90.

——(2013) 'Nuevas geografías migratorias en América Latina: prácticas de ciudadanía en un destino de turismo residencial' *Scripta Nova – Revista electrónica de Geografía y Ciencias Sociales* XVII (439). www.ub.edu/geocrit/sn/sn-439.htm.

McIntyre, N. (2009) 'Rethinking amenity migration: Integrating mobility, lifestyle and social-ecological systems' *Die Erde* 140(3): 229–50.

McWatters, M. (2009) *Residential Tourism: (De)Constructing Paradise*. Bristol: Channel View Publications.

Oliver, C. and K. O'Reilly (2010) 'A bourdieusian analysis of class and migration. Habitus and the individualizing process' *Sociology* 44(1): 49–66.

O'Reilly, K. (2000) *The British on the Costa del Sol: Transnational Identities and Local Communities*. London: Routledge.

——(2007) 'Intra-European migration and the mobility-enclosure dialectic' *Sociology* 41(2): 277–93.

Rosa, H. (2012) *Weltbeziehungen im Zeitalter der Beschleunigung. Umrisse einer neuen Gesellschaftskritik*. Berlin: Suhrkamp.

Sheller, M. and J. Urry (2006) 'The new mobilities paradigm' *Environment and Planning D: Society and Space* 38: 207–26.

Urry, J. (2007) *Mobilities*. Cambridge: Cambridge University Press.

Weber, M. (2010) *Die protestantische Ethik und der Geist des Kapitalismus.* Munich: Beck.

Williams, A. and C. Hall (2002) 'Tourism, migration, circularity and mobility. The contingencies of time and place' in C. Hall and A. Williams (eds) *Tourism and Migration: New Relationships between Production and Consumption.* Dordrecht: Kluwer, 1–52.

Part I

Conflicts and frictions in Paradise

2 The gendered spatialities of lifestyle migration

Sheila Croucher

On 27 November 2009, a Mexican judge sentenced Jose Luis Alvarez Gonzalez to 60 years in prison for the rape of five women in the Mexican state of Guanajuato between October 2005 and June 2006. Rape is an all too common crime in Mexico, the United States, and throughout the world, but a number of factors rendered this case notable. All of the victims were foreigners (four Americans and one Canadian), over 55 years in age, and living permanently in a colonial town far from any beach or border. The 58-year-old perpetrator was a Mexican national who had served five years in a Texas prison for burglary; he broke into the women's homes late at night, sexually assaulted them, and then spent hours in the homes seeking to converse in English. Beyond its most significant impact—the personal trauma inflicted upon the women—this incident highlights how gender, in complex intersection with other socio-cultural and political identities, influences the contested spatialities of lifestyle migration. Specifically, the media coverage of the rapes, exchanges on listservs and blog posts, and the author's own fieldwork experience in San Miguel during the summer of 2006 reveal a complex, contested, and heavily gendered set of cultural and political narratives regarding the lifestyle aspirations of relatively affluent transnational migrants.

This chapter begins with a discussion of the events surrounding the rape of foreign women living in Mexico, in order to highlight issues relevant to the study of gender and lifestyle migration. Despite its emphasis on identity, belonging, and self-actualisation, the scholarship on lifestyle migration has paid little explicit attention to the role of gender in this growing migration trend. Other bodies of scholarship, reviewed in the second section and including international migration, transnationalism, expatriate communities, and travel and tourism, have addressed the issue of gender to varying degrees, and offer insights that can be extended to the study of lifestyle migration. Drawing on those insights, the third section of the chapter outlines ways in which gender is implicated in the migration decisions and settlement experiences of relatively affluent border crossers. Examples are drawn largely from lifestyle migrants in Mexico, but include the cases of Spain, Italy, and India. The conclusion makes a case for foregrounding gender as a variable in the study of lifestyle migration, and identifies areas for further investigation.

Serial rapes in San Miguel de Allende

Nestled in the arid mountains of Central Mexico, San Miguel de Allende is widely known as a popular settlement site for North Americans migrating south from the USA and Canada. The town's appeal to 'gringos' is not new, but in recent decades the increase in this migratory flow has resulted in the foreign-born comprising an estimated 15 per cent of San Miguel's population. Local officials estimate that 70 per cent of foreign settlers are from the USA, 20 per cent from Canada, and the remainder mostly from Europe (Schmidt 2006). As is the case in other lifestyle migration destinations, the foreign residents of San Miguel report being drawn to this picturesque colonial town by its warm climate and culture—both of which they claim offer a welcome reprieve from the less hospitable lifestyles they left behind. In October 2005, this sense of comfort was shattered when a serial rapist began attacking American women living in San Miguel. In each case, the woman lived alone and the rapist forcibly entered her home in the middle of the night. By February 2006, the perpetrator had committed four rapes and attempted a fifth; and the events, which had for months consumed the foreign community in San Miguel, caught the attention of the US media.

National Public Radio's Lourdes Garcia-Navarro travelled to San Miguel in March 2006 to cover the story. She opened her report by noting that, 'what was a safe inviting haven for the many single older women who come to live here has become a place of fear' (Garcia-Navarro 2006). Americans in the town, including two of the women who had been raped, described fear so rampant that in one case a woman was barricading herself in her bedroom at night with a chamber pot (Garcia-Navarro 2006). With the report of each new attack, the listservs, Yahoo groups, and blogs that connect the town's foreign residents were rife with posts about the rapes—including speculations about the identity of the perpetrator, condolences for the victims, advice about how to properly secure a home, and criticism of local officials' response to the crimes.

Criticism of local law enforcement not only brought the foreign community into conflict with the town's officials, but also with the local Mexican population. Many foreign residents questioned whether enough was being done to apprehend the rapist, and some expressed distrust of the Mexican legal system. Two of the women who were raped recounted troubling details of a lack of professionalism on the part of the Mexican police, while they reported the crime (Corchado and Kocherga 2006; Garcia-Navarro 2006). The local attorney general, Pablo Gonzalez, defended the Mexican authorities' handling of the investigation, and countered with this: 'A girl comes and tells us she was raped, but in a second declaration, perhaps two hours later, she says the person that raped her was her boyfriend, that she went voluntarily into his car' (Garcia-Navarro 2006). Gonzalez's general scepticism regarding accusations of rape was echoed among other locals in response to the crimes. Some native residents, including the rapist, were willing to blame the victims. In a shuttle ride from the Leon airport to San Miguel in June of 2006, the Mexican driver told me that the rape victims were 'American women known to hang out in bars with younger men,' and he chastised the local police for detaining innocent Mexican men in an effort to appease the powerful foreign community (Croucher 2009a: 61). Reactions such as these at least partially reflect the discomfort and unfamiliarity of many Mexicans in San Miguel with the lifestyles of the town's foreign residents. Local Mexican women, for example, rarely reside alone or patronise restaurants and clubs without family and friends.

Even among local Mexicans who were otherwise sympathetic to the criminality of the rapes, perceptions of, and resentment toward, the disproportionate power of foreigners in San Miguel were prevalent. Alejandra Saucillo, director of the city's Prevention of Violence Program, commented that, 'If this had happened to a Mexican woman, I don't think authorities would have made such a big deal' (Corchado and Kocherga 2006). Rosalinda Chavez, a 40-year-old food vendor concurred, 'A Mexican woman would not have received that type of attention. It was the dollars that Americans bring here that mobilized authorities' (Corchado and Kocherga 2006). Meanwhile, several of these Mexican women also expressed admiration for the American women's willingness to speak openly about the crimes. Chavez, who lamented the undue influence of the Americans' wealth, applauded the expatriate women for speaking out and holding law enforcement officials accountable (Corchado and Kocherga 2006). Mercedes San Martin, a native of San Miguel exclaimed, 'The people of San Miguel will tell you: "Don't talk about it. Our dirty laundry should be washed at home." … But we must say what is happening, too. I profoundly respect these women who have spoken out' (Garcia-Navarro 2006).

In the early morning hours of 23 June 2006, the rapist attacked his final victim. This resident, an American woman writer, decided to publish her account of the crime in the town's local English-language weekly. She confirmed that the rapist wanted to speak English, and shared that by praying aloud, in Spanish, she believes she lessened the length of time he remained in her home. She and close friends used a listserv popular among the foreign community living in San Miguel to spread the Spanish translation of the Hail Mary. This woman also praised the responsiveness of Mexican officials and noted, 'We need to stop condemning our police' ('Personal ordeal' 2006). Twelve days later, and with the help of the US Federal Bureau of Investigations, Alvarez was arrested in San Miguel's central downtown. He admitted to having had sex with the women, but claimed that it was consensual based on their 'liberal views' (Corchado and Kocherga 2006).

Much in this story is familiar: persistent sexual violence against women and the terror that accompanies it, the tendency to 'blame the victims,' and ignorance on the part of some law enforcement officials. What is particular about this saga is that it cannot be properly understood without reference to globalisation, transnational migration, and the intersection of gender, race, class, and nation. Why, for example, is this sizeable population of American women living (often alone) in central Mexico? What gender-specific opportunities and challenges does migration present for them? How do sex and gender intersect with other identities and social hierarchies, and what are the implications of this intersection for the migrants and the communities where they settle?

The emerging field of lifestyle migration offers exciting fodder for the exploration of these questions, but gender as a specific analytical variable is nearly absent from the current literature on this topic. Studies of migration and transnationalism more generally (Goldring 2001; Hondagneu-Sotelo 1994, 2003; Pessar and Mahler 2003), travel and tourism (Grewal 1996; Mills 1991; Pratt 2008), and expatriate communities (Callan and Ardener 1984; Fechter 2008; Leonard 2010) have made valuable contributions with regard to incorporating gender. The following section culls that scholarship for insights applicable to lifestyle migration.

Mobile women

Noting the curious lack of attention paid to gender by scholars of global migration, Pierrette Hondagneu-Sotelo insists, 'gender is one of the fundamental social relations anchoring and shaping immigration patterns, and immigration is one of the most powerful forces disrupting and realigning everyday life' (Hondagneu-Sotelo 2003: 3). In recent decades, her scholarship (Hondagneu-Sotelo 1994, 2003) and that of many others, has gone far toward filling this analytical void. Among the notable findings have been the different attitudes of female and male migrants with regard to permanent settlement in the receiving society. For many women, migration, even if motivated by economic hardship, provided an escape from patriarchal structures (Anthias and Lazaridis 2000). Because women tended to feel that their social status improved post migration, they more openly embraced permanent settlement in the destination country than did men who were more disposed to return to their country of origin (Goldring 2001; Jones-Correa 1998).

By the mid-1990s, the study of international migration took a profound transnational turn. No longer was migration conceptualised in terms of a rupture between 'there' and 'here,' but instead migrants were recognised as 'taking actions, making decisions, and developing subjectivities and identities embedded in networks of relationships that connect them simultaneously to two or more nation-states' (Basch *et al.* 1994: 7). As this analytical perspective took hold, some scholars stepped up to incorporate gender. Sarah Mahler and Patricia Pessar developed a framework, 'Gendered Geographies of Power,' for examining gender across transnational spaces. Their model highlighted how gender relations are negotiated across national borders and how gender articulates transnationally with other modes of identity. One of the questions generated by Mahler and Pessar's framework concerns whether the distribution of gender regimes across transnational space reinforces prevailing gender ideologies and norms or, conversely, provides opportunities for women and men to challenge hegemonic notions, and entertain competing understandings of gendered lives (Pessar and Mahler 2003: 819). A second component of Mahler and Pessar's framework highlights the influence of interconnected hierarchies of class, race, sexuality, ethnicity, nationality, and gender on an individual or group's social location. The 'playing field', these authors caution, 'is not level for all participants, and this is particularly true for international migrants whose desire for and actual border crossings initiate them into new power hierarchies' (Pessar and Mahler 2003: 822). Finally, this model acknowledges a key role in these transnational processes for social imagination and cognition.

Pessar and Mahler and others shed valuable light on how gender is negotiated within and across boundaries, but like the study of transnational migration generally, the analysis tends to be premised on assumptions of marginality. Migrants are conceptualised as occupying positions of economic and cultural disadvantage relative to members of the host society, and countries of origin are presumed to be less powerful in the international system than the countries of settlement (Croucher 2009b). By focusing on mobility of a distinctly privileged sort, literatures on colonialism, tourism and travel, and expatriate communities offer additional clues for gendering lifestyle migration. The roles of Western women in colonialism have been widely analysed, as has the significance of gender in travel literature (Grewal 1996; Mills 1991; Pratt 2008; Robinson 1990). Similar to the findings above regarding the sense of emancipation on the part of female labour migrants moving to developed countries, colonialism has been characterised as providing Western women who settled in the colonies with 'opportunities and access to the public sphere hitherto unavailable to them at home' (Mohanty 1995: 1059). Some colonial women reportedly gained a sense of liberation and empowerment from their journeys (Grewal 1996; Pruitt and LaFont 1995: 425), and travelling itself is described as a means through which women constituted their subjectivity (Pratt 2008).

Historically seen as the purview of men, travel today is increasingly marketed to women as a form of empowerment and a means by which to break free of 'traditional feminine restraints' (Robinson 1990: 6). Through travel, women have the opportunity to 'expand their gender repertoires to incorporate practices traditionally reserved for men' (Pruitt and LaFont 1995: 425). One contemporary illustration of these dynamics can be found in the practice of 'romance tourism' (Pruitt and LaFont 1995) or 'sex tourism' (O'Connell Davidson and Sanchez Taylor 1999). Largely focused on North American and European tourists (women and men) who travel to the Caribbean, these studies describe romantic and/or sexual encounters between travellers and 'natives.' Beyond merely romance or sex, this form of mobility offers Western women, whose gender can be disempowering at home, an opportunity to gain a sense of power and control over themselves and the locals with whom they interact (O'Connell Davidson and Sanchez Taylor 1999: 47–48).

The topic of 'expatriates,' per se, has generated a less robust body of scholarship than travel and tourism. Valuable contributions exist (Cohen 1977; Fechter 2008; Leonard 2010; Wennersten 2008), however, and in its evolving incarnations this literature has featured gender as a theme. The seminal work, *The Incorporated Wife* (Callan and Ardener 1984), explored various roles women fulfill as 'wives' of corporate husbands employed overseas. More recent studies of 'expat girls' reveal improvements in the options available to relatively affluent women living and working abroad, but also point to the persistent restrictiveness of transnational gender norms and ideologies (Fechter 2008). These studies of privileged mobility reveal that movement affords women a degree of empowerment, but also highlight the fact that gender is not lived in isolation from other identities and social hierarchies. In the case of relatively affluent women migrants (travellers, colonialists, expatriates), the emancipation they experience with regard to gender intertwines closely with the privilege they enjoy in terms of race, class, and nationality. Studies of colonialism reveal that Western women traded on their constructed racial, national, and economic superiority to compensate for their assigned sexual inferiority (Grewal 1996; Chaudhuri and Strobel 1992). Analyses of women and travel illustrate similar dynamics. Women who engage in romance or sex tourism gain a sense of control not only over themselves, but also over exoticised 'others'—an exoticisation that allows these women to affirm their own privilege as Westerners (O'Connell Davidson and Sanchez Taylor 1999: 49–50). In her study of expatriates (retirees and Western workers), Pauline Leonard emphasises that as transnational organisations mushroom, so too do transnational productions and performances of difference—including those of gender. In opposition to popular fixations with placelessness and hybridity, Leonard insists that gender, race, and nation are 'regularly drawn upon in the construction and performance of migrant lives and identities, albeit in uneven and fragmented ways' (2010: 4).

This varied scholarship produces a number of relevant findings. First, gender matters in understanding patterns and dynamics of human mobility. This is the case in terms of the factors that motivate migration and with migrants' settlement experiences. Mobility, for example, appears to offer migrants—especially women—a form of liberation from socially imposed gender constraints in their home countries. Secondly, what is revealed is that the workings of gender intersect closely with other forms of identity and social hierarchy (Alexander-Floyd 2012). How can these insights inform the study of lifestyle migration?

Gendering lifestyle migration

As a field, lifestyle migration directs needed attention to a relatively understudied trend in human mobility. Specifically, it takes as its subject matter relatively privileged individuals whose border crossing is motivated more by existential longings for an alternative way of life than by economic hardship (although financial motivations can be a factor). The scholarship on lifestyle migration, much of it ethnographic, has seized upon the self-reflexive and quasi-spiritual tendencies of this migration trend, and highlighted themes of identity, community, belonging, home, and ethnicity (Benson 2011; Benson and O'Reilly 2009; O'Reilly 2000a). Less recognised is that these themes are heavily gendered ones. Gender, in fact, exerts a profound and pervasive influence on lifestyle and frequently acts as a signifier for 'lifestyle,' and vice versa. What is needed, then, is more explicit analysis of how gender as a set of socially constructed norms and expectations is implicated in lifestyle migration. In discussing their motivations for relocation, lifestyle migrants make repeated references to their longing to break free of various social and cultural expectations. The roles and constraints from which they seek emancipation frequently relate to gender and this is particularly true for women. In a collection of essays titled, *Midlife Mavericks: Women Reinventing their lives in Mexico*, Karen Blue interviews other middle-aged and older American and Canadian women living alone in Mexico about their decisions to migrate. One 63-year-old Canadian woman who had been living in Mexico for six years explained: 'When Mom passed away, I felt alone. My marriages had been unsuccessful and I have no children or siblings. … I was a caregiver who had no more care to give' (Blue 2000: 79). An American woman, 44 years old and living in Mexico for five years remarked, 'I was a very fortunate yuppie wife. I had everything I could ask for. … I didn't have a very good reason for asking for the divorce. I think I was just bored' (Blue 2000: 98). At 71 years old, a former nurse from New England, living in Central Mexico, proclaimed, 'I've been married three times—most of my life. But no more. This dance is mine' (Blue 2000: 133).

Similar sentiments are echoed on numerous websites and blogs. In one online essay entitled *Gringa Unplugged* Lee Valenti, an American woman who had lived in Mexico for 15 years, explained the circumstances that conditioned her migration: 'I had divorced the year before and the children were grown and had lives of their own. All that remained was to resign, rid myself of accumulated possessions and leave' (Valenti 2012). In a blog about conversations with the expatriate community living in San Miguel, an American woman observed: 'Clearly these women see the move away from the U.S. and the obligations and expectations of society, their families, and (in many cases) the ex-husbands they left behind as a means to express themselves in a way that they found impossible in the U.S.' (Lattanzi 2006).

Women 'finding themselves' in Mexico is the central theme of a video-documentary about foreigners living in San Miguel produced by American lifestyle migrant, Karen Cross. One of the women interviewed contrasted her sense of comfort and belonging in Mexico to an opposing experience in the USA: 'I find it [the U.S.] a fairly masculine, kind of point to point culture. … I don't really fit in and when I came here it's like sitting down on, you know, your favourite old chair. It's like I'm home' (Cross 2007). Similarly, a native of Philadelphia who had moved to Mexico 11 years earlier, described her experiences in the USA as 'growing up in a very male, intensely male culture … I was looking to escape being a nobody because I'm female, and I didn't have a place in that culture … that whole culture let me down' (Cross 2007). Through frequent references to marriages, divorces, parenting, and other family or career obligations, gender surfaces as a pervasive theme in the narratives of lifestyle migrants. Gender figures into their motivation to move, but also surfaces in descriptions of their settlement experiences. Freedom from gender expectations of dress and behaviour is a familiar refrain. One 70-year-old British woman living in Southern Spain, and sporting shorts and a brightly collared T-shirt, exclaimed: 'If I dressed like this in England, people would just stare at me. I wouldn't dare do it' (O'Reilly 2000b: 231). An American woman described her feeling of liberation in Mexico this way: 'You don't have to behave in a certain way' (Cross 2007). Another migrant commented on how British women living in Spain feel emancipated from pressures to cook, clean, sew, and entertain: 'We've come here to enjoy ourselves, not get stuck in the kitchen' (O'Reilly 2000b: 231). British mothers living in Spain report feeling less confined to the home. Single women feel less excluded from social life, and widows feel less isolated (O'Reilly 2000b: 231–33).

Women lifestyle migrants of all ages and in various settlement sites (Mexico, Spain, India, and Italy) also report feeling safe. A European woman living in Varanasi, India mused: 'Here I feel maybe better in the street than in my home country. I think in the West, I feel more fear' (Korpela 2006). A divorced woman and native of California living in Chapala, Mexico, remarked: 'I feel protected and safe here' (Blue 2000: 115). As women describe their settlement experiences, countries themselves become gendered. Bemoaning the serial rapes in San Miguel, one American woman explained: 'The United States to me is like an adolescent. Mexico is like a grandmother—and it's safe, and nurturing, and warm—that's why we moved here' (Garcia-Navarro 2006). An American woman living in Italy portrayed her adopted home this way: 'Italy is a place to start over, not in an American sense of finding a new job, but to start over by getting closer to rhythms containing life's secrets. … Italy is a country that is about mothers and mothering, far more than about fathers, rules, success, meeting high goals' (Wilde-Menozzi 2003: 161).

Similar to the experiences of low-skilled migrants, women lifestyle migrants appear to embrace permanent settlement abroad more fully than do men. In her study of foreigners living in Italy, Wilde-Menozzi observes that the majority who stay are women (2003: 158–59). Similarly, several of the American women interviewed in Cross's documentary comment on their husbands' reluctance or refusal to make the move to Mexico. One woman whose husband returned to the USA explained: 'It's not for him'; and Cross's husband said of his wife's initial plan to migrate: 'It wasn't really my cup of tea' (Cross 2007). O'Reilly's (2000a) ethnography of Brits in Spain also reveals the complex negotiations between spouses in making migration-related decisions. Men do participate in lifestyle migration, and their experiences are also gendered. Cross's video features a lengthy monologue by a middle-aged

American man who left a lucrative law practice to escape the 'rat race' and pursue a simpler, more fulfilling lifestyle in Mexico. Implicit in his and other narratives is pressure associated with what constitutes 'success' for men—particularly in terms of being assigned the gendered role of 'breadwinner' (Wilde-Menozzi 2003: 159). It is not uncommon for white middle-class heterosexual men from the American Midwest to describe how life in Mexico helped them overcome social and cultural constraints associated with gender, including their initial hesitance to indulge in the pleasures of a pedicure (Croucher 2009a: 62). One American woman whose husband only reluctantly joined her lifestyle journey to Mexico, praised him for owning his first-ever pair of sandals (Cross 2007). Some of these men also comment on the newfound ease with which they form friendships with fellow lifestyle migrants who are gay and with whom they would have been unlikely to socialise in the USA (Croucher 2009a: 62).

As was the case with other forms of privileged mobility, gender liberation and empowerment for lifestyle migrants tends to take shape in opposition to raced and classed 'others.' Korpela's (2006) analysis of Westerners in India illustrates that the empowerment European women experience living abroad is a product of the distinctions they draw between themselves and Indian women who they perceive as backward and oppressed. A similar dynamic is apparent among Americans in Mexico, particularly women, who often establish paternalistic relationships with their Mexican 'help' (Croucher 2009a: 137–74). Some lifestyle migrants also share with romance tourists the tendency to exoticise the 'locals' or 'natives' among whom they live. In one study, Anglo women living in Italy (a majority of whom were American) acknowledged that their migration was initially influenced by fantasies of sexual exoticism and the perceived appeal of a 'Latin lover' (Trundle 2009: 56). This 'othering' of locals reflects and sustains the race, class, and national privilege of lifestyle migrants, but so too does their construction of social worlds that tend to elide the material and political realities of specific places and the people who inhabit them. As Korpela observed, for example: 'It is ironic that the place where these Europeans choose to free themselves as women is India where gender roles seem to be even stricter than in Europe' (2006). Freedom afforded women, for instance, is not a cultural trait with which India, Italy, Mexico, or Spain is most closely associated. That many lifestyle migrants experience such freedom is a function of their own state of liminality—and in this case, a particularly privileged form of liminality. Liminality, a state of being 'betwixt and between,' born out of a separation from familiar routines, spaces, and social structures (Turner and Turner 1978), is a featured theme in lifestyle migration studies (Benson 2011; D'Andrea 2007; O'Reilly 2000a). Migrant Karen Cross captured this condition perfectly when she remarked: 'I am no longer a part of the U.S. culture and I'm not a part of the Mexican culture. It kind of leaves me free' (Cross 2007).

Several issues warrant further emphasis with regard to the liminality associated with lifestyle migration: women and men appear to experience it differently, it is distinctly linked to privilege, and it can, as the term 'liminal' implies, be transitory. In her study of Anglo romance tourists turned migrants in Italy, Trundle reveals that once these women become more fully integrated into the host culture they experience social restrictions in direct conflict with the desire for freedom and individualism that propelled their border crossing (Trundle 2009: 58). In her ethnography on the British in Southern Spain, O'Reilly addresses the image, and to a significant extent reality, of the immigrants' carefree lifestyles. Despite abundant sunshine and socialising, however, the state of being 'betwixt and between' takes a toll. Some British women, in particular, admitted privately to being lonely or sad in Spain (O'Reilly 2000a: 4). In India, Korpela found that, interspersed with their narratives of empowerment, Western women described multiple challenges. One remarked: 'being a Western woman in India is a lot more complicated than being a Western man' (2006). Finally, the rapes in San Miguel offer a poignant example of a rupture in the sense of security that can accompany lifestyle migration. The concept of liminality captures well the ambiguity associated with lifestyle migration and, by extension, helps elucidate contested spatialities of lifestyle migration. In order for an existence 'betwixt and between' cultures to be experienced as empowering, the status is likely a voluntary one that affords the subject an opportunity to evade the constraints of one society and her place in it while remaining relatively disconnected from another and her place in it. This disconnectedness and the privilege underlying it, facilitates, at least temporarily, a constructed reality largely of the participant's choosing. Such status is akin to the bubble Fechter (2007) uses as a metaphor for the lives of expatriates in Indonesia. But thresholds and bubbles are inherently unstable spaces and the narratives that sustain them inevitably come into contact with competing social and material realities. American women in San Miguel assigned Mexico and Mexicans the role of protective grandmother. Their reaction to the rapes signalled disappointment, but also exposed negative cultural stereotypes they held about Mexicans and the legal system in Mexico. The locals in San Miguel tend to acknowledge and skilfully navigate their dependent relationship on the foreign community (Croucher 2009a), but the events and coverage surrounding the rapes also revealed suspicion and resentment of that community. For their part, Mexican women were shown to inhabit a space of simultaneous resentment and admiration regarding the women immigrants residing in their town. Fortunately, episodes like this one in San Miguel seem rare in the world of lifestyle migrants; but the events are a powerful testament to the need for broadening the lens to capture the gendered and contested realities of lifestyle migration.

Conclusion

As a still-emerging field, lifestyle migration intersects with scholarship on international migration, transnationalism, and forms of privileged movement (Amit 2007; D'Andrea 2007), but it seeks to make sense of a particular form of mobility. What distinguishes this migration trend is 'its emphasis on lifestyle choices specific to individuals of the developed world,' for whom migration is often a 'self-realisation project' or search for the 'good life' (O'Reilly and Benson 2009: 1). Gender is inscribed everywhere in the constitutive narratives and experiences of these migrants, but has been rendered nearly invisible in much of the analysis—its obviousness perhaps contributing to its obscurity. Bringing gender more centrally into the study of lifestyle migration will deepen understanding of this burgeoning phenomenon. Meanwhile, incorporating privileged forms of mobility such as lifestyle migration into general studies of gender and migration will (1) contribute insights into how gender acts as 'one of the fundamental social relations ... shaping immigration patterns' (Hondagneu-Sotelo 2003: 3), and (2) deepen the examination of how gender articulates transnationally with other modes of identity (Pessar and Mahler 2003: 814).

Borrowing from a large body of related scholarship, this chapter identifies some of the ways gender is implicated in lifestyle migration and points to fruitful areas for further investigation. When the story of the rapes in San Miguel broke, among the many questions it prompted were: who are these women living alone in Mexico, why, and how many are there? Regarding the question of 'how many,' scholars of lifestyle migration regularly bemoan the challenges associated with gathering reliable demographic data on these migrant populations. Improved availability and access to such data are high priorities, but so too is including the migrants' sex as a featured variable alongside age, national origin, and income. Anecdotally, at least, women appear to comprise a larger proportion of this migrant population. As one American in Mexico observed: 'Women who move to a Third World country are generally independent, fully expecting to take care of themselves. Men come here, I think, looking for someone to take care of them. *And at a ratio of ten women to one man, the odds definitely favor them*' (Blue 2000: 72–73, emphasis added). As suggested by this quotation, scholars also need to consider more closely how gender is implicated in the motivations for migration and experiences with settlement. To what extent are female and male lifestyle migrants seeking and/or finding different outcomes, and are those aspirations and experiences influenced by gender? The scholarship of O'Reilly (2000a) and Benson (2011) is exemplary in moving beyond sensational headlines and superficial renditions of the lifestyle migration experience to probe how these migrants actually fare. Their studies and others reveal that liminality is both a privileged state, and a precarious one. What must be probed further, however, are the ways in which neither liminality nor lifestyle can be separated from the workings of gender.

A third area for further investigation concerns the impact of this migration trend on the receiving societies. Much remains to be understood regarding the economic and political implications of lifestyle migration, and so too with its socio-cultural impact (including attitudes and practices related to gender). As Pessar and Mahler emphasised, cognition plays a role in transnationalism and may affect prevailing ideologies and hierarchies. For example, on the one hand, the immigrant women's relatively open and assertive response to the rapes in San Miguel may have altered the imaginings of some Mexican women and men. Yet, on the other hand, the gender emancipation that lifestyle migrants seek, or appear to have achieved, may be more a function of their privileged liminality than the empowering capacity of transnationalism to challenge hegemonic notions or prevailing ideologies (Pessar and Mahler 2003).

In her study of Anglo migrants to Italy, Trundle cautions scholars of lifestyle migration that, 'in creating a new category of migrant we should be wary of such a category's strength to hide the life span developments and changes that migrants experience' (2009: 64). To her concern about disregarding the significance of lifespan variations in migrants' subjectivities and practices, should be added a caution about overlooking the role of gender. Trundle notes that the quest for personal fulfilment that characterises lifestyle migration is, after all, rarely complete. This chapter contends that not the quest, its fulfilment, nor its consequences can be abstracted from the ideological and material workings of gender.

Bibliography

Alexander-Floyd, N.G. (2012) 'Disappearing acts: Reclaiming intersectionality in the social sciences' *Feminist Formations* 24(1): 1–25.

Amit, V. (ed.) (2007) *Going First Class? New Approaches to Privileged Movement*, New York: Berghahn Books.

Anthias, F. and G. Lazaridis (eds) (2000) *Gender and Migration in Southern Europe*, Oxford: Berg.

Basch, L., Glick Schiller, N. and C. Szanton Blanc (1994) *Nations Unbound*, Langhorne: Gordon and Breach.

Benson, M. (2011) *The British in Rural France*, Manchester: Manchester University Press.

Benson, M. and K. O'Reilly (eds) (2009) *Lifestyle Migration: Expectations, Aspirations and Experiences*, Surrey: Ashgate.

Blue, K. (2000) *Midlife Mavericks: Women Reinventing their Lives in Mexico*, Parkland, FL: Universal Publishers.

Callan, H. and S. Ardener (1984) *The Incorporated Wife*, Kent: Croom Helm.

Chaudhuri, N. and M. Strobel (eds) (1992) *Western Women and Imperialism*, Indianapolis: Indiana University Press.

Cohen, E. (1977) 'Expatriate communities', *Current Sociology* 24(3): 5–90.

Corchado, A. and A. Kocherga (2006) 'Mexican city's rape saga has lessons for locals, expatriate Americans alike', *Dallas Morning News* (July 26). www.banderasnews.com/0607/nr-rapesaga.htm (accessed 11 June 2012).

Cross, K.(2007) *Lost and Found in Mexico* (film). www.lostandfoundinmexico.com. (accessed 18 October 2012).

Croucher, S. (2009a) *The Other Side of the Fence: American Migrants in Mexico*, Austin: University of Texas Press.

——(2009b) 'Migrants of privilege: The political transnationalism of Americans in Mexico', *Identities: Global Studies in Culture and Power* 16: 463–91.

D'Andrea, A. (2007) *Global Nomads*, London: Routledge.

Fechter, A.M. (2007) 'Living in a bubble: Expatriates' transnational spaces' in V. Amit (ed) *Going First Class*, New York: Berghahn Books, 33–52.

——(2008) 'From "Incorporated Wives" to "Expat Girls"', in A. Coles and A.M. Fechter (eds) *Gender and Family among Transnational Professionals*, New York: Routledge.

Garcia-Navarro, L. (2006) 'Rape stirs up controversy over justice in Mexico,' Transcripts, National Public Radio, Morning Edition, Washington, DC: 13 March.

Goldring, L. (2001) 'The gender and geography of citizenship in Mexico-U.S. transnational space', *Identities* 7(4): 501–37.

Grewal, I. (1996) *Home and Harem*, London: Leicester University Press.

Hondagneu-Sotelo, P. (1994) *Gendered Transitions: Mexican Experiences of Immigration*. Berkeley: University of California Press.

——(ed.) (2003) *Gender and U.S. Immigration*. Berkeley: University of California Press.

Jones-Correa, M. (1998) *Between Two Nations: Latinos in New York City*, Ithaca, NY: Cornell University Press.

Korpela, M. (2006) '"I'm Not Like Indian Women." Reflections of Young European Women in Varanasi, India.' *J@RGONIA-Elektroninen Julkaisusarja*. http://research.jyu.fi/jargonia/artikkelit/jargonia9.pdf (accessed 23 March 2012).

Lattanzi, D. (2006) 'Reinvent yourself in Mexico' Blog entry. *Living Ethnography*. Available online at: http://livingethnography.wordpress.com/2006/07/24/reinvent-yourself-in-mexico/ (accessed 3 May 2012).

Leonard, P. (2010) *Expatriate Identities in Postcolonial Organizations*. Burlington, VT: Ashgate.

Mohanty, C. (1995) 'Book review on gender and colonialism', *SIGNS* (summer): 1058–61.

Mills, S. (1991) *Discourses of Difference: An Analysis of Women's Travel Writing and Colonialism*, London: Routledge.

O'Connell Davidson, J. and Sanchez Taylor, J. (1999) 'Fantasy islands', in K. Kempadoo (ed.) *Sun, Sex and Gold: Tourism and Sex Work in the Caribbean*, Lanham, MD: Rowman and Littlefield, 37–54.

Oliver, C. (2008) *Retirement Migration: Paradoxes of Ageing*, New York: Routledge.

O'Reilly, K. (2000a) *The British on the Costa del Sol*, London: Routledge.

——(2000b) 'Trading intimacy for liberty: British women on the Costa Del Sol', in F. Anthias and G. Lazaridis (eds) *Gender and Migration in Southern Europe*, Oxford: Berg, 227–48.

O'Reilly, K. and M. Benson (2009) 'Lifestyle migration: Escaping to the good life' in M. Benson and K. O'Reilly (eds) *Lifestyle Migration: Expectations, Aspirations and Experiences*, Surrey: Ashgate.

'Personal ordeal with the rapist' (2006) In *Atención*, San Miguel de Allende, Mexico. previously available: www.atencionsanmiguel.org/archives/feat_2006_jun_30_eng.html (accessed 19 August 2012).

Pessar, P. and S. Mahler (2003) 'Transnational Migration: Bringing Gender', *International Migration Review* 37(3): 812–46.

Pratt, M.L. (2008) *Imperial Eyes: Travel Writing and Transculturation*, New York: Routledge.

Pruitt, D. and S. LaFont (1995) 'For love and money', *Annals of Tourism Research*, 22 (2): 422–40.

Robinson, J. (1990) *Wayward Women: A Guide to Women Travelers*, New York: Oxford University Press.

Schmidt, C. (2006) 'Count of expats in town increases.' *Atención*, San Miguel de Allende, Mexico: 23 June.

Trundle, C. (2009) 'Romance tourists, foreign wives or retirement migrants?' in M. Benson and K. O'Reilly (eds) *Lifestyle Migration: Expectations, Aspirations and Experiences*, Surrey: Ashgate.

Turner, V. (1967) *The Forest of Symbols*, Ithaca, NY: Cornell University Press.

Turner, V. and E. Turner (1978) *Image and Pilgrimage in Christian Culture*, New York: Columbia University Press.

Valenti, L. (2012) 'Gringa unplugged.' *The People's Guide to Mexico*. www.peoplesguide.com/1pages/retire/where/guate/lee/unplug.html (accessed 11 April 2012).

Wennersten, J. (2008) *Leaving America: The New Expatriate Generation*, Westport, CT: Praeger.

Wilde-Menozzi, W. (2003) 'Grafting on Italian roots', *The Literary Review*, 47: 157–65.

3 Marrakesh Medina

Neocolonial paradise of lifestyle migrants?

Anton Escher and Sandra Petermann

Although Morocco is only separated from Europe by the narrow Strait of Gibraltar, most Europeans view the country as another world: an unknown realm from centuries past, a distant desert kingdom full of adventure and an oriental fairyland as glamorised in the 'Arabian Nights'. These appealing characterisations also apply to Marrakesh, the urban symbol of Morocco, and have reinforced its exotic image with the numerous media-presented narrations about Marrakesh. If one were to believe newspaper articles, travelogues and filmed reports, you would find the 'real and authentic orient in Marrakesh in particular and get caught up in the "whirlwind of events"' (Kirchhoff 1999: 28). We are now witnessing a process here that has been taking place over two decades and which would have been unfeasible in the early 1990s for the relevant academic community: Morocco has evolved into a destination for lifestyle migrants from all over the globe who travel to the old city of Marrakesh to buy overcrowded or neglected and/or vacant buildings and then transform them into magnificent residences based on orientalising designs with extended rooftop terraces and swimming pools. The question is, however, why have foreigners bought more than 2,500 properties in Marrakesh's medina so far? What are they looking for? What type of lifestyle do they lead? And how does their migration affect the life of the local Moroccan population?

Lifestyle migration and lifestyle migrants

John Locke (1632–1704) is regarded as the first (pre)-modern thinker to define the basic 'right a man has to subsist and enjoy the conveniences of life' (Locke [1689] 2005: 44). For the philosopher that meant enjoying the pleasures of life as they occur and not making happiness and indulgence one's aim in life, and thus arranging day-to-day activities accordingly. Thomas Jefferson (1743–1826) asserted the claim for the indisputable natural law that was later incorporated in the US Declaration of Independence as 'pursuit of happiness': 'We hold these truths to be self-evident, that all men are created equal, that they are endowed, by their Creator, with certain unalienable Rights, that among these are Life, Liberty, and the pursuit of Happiness' (Stimson [1908]

2004: 76). Bliss or the pursuit of happiness refers to a balanced state of well-being at the end of life, a 'state where there are no longer any problems or wishes' (Farlex Inc. n.d.). In this age, the pursuit of happiness has become an aim in life (for instance, striving for good health and belongings) and does not imply a feeling of happiness at a given moment.

At the end of the twentieth century, when most people living in countries of the North considered their needs in terms of health and belongings as being satisfied for the most part, these intersubjectively tangible qualities no longer formed the focal point of the pursuit for happiness. Instead emphasis is placed more on subjectively intentional qualities like pleasure and sentiment and is accompanied by an increasing individualisation of people and differentiation of hedonistic lifestyles of opulence (see Beck 1983, 1986). Selfishness and emphasis on ascribing meaning to the here and now and an increasing loss of transcendental interpretation of meaning place self-portrayal, self-actualisation, satisfaction of basic individual needs and pleasure at the heart of post-modern pursuits. 'Happiness and pleasure' represent the desirable objective of almost every action. In addition to that, globalisation, (neo-)liberalisation and digitalisation at the end of the twentieth century are responsible for a blurring of spatial and temporal boundaries for the actions of people living primarily in industrial countries. The resulting framework conditions of everyday life have developed dramatically during the ensuing years especially with regard to the dimension of one's actions and have thus resulted in migration increasingly becoming a strategy for shaping and improving the quality of everyday life based on individual preferences. Currently, broad sections of population, especially those living in first-world countries, are always looking for a better and different life. In the past, this form of migration was only a privilege reserved for the wealthy and those who chose to escape for one reason or another. Besides migrating for economic or political reasons or to survive and have a safer or better way of life, people have also moved in search of a more satisfying and more pleasurable way of life.

The most important publications addressing lifestyle migration as a topic come from Benson and O'Reilly (2009a,b). As part of their research, the two authors focus on locations that promise the possibilities of a better way of life: ' … lifestyle migration is the spatial mobility of relatively affluent individuals of all ages, moving either part-time or full-time to places that are meaningful because, for various reasons, they offer the potential of a better quality of life' (Benson and O'Reilly 2009a: 2). From the standpoint of migrants, relocating one's residence is like a project ' … that encompasses diverse destinations, desires and dreams' (Benson and O'Reilly 2009b: 610). It is based on subjective analysis and evaluation of one's current living conditions in their home country: ' … migration for these migrants is often an anti-modern, escapist, self-realization project, a search for the intangible "good life"' (Benson and O'Reilly 2009a: 1). Taking Benson and O'Reilly (2009a,b) into consideration and integrating ideas from Hoey (2005) led Torkington (2010: 102) to the following idea:

> Whilst the lifestyle orientations and motivations of these migrants may differ, perhaps the one unifying factor of this group is their belief that a *change of residential place* will lead not simply to better opportunities in life, but rather to something which might be described as a better *lifestyle* and/or a more fulfilling *way of life*.

In this chapter, we would like to further characterise the rather general definitions of lifestyle migration by focusing on the lifestyles that are pursued at the given locations. This chapter also aims to illustrate the extent in which the lifestyles are linked with the migration process, whereas Zapf *et al.* (1987: 14) have already made reference to the 'mobile welfare society' for shaping lifestyles. To present the lifestyles in greater detail, it would first be helpful to take a look at sociology as it is taught in Germany. Hradil (2005: 46) defines lifestyles as the attitudes, actions and practices adopted by persons in the overall context of everyday life, whereas Geißler (2002: 126) identifies ' … recreation, leisure and consumerism as the main focus. In addition to that, reference is also made to family life, tastes and cultural interests and sometimes to work and politics, if only marginally at that.'

Migration in this context is frequently influenced by a way of life, where the lifestyles are often extremely hedonistic and egocentric as the described trends of the last 30 years bear testament. With that we are making 'the more or less conscious self-portrayal (stylization) of a given individual in terms of taste and cultural interests' (Geißler 2002: 126) the focal point of our study. According to the authors, it is possible to classify, from a pragmatic standpoint, lifestyles into the following four dimensions: (1) conscious physicalness, (2) differentiated and civilised satisfaction of basic needs, (3) tailored, direct physical residential environment and (4) selected social and media-based common life areas (Figure 3.1).

The described dimensions can be broken down in different categories, as is in part presented especially in so-called 'lifestyle magazines'.[1] Physicalness is covered by 'Fashion and Beauty' and 'Wellness and Fitness'. The basic primary needs can be described with the areas 'Food and Drink' and 'Eroticism and Sex'. The tailored, direct physical residential environment can be defined

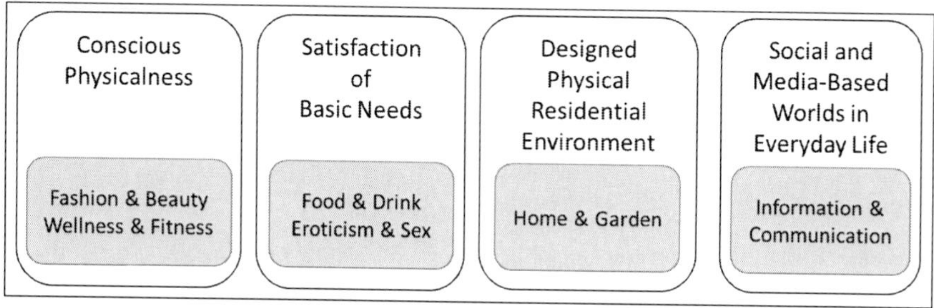

Figure 3.1 Dimensions and categories of lifestyles of lifestyle migrants

with 'Home and Garden', and the selected social and media-based society can be characterised with 'Information and Communication'.[2] The individual categories do not necessarily have to be experienced or consumed to a greater extent or in a more exotic manner. They can also be characterised by a reticence in consumption based on the idea of a simpler way of life at the newly adopted home (for an example, see Therrien this volume).

This chapter consequently treats lifestyle migration as a permanent change in place of residence or the selection of an additional temporary place of residence, where the main purpose is to find a 'better life' for the purpose of self-actualisation, self-portrayal and satisfaction of basic needs. Lifestyle migration frequently unfolds at a location where there are different economic prerequisites and other political conditions or where other social rules or different rules of social control apply that offer migrants as foreigners a legal and social interstice and open up additional potential for action. The lifestyles practised at such locations are marked by a purposeful change and subjective enhancement of the capacity to deliberately influence physicalness, to satisfy basic needs in a civilised manner and to individualise physical and social environments. All in all, lifestyle migrants tend to experience an increase in options for individual self-actualisation, since the socio-economical foundation usually remains embedded in the respective countries of origin.

Ultimately, lifestyle migration differs from other forms of migration in that the migrants choose to move from a relatively good life to an even better and more gratifying life. The objective of lifestyle migration is to create opportunities, to overstep or push boundaries in many different ways. That said, these boundaries are not only physical like the borders of a country but may also be symbolic, moral and/or legal boundaries. While lifestyle migration may be temporary or permanent, it always illustrates the difference between the (former) places of residence and highlights the advantages, the freedom and happiness that lifestyle migrants continuously enjoy by opting for a different or additional place of residence. Lifestyle migration always represents a migration to places that have aesthetic characteristics within the meaning of 'beautiful landscape' (see Lacoste 1990) or 'old cultural location' (see Cosgrove 1998) or cultural landmarks that are worth preserving like historic districts or neglected villages. Lifestyle migrants therefore pick specific landscapes, cities and countries that are able to provide the setting or platform for the intended lifestyle. The shaping of the locations by the lifestyle migrants who take possession of the location cannot be overlooked and easily forms the basis for empirical study.

In search of a better life in Marrakesh's Medina[3]

In order for a location to become the destination of lifestyle migrants, it requires a series of framework conditions, prerequisites and qualities that initiate, stimulate and stabilise the process. These factors are either already present or are created during the course of the migration process. The empirically examined migration process to Marrakesh is plainly enabled by the cultural, economic and political globalisation as preconditions. For instance, UNESCO, the WTO and Morocco's king can be cited as representative protagonists. UNESCO designated the Medina of Marrakesh as a World Heritage site in 1985 and placed the city's central square (Djemaa el-Fna) on the List of 'Masterpieces of the Oral and Intangible Heritage of Humanity' in 2001. The WTO encourages the dynamisation of cross-border financial and freight services with the global measures of the Uruguay Round, which ended in 1994 with the Marrakesh Declaration. In addition, the Moroccan King Mohammed VI declared in 2001 that international tourism was the country's growth sector that deserved the most support and stated in 2010 that Morocco's tourist infrastructure will be further developed. The declared aim is to become one of the top 20 tourist destinations in the world with 20 million tourists by 2020 (Najjar 2011). Even the geographical location of Marrakesh makes the city very attractive. The landscape is characterised by the mountains surrounding the Haouz,[4] first and foremost by the High Atlas with its long, frequently snow-covered peaks. Casablanca in the north, the Atlantic Ocean to the west and the desert to the south are easy to reach within a couple of hours of driving. The ability to fly to almost every European capital in just a couple of hours also plays a key role in the process. In addition to that, there are the climatic conditions that are locally influenced by the Mediterranean and sub-Sahara (Escher and Petermann 2009).

The most important prerequisite for the lifestyle migration is the old city that is relatively well preserved as a monument. This can be attributed to a large extent to the politics of the French protectorate (1912–56), which constructed the new city (ville nouvelle) at a physical and functional distance from the old city (see Escher 2012). As a result of the migration from rural areas to cities at around mid-twentieth century, the old city became an overcrowded domicile for the rural and poor segments of population residing in buildings that are characterised by segmentation, obstruction and neglect (see Petermann 2012). The residential buildings in Marrakesh – especially the so-called riads, which are traditional Moroccan houses with interior courtyards with fountains and a garden split in four quadrants – are attractive and desirable buildings for migrants. The riads are regarded as a copy of paradise on earth, as is described in the Qur'an with two gardens and four rivers (of milk, water, honey and wine) and birds (see Leisten 1993, Escher and Petermann 2009). For lifestyle migrants, a riad is an earthly paradise that can be bought, an affordable house of oriental design that cannot be found in Europe. This 'small paradise' guarantees an entitled freedom and interstice between its walls. On top of that, this paradise is reasonable: from a European perspective, Marrakesh promises low cost of living and low staff costs as a result of the economic gap between countries of the North and Morocco. According to one European migrant, you find ' … great value for money here and you get, you can live a life where, you know, people can clean and cook for you … '. Consequently, the city appeals to members of Europe's middle class. If, however, the resources fail to be sufficient, there is always the possibility of using the riad as a guesthouse and listing the rooms in the internet. Thus, buying the house can (seemingly) be seen as a way to finance the upkeep of the property at the same time.

The existence of the Western 'Marrakesh myth' is equally important for lifestyle migration (Escher and Petermann 2009). The myth was inspired by Western artists like Jacques Majorelle, the 'painter of Marrakesh', who came to the 'pearl of the south' in the 1920s and who created his famous Majorelle Garden here. The Hotel La Mamounia, which was built during the same period and has been remodelled numerous times, accommodates famous politicians, eccentric Hollywood actors and international jet set and thus links Marrakesh with unending luxury. Influenced by the beat generation of the 1940s, hippies travelled here with the 'Marrakesh Express' during the 1960s and 1970s and experienced their utopia beyond the constraints of Western societies. They spread word about the fairytale-like city of the Arabian Nights and some of them come back later on as lifestyle migrants.

Media like newspapers, books, feature films and documentaries play a significant role in the development process of lifestyle migration on various levels, for without them, the myth of Marrakesh would never have spread so fast nor so far in the Western world. The date 14 June 1998 represents a key moment, which broke all dams: the documentary entitled 'Villas in Morocco: Luxury at your fingertip' was broadcast at that time on French TV. The message was plausible and said that Europeans could easily buy oriental palaces for about FRF 150,000 in the medina of Marrakesh and Essaouira. That caused a stampede headed towards the medina of Marrakesh, which in turn was covered in many newspapers and magazines with headlines such as 'Marrakech: The rush towards the riads' (Scemama 2001), 'Ryad – the new must' (Khizrane 2000) or 'Building boom in Marrakesh. Real estate prices skyrocket, Investors scramble to get building permits' (Müller 2007: 4). Even the internet plays an important role in propagating the myth and the development of lifestyle migration. For instance, there was an explosion in the number of websites operated by real estate agents, property developers, guesthouse operators and many other service providers that continuously talk up this so-called paradise on earth.

In addition, a legal security that is guaranteed by an official entry in the land registry (titre foncier) is important for migrants. Foreigners are more or less entitled to freely buy, sell or rent real estate in Moroccan cities. This provided the framework that allowed an international real estate market to establish itself at the end of the 1990s. At that time there were primarily bi-national real estate agencies like Marrakech–Médina, which was an enterprise founded by a Belgian architect and his Moroccan partner.

Under the conditions described, the adopted location must allow lifestyle migrants to have a 'better life', i.e. a positive subjective attitude towards life and happiness as well as the positive experience of the categories addressed in the first section with regard to physicalness, physical and social environments as well as gratification of basic needs. Based on the perception of the migrants, this is mainly granted in the four different subjective spheres: colonial sphere, Arabian Nights sphere, comfortable sphere of life and local social sphere.[5] They consist of tangible and intangible aspects (Figure 3.2).

The colonial sphere is reminiscent of past times: there is still ' … a bit of a colonial atmosphere. It's the sort of the thing I love about Morocco. There is still that sort of gracious colonial atmosphere.' The neocolonial[6] activities of no less than lifestyle migrants have surfaced in the colonial sphere, which are evident in the master–servant relation to the Moroccan population and especially towards service personnel (Escher and Petermann 2000, Petermann 2001). The staff are often financially dependent on the migrant and hardly in the position to negotiate their pay (Petermann 2001). What is striking, however, are neocolonial aspects, especially in the way of daily management of the service staff, which is often limited to a ' … colonial kind of "hey man, go, get me my cup of tea and wipe my table"'. For instance, as one female migrant puts it: 'Well, regarding their domestic staff, they are in one or another way acting in a colonial style for sure.' Reports especially about French migrants also show that they have ' … some kind of neocolonial mentality. I think that's very striking. Not everybody, but all of the people who buy riads. These are people arriving with the idea of living here like a pasha, like a king.' As a form of cultural dominance can be interpreted the fact that only very few migrants are willing to learn the local language, but they communicate in the language of the former protectorate with their employees and neighbours (see Torkington in this volume).

Closely tied with the availability of service personnel is also the presence of male and female adult and child prostitutes. A European reported on the

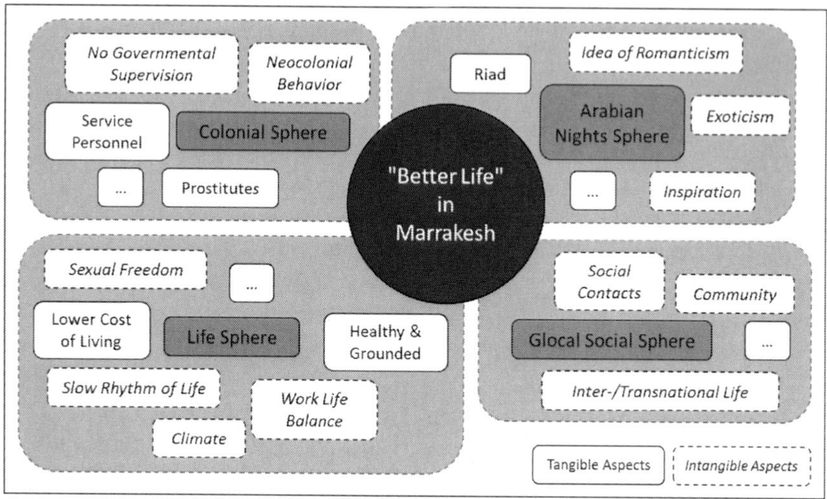

Figure 3.2 'Better life' in Marrakesh

situation as follows: 'There are even kids here; people are coming because of the kids. Sometimes when you walk down the streets at night, there are children at the age of ten or twelve offering you sex.' Or as another migrant summarised:

> Marrakesh is a huge brothel. Especially (homo)sexual and pedophile services are always in demand: … it's like paradise for Europeans. There are a lot of 'easy' cute little Arabs. A lot of French homosexuals come here. There are a lot. If you go to a dinner party, 20 to 30 per cent are gay. That's disproportionate.

Even many newspapers and magazines focus on Marrakesh's role as tourist destination for homosexuals (Anon. 2008). Here it is possible to experience almost every fantasy, since the migrants are able to act within the four walls of their houses where they are isolated from the outside world and are thus out of reach of the police or authorities. This liberty and/or release from any individual and social constraints was summarised by one interviewee as follows: ' … once you're in your house, you're in your own little kingdom'.

The Arabian Nights sphere is characterised predominantly by the exoticism, magic and the idea of romanticism that can be felt in Marrakesh. 'When you walk for the first few times – and still today – through the world of this fairytale Medina, it really seems to me like The Arabian Nights: Everything's sparkling and glittering and smelling and there are surprises everywhere. You think "now this is happening" and then something completely different appears.' Even the houses of migrants, regardless of whether they are private houses, guesthouses, restaurants or hammam or spa, are primarily designed to reflect the style of the Arabian Nights and are advertised as such in the media.

The comfortable life sphere in the sunny climate comprises many different components. It is frequently the slow rhythm of life that attracts the migrants who come primarily from industrial countries to rethink their perception of time. For instance, one migrant described the situation as follows: 'I fell in love with this country … . And I love particularly the rhythm of life here.' Even a French woman who migrated to permanently live in the medina in 2006 agreed with the statements. She came here for 'a desire to change life, change profession, rhythm of life … or "way of life" as you say in English'. Here there is a relatively balanced relation between work and recreation, provided that the migrants do work here at all. This is possible in particular because service personnel are inexpensive based on the lower costs of living, and many tasks even in the private household are assumed by Moroccan personnel. Other aspects contributing to this easy life include the aforementioned sexual freedom and the feeling that one is down-to-earth and living healthily thanks to the slower rhythm of life and the local agricultural products.

The glocal social sphere of the migrants is anchored locally within the community of foreigners and linked globally or transnationally through the internet and mobility (Arnold 2010). The entire world meets here in Marrakesh. Even if only temporarily, people from all over the globe gather here: 'I love Marrakesh because it's so international. … people constantly come through here. And so that amuses me.' Social contact with Moroccans is maintained only in very exceptional cases (see When lifestyle migrants meet locals).

Idealised lifestyles of migrants in Marrakesh

Lifestyle migrants generally want to leave behind their old life and daily routine (at least temporarily) by moving. They settle in Marrakesh's medina in order to shape their everyday life and fulfil themselves as individuals in a way that they could not have done or only to a limited extent at another location. They relocate their place of residence to realise a certain lifestyle, an existence that is better than would have been possible in their old way of life. They want to redefine or reinvent themselves and change their place. They want to act out their talents and needs as much as possible without the constraints of rules and morals. The vast majority of lifestyle migrants living in Marrakesh are circular migrants. In other words, they spend periods of various durations in the home country time and again. Most lifestyle migrants avoid Marrakesh especially during the very hot summer months from June to August.

To form the ideal types,[7] it is necessary to examine various elements of the hedonistic lifestyles already addressed in the theoretical section. In this case, the dominating motive for migration and subsequently determining how to lead one's life serves as analytical guidance and definitive for the lifestyle.[8] The elements 'Home and Garden', 'Eroticism and Sex' and 'Information and Communication' play an even greater role as catalysts than the categories 'Food and Drink', 'Wellness and Fitness' and 'Fashion and Beauty', which can be addressed at any location. Based on the empirical analysis, it is possible to distinguish analytically seven lifestyles among the foreigners living in Marrakesh: Riad style, Self style, Homo style, Mobile style, Social style, Setting style and Posing style. The last two styles do not really designate lifestyles of migrants who have changed their place of residence for several months but rather those of very mobile persons who only stay for short periods. The different lifestyles of migrants interlock, overlap and permeate one another in the forms of their everyday life. The order of the list normally corresponds with the descending order of the length of stay in Marrakesh in a given year.

Riad style

This lifestyle is characteristic for many migrants in Marrakesh's medina and is determined by the combination of elements 'Home and Garden' as they can only be found in this form in the 'Red City'. The created, direct physical environment forms the focal point of this lifestyle; here everyday life revolves around one's own riad. The purchase of the house, the finishing and/or renovation not only cost money but also demand in particular time and energy. As of that point in time, the preservation and the interior design of the riad with its frequently oriental design elements play the most important role in the life of Riad-style migrants. Owing to the high maintenance costs and the additional charges for water, electricity and upkeep, almost two-thirds of the lifestyle migrants decide in favour of opening a guesthouse. Their lifestyle is always closely linked with the operation of the house: sunset years, recreation, hotel business and gastronomy merge together smoothly. The elements 'Food and Drink' and 'Wellness and Fitness' also play an active part: more and more guesthouse operators integrate restaurants and wellness centres in their buildings or open them up in new premises. Even during private time, much of their life revolves around meals and physical well-being. For instance, Riad-style migrants regularly meet with like-minded people to eat together. The lifestyle elements 'Information and Communication' are influenced to a considerably extent by these get-togethers, and in the event of guesthouse operators by their communication with customers. The canvassing of potential clients and communication with friends back in their home country takes place for the most part via the internet. The necessary functional and communicative connection to Morocco's everyday world in Marrakesh is frequently implemented by the wage-dependent service personnel who prepare the meals, take care of the garden and watch the riad.

Self style

Self-actualisation plays a key role in the everyday routine of these migrants. They are frequently artists and producers of culture such as authors, graphic artists, photographers, craftsmen and film makers who have migrated to Marrakesh by following the footsteps of painters and poets of the nineteenth and twentieth century. Even self-appointed 'architects' are able to act out and realise their creative ideas in building and designing structures for foreign customers in Marrakesh. They are inspired by the Red City with its lighting and vibrant life on the streets. In 'Home and Garden' they find the requisite peace and quiet in order to be able to live out their creativity. Their everyday life revolves primarily around themselves, their products and their marketing. Insofar as 'Information and Communication' is concerned, the Self-style migrant is rarely integrated locally in the general populace of the foreign community. Instead these migrants maintain intensive contact with their customers as well as with artists and intellectuals who are present locally and globally. This lifestyle group is characterised more than any other by friendly contact with the Moroccan community.

Homo style

'Eroticism and Sex' are primary factors motivating male homosexual migrants in particular to move their place of residence to Marrakesh, since

Morocco is regarded as an open, friendly country, even though homosexuality is actually prohibited by law there. Owing to social rules in Morocco's gender-segregated society, Homo-style migrants frequently view cultural practices like individuals of the same sex holding hands in public as pleasant and liberating. They enjoy in particular the individual freedoms and sexual offerings that exist within the 'Home and Garden' group. With regard to 'Information and Communication', this lifestyle is often characterised by integration locally into a large gay community and online. The categories 'Food and Drink', 'Wellness and Fitness' and 'Fashion and Beauty' play a significant role in self-portrayal. Looking for physical gratification and new contacts has a major part in this lifestyle.

Social style

The search for social integration draws many migrants to Marrakesh, especially older people who are retired. They enjoy the attention, the feeling of recognition and respect that they get from the Moroccans in Marrakesh. The elements 'Information and Communication' are especially characteristic for the Social-style group. Many active retirees very much appreciate that the people of Marrakesh make time for tea and chatting. They are frequently able to offer the experience and skills that they have acquired during their careers and are thus valued because of that. Especially the extensive group of French elderly people is looked after and taken care of by different (in part state) organisations. In Marrakesh they are also frequently able to afford a standard of life with service personnel in 'Home and Garden', something denied to them in their home country. This lifestyle involves social recognition and the desired respect for one's age and skills.

Setting style

Marrakesh is construed as the counterpart to Europe's working world and as an exotic backdrop for a better life. This lifestyle is enjoyed primarily by the European middle class, which strives to go back in time and space. In Marrakesh the Setting-style migrant finds a better climate and cultural aspects that have been lost. 'Home and Garden' are for this group a secondary residence, where they tend to stay for shorter periods than the migrants of the previously addressed lifestyles. 'Information and Communication' here is realised with other Europeans who have common interests and speak the same language during 'Food and Drink' or 'Wellness and Fitness'. Digital media allow the migrants to integrate in Europe's communication landscape. This lifestyle is well informed about world events; actual events in Morocco usually interest this group only if they directly concern the migrants. In the Setting style, everything revolves around the permanent change between the conventional, known place of residence and work and the exotic location for relaxing.

Mobile style

This lifestyle is marked by even shorter and less frequent stays. Mobile-style migrants may be described as permanent repeat visitors, who are similar to cosmopolitans due to the technical travel options and potential communication capabilities. Marrakesh is a location, among other places in the world, where one can easily live out one's own lifestyle. 'Home and Garden' are handed over to an administrator, and 'Information and Communication' with friends and acquaintances in the world play a greater role as a catalyst for mobility than 'Eroticism and Sex', 'Food and Drink', 'Wellness and Fitness' and 'Fashion and Beauty'. Marrakesh is a location among many others that the Mobile-style migrant knows well, where one seeks closeness to other lifestyle migrants and Moroccan 'Europaphiles'. The lifestyle is characterised by the permanent change of place of residence and thus associated with a transnational network.

Posing style

Even if the Posing-style migrants do have 'Home and Garden' in the medina or real estate in the *ville nouvelle* or in the palm oasis, they usually come to Marrakesh for a short period of time. While 'Fashion and Beauty' and 'Wellness and Fitness' are paramount, 'Eroticism and Sex' cannot be omitted from this lifestyle. For the most part this group involves jet-setters, for whom Marrakesh is a 'must' like many other locations in the world so long as they are popular in their community. If the persons do not possess a riad, they stay primarily at the most expensive hotels in the city. Marrakesh is 'le dernier crie' for European and US 'high society' and a 'dirty weekend' in the pearl of the south always provides a good change. 'Information and Communication' are essential aspects of this lifestyle, since their presence would otherwise pass unnoticed. In this regard, it is very important for the self-portrayal of these visitors to Marrakesh that they are always mentioned in the 'yellow press' of various countries.

When lifestyle migrants meet locals

The mass sale of residential houses to foreigners, the way of life led by the lifestyle migrants and the presence of tourists in the guesthouses impact the existing residential buildings and the local population there in a variety of ways, as described above. For instance, residential buildings are renovated and then used in part in a different manner. The local real estate sector, job market and conditions in neighbourhoods have changed. Although, according to statements made by local population, many locals recognise advantages in the change processes unfolding in the old town, disadvantages are also cited almost in the same breath and conflicts do appear.[9] Parallels are frequently drawn to an apparent non-violent neocolonialisation of the country, emphasising one's own positive personal experience with the new arrivals from abroad and presented as opinion of the other, mainly older, generation.

As was already mentioned, many Moroccans have been directly affected by the move of lifestyle migrants to Marrakesh due to the changes on the local real estate market. While, from the viewpoint of the interviewees, buying a house was once a quick, verbal and thus unbureaucratic process that was based on trust, now tedious, bureaucratic processes are in part standard due to the legal security required by foreigners and thus involve higher costs today. The foreigners want to have a government-guaranteed land registration process (titre foncier) for security's sake and therefore surveying of the property and multiple administrative acts have become necessary. The traditional real estate agent (simsar) has been replaced by domestic and international realtors. Owing to the high profit margins, inexperienced locals are trying their hand as realtors in the hope of better earnings opportunities. Almost every piece of real estate in the medina is for sale now.

The demand on the part of comparably financially strong foreign lifestyle migrants for riads has led to a tremendous price increase on the real estate market. Many Moroccan building owners have in the hope of obtaining a high return on sales now decided to sell their properties to foreigners for profit and thus leave the medina as a place of residence or terminate existing tenancies. This has resulted in a lack or greatly reduced supply of affordable 'Rhan' tenancy agreements in the medina.[10] Many tenants in the medina are consequently forced to look for a building in residential areas outside of the medina, where Rhan tenancy agreements are still possible (see Bastos in this volume, who speaks according to Harvey of 'accumulation by dispossession'). Moroccan real estate owners in the medina profit considerably by selling residential buildings. The losers are the Moroccan tenants. Affordable rental prices can no longer be found in the medina and in the surrounding urban area.

The direct contact between the Moroccan populace and the incoming foreigners occurs mainly in the form of work and/or business relations that are based primarily on purpose. Get-togethers between neighbours are rather rare.[11] Many lifestyle migrants are employers, e.g. of workers in restaurants, private residences and guesthouses, direct or indirect employers in the renovation of a riad and/or customers of souvenir vendors, artisans, tour guides or real estate agents. While those working independently on behalf of a foreign migrant are satisfied with the negotiated pay, employees frequently complain about inadequate pay and poor work conditions (e.g. having to serve guests at 40°C on a roof terrace). Local low-skilled unemployed persons strive relatively often to develop friendly relations with foreigners, since they hope to find opportunities for work and earning money through the networks of foreigners. According to the Moroccans interviewed, the friendships do not really become close as a result of existing language barriers and different cultural perceptions. Migrants are frequently of the opinion that close relationships with Moroccans are impossible: 'You can't be friend–friend really. Having friends or deep relationships with Moroccans is impossible in my opinion.' This was also confirmed by a migrant woman from Belgium: 'The only thing that (Moroccans) are interested in is how they can make money easily without doing anything'. She further added: 'Friendship with Europeans does not exist between Moroccans … because there is always a conflict and financial interest in the back of the head of the person.' This circumstance is attributed to cultural differences and different attitudes (e.g. language, concept of time, gregariousness, propensity to talk). Many migrants seem to feel an underlying lack of acceptance or even rejection on part of the Moroccan people. In light of this, the majority of non-commercial contact between foreigners and the local population remains very distant. The Moroccans interviewed note that the often claimed hospitality and generosity of the foreigners tends to disappear with the long stay in Morocco or as a result of Moroccan spouses and that they become 'unfriendly, egoistical or just bad'. In addition to that, there are conflicts triggered by the lifestyles of foreigners who live in Morocco without family or who are homosexual or paedophilic.[12] The use of roof terraces by men and women as extended leisure areas for breakfast, eating and sunbathing is considered annoying, since such uses conflict with the traditional use of roof terraces as area reserved for women.

In turn, many lifestyle migrants have adapted their everyday behaviour outside of their residences in the medina and their contact with local neighbours over the course of the past 10 years to the generally applicable rules and regulations of the Moroccan community in the medina.

Marrakesh, paradise for lifestyle migrants on earth?

Lifestyle migrants from all over the world come to Marrakesh because they are able to fulfil, based on a subjective point of view, their search for a more satisfying and more pleasurable way of life in an individually shaped paradise. The geographic location, the old city with its neglected residential buildings, the myth of the exotic that is idealised by the mass media and the government-guaranteed legal security for real estate investments have contributed in making Morocco a top destination for lifestyle migrants. Residential buildings purchased in the medina and thus the direct physical environment are shaped with an 'oriental, exotic and idyllic touch'. For the migrants, even the intersecting social and media-based worlds of everyday life are (apparently) subject to unrestricted individualisation. The process is facilitated and encouraged by the country's colonial history, since the transformation that the state and society have experienced (European language, everyday practices and acceptance by the host community) ensure recognition and acceptance of the foreign migrants. The migrants live in a world between communities and cultures. They have settled down, isolated from the everyday life of the medina's local population in colonial, comfortable and global spheres based on the tales of the 'Arabian Nights'.

Providing the necessary living and prepared stage for helping the lifestyle migrants realise their desired ways of life, the local population and the old city of Marrakesh have undergone significant change and detriment. The structural and infrastructural transformation of the medina is usually regarded as positive, just like the creation of a new job market in the building, trade and service sectors. On the other hand, it is not possible, however, to ignore a displacement of poorer sections of the medina's population with the disappearance of inexpensive living quarters. In addition, a master–servant relationship has evolved between the lifestyle migrants and the Moroccan population, resulting in considerable interaction problems affecting aspects of daily life. The sexual exploitation especially of Morocco's youth should not go unmentioned either. Hence, the question remains to what extent these 'shadows of paradise' cloud the spheres of the lifestyle migrants in Marrakesh's medina?

Notes

1 Many of Germany's tabloid newspapers like *Bunte*, *Bild*, *Gala*, *Stern*, etc., contain a section entitled 'Lifestyle', where relevant information is provided to assist readers in shaping their lifestyles. Reference to everyday usage of the term in the German language can be seen on a wide variety of internet pages (see, for example, Digital Institut n.d.).

2 It is evident that the various analytical categories, which have been addressed and focus on 'habits, cultural practices and symbolic significance' (Postel 2005: 2), are accessible partially or to a varying degree empirically speaking (for instance public statements about sexual preferences and practices).

3 The empirical research of the German Research Foundation (DFG) funded research project "Gentrification in the Medina of Marrakech" was conducted in the years 1999, 2000, 2003, 2006, 2009 and 2012 also by interviews with student teams. More than 150 interviews in French, English, German, Italian, and Spanish with foreign migrants were carried out, recorded and analysed. Additionally, during all campaigns the property of all foreign migrants was recorded cartographically and entered into a geographical information system (GIS) (see e.g. Escher and Petermann 2009). In addition, the two authors were several times every year in the field for interviews and observations of key persons, migrants and residents).

4 Haouz is the traditional designation of the region around Marrakesh (cf. Pascon 1977). Nowadays, El Haouz stands for an administrative province to the south of Marrakesh.

5 The spheres correspond in many parts with the previously mentioned 'Marrakesh myth'. Additional spheres could exist. They do tend to overlap within everyday life.

6 Neocolonialism is more broadly understood as the continuation of mostly economic and technological dependence from politically independent countries with the Western industrialised countries (colonialism without colonies) and in a narrow sense as the continuation of direct political, economic and military presence by the old colonial power (Elsenhans 1985: 599, see Petermann 2001). In the present case, it is not so much about dependence and dominance by the state rather than on the individual–private level.

7 In this regard, they are ideal types of lifestyles that cannot be found in the clearness of the described characteristics locally. According to Weber ([1904] 1995) and Gerhardt (2001), the prevailing social reality is modelled and overdrawn such that the difference of the various styles is clear. The lifestyles are presented on the basis of empirical data, where not all aspects could be addressed and the aspects covered may be ascribed greater significance than in actuality.

8 Motives for migration are frequently distinguishing for the described phenomenon such as the concepts 'retirement migration' (Gustafson 2001), 'tourism entrepreneurship' (Lardiés 1999) or 'residential tourism' (McWatters 2009) make clear.

9 The information is based on observations made as part of a research project (1999–2012) and an empirical study from 2003, during which 32 locals were interviewed qualitatively in Arabic with regard to the relationship that the Moroccan population has to the transformation process and foreigners.

10 A 'Rhan' tenancy agreement is based on a loan transaction between the tenant and the landlord with a written loan agreement, where the tenant lends the landlord a larger sum of money for the duration of a year and receives in return a reduced rent.

11 Informal and accidental contact between the Moroccan people and foreign migrants is also complicated by Moroccan authorities. If locals have a non-professional relationship with a foreigner, they must obtain an authorisation issued by the local police authorities in order to interact with the foreigners.

12 A coalition called 'Touche pas à mon enfant' was founded in July of 2004 in response to this dictate, among other factors. Its objectives include promoting the rights of children and protecting them against sexual abuse and sexual exploitation (Tanmia 2012).

References

Anon. (2008) 'La foire des enfoirés. Gays et lesbiennes du monde s'exhibitent à Marrakech', *Maroc Hébdo International* 797: 30.

Arnold, G. (2010) 'Europäische Transmigranten in Marrakech: Die Entstehung multi- und translokaler Zuhause durch Pluralisierung von Identitäten und kultureller Hybridisierung', unpublished thesis, Johannes Gutenberg University Mainz.

Beck, U. (1983) 'Jenseits von Stand und Klasse? Soziale Ungleichheiten, gesellschaftliche Individualisierungsprozesse und die Entstehung neuer sozialer Formationen und Identitäten', in R. Kreckel (ed.) *Soziale Ungleichheiten. Soziale Welt (Sonderband 2)*, Göttingen: Schwartz.

——(1986) *Risikogesellschaft. Auf dem Weg in eine andere Moderne*, Frankfurt am Main: Edition Suhrkamp.

Benson, Michaela and O'Reilly, K. (2009a) 'Lifestyle migration: Escaping to the good life?', in M. Benson and K. O'Reilly (eds) *Lifestyle Migration: Expectations, Aspirations and Experiences*, Farnham, Surrey: Ashgate.

——(2009b) 'Migration and the search for a better way of life: A critical exploration of lifestyle migration', *The Sociological Review* 57(4): 608–25.

Cosgrove, D. E. (1998) *Social Formation and Symbolic Landscapes*, London: University of Wisconsin Press.

Digital Institut (n.d.) *Lebensstil*. www.nads.de/lebensstil/ (accessed 8 September 2012).

Elsenhans, H. (1985) 'Neokolonialismus', in D. Nohlen and R.-O. Schultze (eds) *Pipers Wörterbuch zur Politik. vol. 1: Politikwissenschaft. Theorien – Methoden – Begriffe*, Munich: Piper.

Escher, A. (2012) 'Observations sur les 'villes nouvelles' de l'époque du Protectorat dans le Royaume du Maroc du XXIe siècle', in H. Popp and M. Aït Hamza (eds) *Un siècle après le traité de Fès 1912. Bilan de la colonisation française au Maroc. Actes du 8e colloque maroco-allemand Bayreuth 2011*, Bayreuth: Selbstverlag der Naturwissenschaftlichen Gesellschaft Bayreuth e.V.

Escher, A. and Petermann, S. (2000) 'Neo-colonialism or gentrification in the Medina of Marrakech', *ISIM Newsletter* 5: 34.

——(2009) *Tausendundein Fremder im Paradies. Ausländer in der Medina von Marrakech*, Würzburg: Ergon Verlag.

Farlex Inc. (n.d.) *TheFreeDictionary*. http://de.thefreedictionary.com/selig (accessed 31 August 2012).

Geißler, R. (2002) *Die Sozialstruktur Deutschlands. Die gesellschaftliche Entwicklung vor und nach der Vereinigung*, 3rd edn, Wiesbaden: Westdeutscher Verlag.

Gerhardt, U. (2001) *Idealtypus. Zur methodischen Begründung der modernen Soziologie*, Frankfurt am Main: Suhrkamp.

Gustafson, P. (2001) 'Retirement migration and transnational lifestyles', *Ageing and society* 21(4): 371–94.

Hoey, B. B. (2005) 'Place for personhood: Individual and local character in lifestyle migration', *City and Society* 22(2): 237–61.

Hradil, S. (2005) *Soziale Ungleichheit in Deutschland*, 8th edn, Wiesbaden: VS Verlag für Sozialwissenschaften.

Khizrane, A. (2000) 'Ryad, Le nouveau must', *Medina. Maroc Magazine* 2, cover.

Kirchhoff, B. (1999) 'Taumel des Seins', *Merian* 52(2): 28–37.

Lacoste, Y. (1990) 'Wozu dient Landschaft?', in Y. Lacoste (ed.) *Geographie und politisches Handeln*, Berlin: Wagenbach.

Lardiés, R. (1999) 'Migration and tourism entrepreneurship: North-European immigrants in Cataluña and Languedoc', *International Journal of Population Geography* 5: 477–91.

Leisten, T. (1993) 'Die Gärten des Islam. Das islamische Paradies als Idealbild des Gartens', in H. Forkl *et al.* (eds) *Die Gärten des Islam*, Stuttgart and London: Ed. Mayer.

Locke, J. (2005) *Two Treatises of Government and a Letter Concerning Toleration*. Stilwell, KS: Digireads.com Publishing.

McWatters, M. R. (2009) *Residential Tourism: (De)Constructing Paradise (Tourism and Cultural Change)*. Bristol, Buffalo, NY and Toronto: Channel View Publications.

Müller, S. (2007) 'Bauboom in Marrakesch', *Handelsblatt*, 17 August: 4.

Najjar, F. (2011) *Tourismusprojekte in Marokko mit neuem Schwung. Arabische Golfstaaten gründen Tourismusfonds / Touristenzahl soll sich bis 2020 verdoppeln*. www.gtai.de/GTAI/Navigation/DE/Trade/maerkte,did=411420.html (accessed 14 October 2012).

Pascon, P. (1977) *Le Haouz de Marrakech*, 2 vols, Rabat, Tanger: Editions marocaines et internationales.

Petermann, S. (2001) 'Ausländer in der Medina von Marrakech. Gentrification oder Neokolonialismus?', unpublished thesis, University of Mainz.

——(2012) 'L'impact du Protectorat sur la sauvegarde et la valorisation touristique des médinas au Maroc', in H. Popp and M. Aït Hamza (eds) *Un siècle après le traité de Fès 1912. Bilan de la colonisation française au Maroc. Actes du 8e colloque maroco-allemand Bayreuth 2011*, Bayreuth: Selbstverlag der Naturwissenschaftlichen Gesellschaft Bayreuth e.V.

Postel, B. (2005) *Charakterisierung von Lebensstilen durch Wertorientierungen*, Potsdam: University of Potsdam. http://opus.kobv.de/ubp/volltexte/2006/1076/pdf/Potsdamer_Beitrag_Nr._23.pdf (accessed 22 October 2012).

Scemama, C. (2001) 'Marrakech: La ruée vers le riads', *L'Express international* 2612: 58–63.

Stimson, F. J. ([1908] 2004) *The Law of the Federal and State Constitutions of the United States: With an Historical Study of Their Principles, a Chronological Table of English Social Legislation, and a Comparative Digest of the Constitutions of the Forty-Six States*, Clark, NJ: The Lawbook Exchange. http://ia600409.us.archive.org/26/items/federalstatecons00stim/federalstatecons00stim.pdf (accessed 27 October 2012).

Tanmia (2012) *Touche pas à mon enfant*. www.tanmia.ma/article.php3?id_article=6385 (accessed 14 September 2012).

Torkington, K. (2010) 'Defining lifestyle migration', *Dos Algarves* 19: 99–111.

Weber, M. ([1904] 1995) *Die Objektivität sozialwissenschaftlicher und sozialpolitischer Erkenntnis*, Schutterwald, Baden: Wissenschaftlicher Verlag.

Zapf, W. *et al.* (1987) *Individualisierung und Sicherheit. Untersuchung zur Lebensqualität in der Bundesrepublik Deutschland*, Munich: Verlag C. H. Beck.

4 Territorial dispossession and indigenous rearticulation in the Chapala Lakeshore

Santiago Bastos

During these times of globalisation, international retirement migration is an important factor in the development and economic agenda of many countries in the global south, for it combines investments in tourism and real estate capital (Janoschka 2009; Jackiewicz and Crane 2010). Typically, this kind of international migration has been seen as an instrument of 'development' because of its beneficial effects on local labour markets (Truly 2002; Sunil *et al.* 2007; see also MPI 2006 for the Mexican case). However, as Croucher (2012: 5) notes, 'the debate over whether immigration leads to job loss *versus* job creation is a complicated and unsettled one'. For those who have studied the phenomenon from the place where retirement migrants settle (Lizárraga 2008; Janoschka 2009, 2012; Jackiewicz and Crane 2010; Blázquez *et al.* 2011), this uncertainty extends to its economic, political and cultural implications.

To enrich this debate, using the case of the Chapala Lakeshore and specifically, the indigenous community of Mezcala, we will see how the process and effects of residential tourism can be understood through the idea of 'accumulation by dispossession', a phrase coined by Harvey (2004) to describe how capital acts in globalisation. This case will also help us understand how resistance to these activities is a fundamental factor in recreating indigenous identity in Latin America today. My interest in the topic of international retirement migration stems from my work with the community of Mezcala in their efforts to maintain the integrity of their territory during the past four years. By studying the historical and regional framework of this phenomenon, the process experienced in the Chapala Lakeshore can be understood in terms of 'dispossession', an idea advanced by Francisco Talavera, a local researcher, three decades ago. In this way, my focus is not to study retirement migration or residential tourism, but rather to understand the processes of reinforcing identity in the context of globalisation. I hope that I can contribute to the debates in this book with such an approach.[1]

Global tourism and territorial dispossession in Chapala

The Chapala Lakeside is a residential and tourist zone located on the edge of Lake Chapala, just one hour from Guadalajara, the second largest city in

Mexico (Map 4.1). Since the late nineteenth century, the lakeshore has experienced combined processes of domestic and international tourism – expatriates, retirees and seasonal residents (Truly 2002: 262). It is one of the oldest and largest spaces for international retirement migration in Mexico and Latin America. It has the largest nucleus of North American retirees outside their countries: in 1997, Mexico's INEGI found around 7,000 permanent and 12,000 seasonal residents, while the US consulate found some 40,000 (Truly 2002: 262). This precedent was reinforced with the worldwide growth in retirement migration and the opening of the Mexican market with NAFTA and other neoliberal policies at the turn of the century (Sunil *et al.* 2007).

In this way, beginning with the centres of Ajijic and Chapala – the former more 'gringo', the latter more local – the northwest lakeshore was filled with residential projects that now saturate the entire length of the shore, from Jocotepec to Chapala itself. As a consequence, it is safe to say that real estate is the primary business of the lakeshore. North Americans and Mexicans, corporations and independent agents, compete in this market, which is evident in every page of the magazine *Lake Chapala Review* and in every street from Chapala to Jocotepec. Even by the 1970s, Talavera considered real estate to be the mainstay of 'regional development' (Talavera 1982: 10–43).

This real estate development can be understood as a process of 'accumulation by dispossession' that takes advantage of the 'rent and price differential'

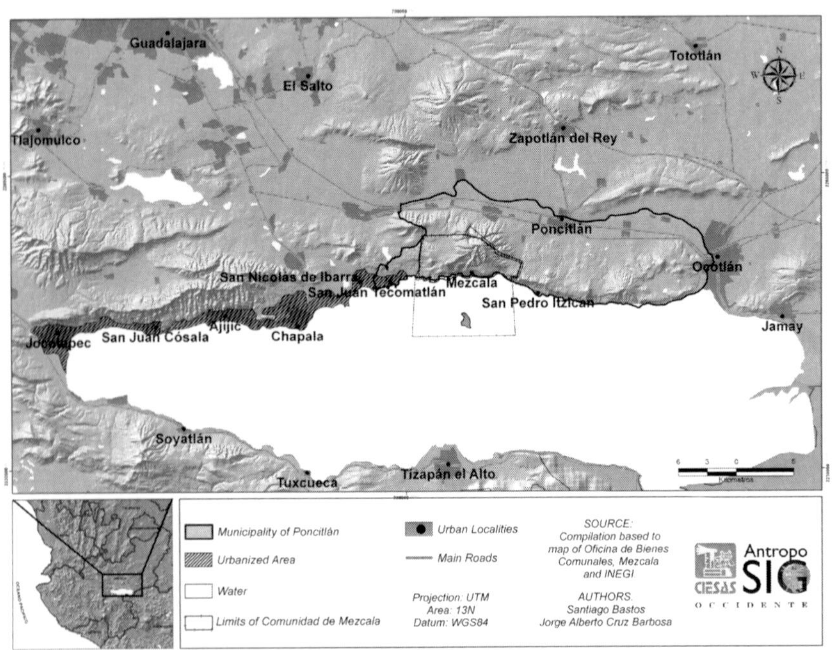

Map 4.1 The Ribera de Chapala and Mezcala

(Blázquez *et al.* 2011: 4) and the economic vulnerability of local property owners. As is usually the case, the business was directly related to the difference between what they pay subsistence farmers for properties and what the firms can extract in capital gains by putting those properties on the real estate market. In Ajijic, properties were purchased at US$1.50 or US$2.00 per square metre; once urbanised, they sold at US$200 to US$400 per square metre, and a summer house could sell for US$45,000 (Talavera 1982: 54). A few decades ago in Tecomatlán, the North American Donald Dwyer paid '12 or 13 million old pesos for an eight-hectare field' where today 'there is a development for retired U.S. Americans and Canadians who live in houses valued between $300,000 and $500,000. But Don has many more lots.'[2] This differential means that we can speak of a 'negative reciprocity' (Garibay and Balzaretti, 2009: 93): what they pay the peasants for their land practically implies giving 'nothing in exchange' in comparison with what they will later receive for that same land.

This strategy is possible not only because of the poverty of the property owners but also because the construction was on lots that were part of *ejidos* – communally owned land. Legal vagueness allowed these lands to be purchased at very low prices or even directly dispossessed with the support of several state authorities who fully backed and benefited from this market (Talavera 1982), which 'exploits the deficiencies in (local) economies' (Jackiewicz and Crane 2010: 23).

This economic path to dispossession is complemented by violations of local laws. There are numerous examples of illegal operations, but the best-known case is the struggle of the indigenous community of Ajijic, lasting from 1945 to the 1970s, against the purchase of part of their territory by a developer from Guadalajara.[3] Although all of the judicial resolutions ruled in their favour, the agrarian and municipal authorities never recognised the indigenous communities as the owners of the land; this land ultimately became *La Floresta*, one of the best-known and most exclusive developments in Ajijic (Talavera 1982: 75–133). The result of this process is that the entire northwestern shore of Lake Chapala is now practically filled with residential tourist developments. The local real estate market has been completely altered by the housing demand of these immigrants: the use of land (Talavera 1982) and prices themselves (Banks 2004: 376) have changed. What is more, the majority of real estate businesses are foreign, usually US owned (Lizárraga 2008: 101). This physical dispossession of territory through structural poverty is complemented by 'ecological displacement' (Talavera 1982: 10 and 59–65): the population has lost its peasant character and depends economically on the jobs generated by residential tourism, such that Ajijic turned into a 'town of domestic workers' (*ibid*: 62). For decades now, these residents have controlled not only the real estate market but also the entire economic sector linked to residential tourism (Talavera 1982: 58). The flourishing businesses are not owned by locals, but by the very immigrants, or at best by locals and *caciques* (*ibid*: 49). As Banks (2004: 376–77) notes:

> The lakeshore economy is dominated by expatriate consumer demands; local fishing commerce has disappeared as opportunities in the service sector have appeared. Local prices for housing (usually in U.S. dollars), restaurants, hotels, and the majority of goods, are higher than prices in areas with retirees.

As for the idea that foreign residents settling in local spaces generates a 'trickle-down' economic effect through consumption and demand for local jobs (Truly 2002; Sunil *et al.* 2007), the evidence suggests otherwise, as in Tecomatlán:

> They were always told that the arrival of investors was good, for there would be jobs and their quality of life would improve. For their wives, they managed to obtain jobs as domestic workers, and for the young people, as gardeners.[4]

The arrival of residential tourism has not meant 'development' for the inhabitants of the Chapala lakeshore. Installing services meant an increase in the cost of life (Talavera 1982: 58), but the jobs generated by the arrival of residents are paid according to the local 'peasant' market, not to the 'modern' market of the residents' home countries.[5] In this way, the Chapala Lakeshore is a symbol of how becoming a centre for residential tourism radically transformed the lives of locals by dispossessing them of their traditional means of subsistence and forms of social organisation. But it did not improve their lives. We can understand what did occur as a 'dispossession of social patrimony (land, resources, wealth, rights) of a social group placed in a specific geography', which is how Harvey (quoted in Garibay 2010: 2) characterises 'accumulation by dispossession'. It is also an 'ecological dispossession ... a violent rupture between the native population and its natural habit ... the definitive break for the Lakeshore locals with regard to their means of production: land, water, flora, fauna, etc. ... The relationship that they now have is exclusively determined by their condition of selling their labor' (Talavera 1982: 10).

Mezcala: community, territory and dispossession

What is happening in Mezcala is a concrete example of how to carry out dispossession in today's world, circumventing a piece of legislation created to prevent such a dispossession. Here, we will describe the concrete strategies used by real estate firms and authorities and the reaction that these strategies have provoked among Mezcalenses. This small town and its two islands – with 6,215 inhabitants, according to INEGI (2010) – are part of the municipality of Poncitlán, and the town is situated on the northeastern shore of Lake Chapala. It is the only case in the region where indigenous identity and social behaviours associated with that identity have been maintained into the present, even though Mezcala has not been recognised as an 'indigenous community' by the authorities because of the lack of certain traits like an indigenous language. The history of permanence in the territory is what sustains this identity – 'we are indigenous because we have been here since time immemorial' (Bastos 2010) – and the Agrarian Community is currently the most important institutional support for this identity, which is manifested in their social organisation and in a dense, ritual festival calendar (Moreno 2008; Bastos 2011).

In 1971, the Mezcalenses obtained recognition as an 'indigenous community' according to agrarian legislation, whereby the post-revolutionary state sanctioned the historically communal character of their territory.[6] Because this territory is 'inalienable', only people from Mezcala can own land within their community. The members of the Agrarian Community (*comuneros*) are responsible for the local territorial integrity. In this way, as opposed to the case of Ajijic, agrarian legislation did serve to protect the territorial integrity of Mezcala, which did remain relatively free from the dynamics of dispossession for several decades thanks to its geographical location. But since the turn of this century, the arrival of new waves of residents (Sunil *et al.* 2007), and the saturation of the constructed environment between Chapala and Jocotepec, contributed to real estate pressure making its way to the municipality of Poncitlán. Mezcala came to be part of the tourist area of the Chapala Lakeshore. This moment coincided with the end of the corporativist state and the enactment of neoliberal policies that seek to put 'social property' on the market and do away with special treatment for peasants (Warman 2003; Hernández *et al.* 2004).

In Mezcala, this meant that a highway to Chapala was finally built in 2002, something that had been requested 30 years before. In 2005, the Secretary of Agrarian Reform tried to apply PRODERE, a programme implemented to favour privatisation of social property.[7] But the assembly of *comuneros* decided not to join this programme, for they did not want to lose their lands (Moreno 2008). Despite this, in 2006, the municipal authorities in Poncitlán unveiled their Plan for Territorial Organisation in Mezcala, which designated areas as 'medium density tourist hotel zones' and 'medium density residential zones' (Gobierno Municipal de Poncitlán 2006).

Despite all of these efforts, real estate capital was not able to enter Mezcala through a strategy based on the economic differential between property markets. Because of this, investors have sought to dispossess through 'predation, fraud, and violence' (Harvey 2004: 112) and by 'obtaining benefits with *impunity*' (Garibay 2010): overstepping both the laws that protect this territory as communal, and the wishes of the property's legal owners.

In fact, real estate pressure arrived through illegal dispossession before it did through government programmes: in 1999, Guillermo Moreno Ibarra, a businessman from Guadalajara, illegally occupied a lot in the summit known as El Pandillo. Because of this, the Community initiated proceedings for restitution of lands through the agrarian tribunals. As locals in Ajijic had done a half century before, locals began a long, difficult and expensive legal process, delayed and boycotted at every step, as the Assembly of *Comuneros* has denounced other abuses and illegal activity in various official channels (Hipólito 2012). This impunity was also visible when authorities revealed their plans to make Mezcala a tourist destination. In 2005, the National Institute of Anthropology and History (INAH), the Jalisco Ministry of Culture (SCJ) and the municipality of Poncitlán began work to restore the island of Mezcala, with the excuse of commemorating the 'defense of the island', a historical event in which Mezcalenses successfully challenged royal power from 1812 to 1816 (Archer 1998; Ochoa 1985, 2006). Again, they did this without respecting the communal nature of the island or even notifying the *comuneros*, who then began a campaign to denounce the tourists' use of their territory and their history that the authorities planned for their island (Moreno 2008; Bastos 2011).

Facing these threats to territorial integrity, the *comuneros* attempted to use agrarian and constitutional legality, and they navigated political channels in nearby Guadalajara and in indigenous spaces to denounce the assault on their territory. A process of generational renewal and expansion of the Communal Assembly also began, mobilising more than 200 people each week for more than two years (Moreno 2008; Bastos 2010), and this process is still under way.

Strategies of impunity

Facing this response, 'the Invader' – as the *comuneros* have dubbed the forces trying to dispossess them of their lands – and the authorities who support urbanising the territory have acted to stop the growing organised opposition. On the one hand, they have sought what Garibay calls the 'communal capture' trying 'to subordinate the local population to interests established by an external power and the dissolution of the community as a "social subject"' (Garibay 2010: 18). In the 2008 Agrarian Community elections, as tensions regarding the projects on the island and the Pandillo summit ran high, surprisingly, a group of candidates supported by the 'pro-development' actors won. The conflict that ensued after the *comuneros* did not recognise these candidates because of lack of activity and managed to dissolve the community's authority and create an internal division with two parallel boards of directors. In the following elections in 2011, they again manipulated loyalty, this time with the clear support of the Agrarian Attorney, to install a new board of directors who would neutralise the *comuneros*' mobilisation. The newly elected board proposed abandoning the Pandillo suit, approving incorporation in PROCEDE, and accepting the Mezcala Municipal Urbanisation Plan. The *comuneros* who met in the Assembly rejected all of this.

These projects show the intent of different actors, who now include the Ministry of Agrarian Reform acting through the Agrarian Attorney, to urbanise the territory. In order to control the communal institutional machinery, they have not only spent money, but also resorted to intimidation and illegal acts: in October 2009, a group broke into the Agrarian Community's office accompanied by 10 police officers from Poncitlán and by Moreno Ibarra himself. In 2011, they turned to physical intimidation and the use of the law to convert many of the *comuneros* into criminals in order to stop them; here Moreno Ibarra participated in a much more direct manner. On 21 April of that year, a group of *comuneros* and *comuneras*, acting on orders from the assembly, went to dismantle a metal structure that Moreno had built on communal territory; they were met with shots fired from their own 'property' and were harassed by a Poncitlán Municipal Police patrol. It was not the first time that people from Mezcala received threats from the group of hired thugs that this person had brought together to watch over his property, nor was it unusual for these men to threaten people passing by the property.[8] This time, though, their actions were more open and more threatening: Moreno himself supervised the entire 'operation', and he threatened and shot at a family who passed by. The *comuneros* filed a complaint against the intimidation, but Guillermo Moreno had filed a complaint first in the Criminal Court against 14 *comuneros* for 'damage to items'. On Tuesday, 6 September, Rocío Moreno – a young *comunera* and leader in the mobilisation – was wrongfully arrested in Guadalajara, even though it had been established that she was never involved in that activity. She was released without charges but 10 *comuneros* remained imprisoned and five of them were not even listed in the complaint. On 25 October, three young *comuneros* were detained in the central plaza in Mezcala by the Poncitlán Municipal Police, and they were accused of having taken some documents from the Communal House. All this time, Moreno Ibarra had arrived in Mezcala surrounded by armed men and women who had intimidated the *comuneros* in the Assemblies. In this way, to break apart the *comuneros*' united opposition to the occupation of their lands, Moreno Ibarra and his allies used a combination of strategies: bribing communal authorities, intimidation, impunities and legal manoeuvring. The punitive aspect of the law has been used as a complement to direct intimidation with weapons, and both of these approaches have been directly supported by judicial and municipal authorities.

Community, conflict and rearticulation

All of these activities have impacted daily life and community dynamics in Mezcala, dynamics already marked by precarious living conditions in the context of globalisation (Bastos 2010). Within the town, there are different positions with regard to the benefits and drawbacks of keeping the lands closed to outside property owners, and these distinct positions have been represented even among the *comuneros* historically. But up to the present, the different opinions on these topics had not led to physical confrontation or legal action between them. Now, the logic of diverse interests has been imposed upon them, to support and draw support from those who no longer wish to maintain the communal designation for the lands because they no longer live there or because they need money.[9] With this, the conflict between real estate interests and agrarian legality became a conflict among the Mezcalense *comuneros*, showing one of the most perverse facets of globalisation: cannibalism as a way in which the excluded devour each other through the violence inflicted on subordinate sectors *by themselves against themselves.*[10] But in the midst of these tensions, after a decade of pressure and conflicts, Mezcalenses have managed to keep residential tourism from occupying their lands. This is due in large part to a shared belief that is frequently expressed: 'We don't want to end up like the people from Ajijic, as servants to those who now have our lands.' Mezcalenses realised that the problem was not only one of losing control over their territory, but also that losing the land meant losing a whole way of life linked to a space imbued with a concrete meaning. This has been expressed in rebuilding the community around the Agrarian Community, which has been reinforced and is transforming its identity.

The institutional and generation renewal began when the *comuneros* realised the magnitude of the threats to the integrity of their territory – the Community's very raison d'être – and they have found support in a group of young people who had been working as the 'Mezcala Collective' since the early 2000s as part of a 'civil' Zapatismo—the 6th Declaration of the Selva Lacandona, the Other Campaign, and the National Indigenous Congress (CNI).[11] Beginning in 2006, a process of renewal and expansion of the members of the Assembly of *Comuneros* was initiated – something that had never been done before. At the same time, they were drafting a new Community Statute. The opposition to the Pandillo invasion and the reconstruction of the island became symbols of a struggle based on memory and indigenous identity. Currently, they are preparing a proposal for 'communal tourism' that would benefit Mezcalenses in a process of autonomous construction. The key to the Mezcala *comuneros*' staunch defence of the territory is that their struggle goes beyond the material. For the investors and the authorities in Poncitlán and Guadalajara, these mountains only have a utilitarian value, as a resource that generates capital gains (Garibay 2010: 8). They act as if what they have before them is an empty space, without people or history (Arias 2009). But of course, there are both: for the Mezcalenses, this history is what gives them strength to oppose the dispossession, and the community land is not a mere resource, it is *their territory*, endowed with a meaning beyond its materiality. It is the base of their identity as Mezcalenses and as indigenous people.

The conflict for the Island reveals these meanings. For the reconstruction team, the space was nothing more than something to take over and give commercial value to. But for the *comuneros,* the Island is 'the heart of the community', and they reclaim it as a central part of their history (Bastos 2012). The symbolic elements are just as important or more so than the merely economic elements in their demands. Indigenous identity anchors them to the land and to the memory of their ancestors, and it gives meaning to their struggle.

> Our ancestors gave us and entrusted the Coca people of Mezcala with water, land, forests, pastures, springs, plants, animals, agriculture, dances; everything that is in the territory, and that says that if we don't do this well, the heart of the land will be paralyzed, and that our past, our present, and our future as a people depends on this.[12]

This identity is in the process of transforming as an effect of the conflict itself. This change is manifested in the Mezcala proposal to be a community belonging to the *Coca People* (Moreno 2008), that is, an *indigenous people* with ancestral rights to the land and to self-government (Bastos 2011).[13] They continue to defend the land as indigenous people, but with a renewed purpose: they defend in the name of the rights of the *Coca People of Mezcala* and supported by the international treaties that defend those rights.

In this way, when the institutions and the legitimacy of the post-revolutionary state are no longer useful for maintaining the territory's integrity, the 'community' can no longer be understood as an agrarian authority, but rather as part of an indigenous people. Being an indigenous people is understood in a new way, in accordance with the projects developed in recent decades by the indigenous movement in Latin America, and in Mexico, specifically by the Zapatistas (Hernández *et al.* 2004). Autonomy becomes the paradigm from which history is reinterpreted and demands are put forth (Burguete 2010), and, in this case, autonomy is a new way of giving meaning to defending the land now combined with the right to self-government. The very pressure on the territory becomes a reinforcing factor for indigenous identity.

Conclusions: dispossession, globalisation and indigenous peoples

In this text, we have seen international retirement migration from a somewhat different perspective. In fact, we have approached this topic from the end of the story: as an element that ends up politically mobilising the indigenous people of Mezcala. By paying attention to the forms of action and the long-term effects of residential migration, we can access perspectives that link the territorial, economic and political, moving beyond the general but short-sighted vision of local job growth. This can help to open new discussions to study this phenomenon in other settings, with at least three possible questions: how does it occur, what consequences does it have, and what reactions might it provoke? What we have seen in the Chapala Lakeshore is how a flourishing residential tourist business is based in part on the great benefits obtained in spaces where structural poverty and peasant culture lead to those peasants selling properties at prices far lower than those obtained by the real estate market. To increase this profit, business is conducted without even a modicum of respect for the land's owners, manipulating the country's laws to put them in the service of particular interests. This is what Harvey (2004) refers to when he defines this form of accumulation as 'dispossession': it is achieved through a combination of economic and extra-economic coercion.

All of this activity is made possible by the participation of some authorities who actively and passively support the investors, although their actions go against the laws in force (Blázquez *et al.* 2011). They use the law as a double standard in which some must obey each and every legal requirement to defend their lands, while others are encouraged to use the laws in an arbitrary and coercive manner. The authorities are an 'interested party' in perverting the rule of law for the sake of capital investment. It is the 'political moment' of accumulation by dispossession (Harvey 2004).

Capitalists and authorities always say that their investments – real estate investments, in this case – are going to 'deliver the local population from backwardness' and 'bring them progress'. Dispossession needs this discourse: thanks to this appeal to development, circumventing the law and the will of individuals is permitted and even garners society's approval, for the discourse makes the opposition seem backward or criminal. But we have seen that developed investment does not guarantee 'progress' for these communities. On the contrary, they suffer a second dispossession, the 'ecological' one (Talavera 1982), when they lose control of their ways of life and begin to depend on others. And they do not manage to overcome poverty. As the *comuneros* from Mezcala have already realised, the people of Ajijic are now the servants of those who possess the lands that they once owned. That is what is perverse about the 'progress' argument: to be profitable, the tourist real estate business does not need 'modern' citizens on the same level as the residents, but rather poor peasants who ultimately become servants, always poor.

These behaviours are based on a vision of space as a product, something evident from the lens of capital. But the 'Indians' – like many other local groups – have another version of their territory: for them, it is a source of identity and of their very existence. From this perspective, they oppose practices of dispossession, in an unforeseen way, and they are able to put the brakes on the capacity of capital dispossession using these new understandings of legitimacy.

When the institutions and the legitimacy of the state are useless for maintaining the integrity of the territory, the Mezcalense *comuneros* recreate and update their understanding of being indigenous. They identify themselves as part of a *pueblo originario*, an original people, which has the right to self-government, to protect its territory, and to an autonomy that they are willing to defend. Mezcala's resistance and capacity for mobilisation is shared with many indigenous communities on the continent who fight to defend their territory and their identity against the onslaught of global capital. In contrast to the multicultural recognition projects of the States (Burguete 2010), the contents of this project endow the indigenous person with a renewed resistance, construction of autonomy and questioning of the neoliberal model.

Thus, viewing retirement migration from the effects it unleashes on the places where retirees settle, we can bring several topics to the debate. From an economic perspective, we can see this migration as part of the dynamics of this globalised world that, in its current phase, can certainly be characterised in terms of 'dispossession'. From a political point of view, beyond the concrete actions of the migrants, residential tourism can be understood as a phenomenon that implies a series of aggressions and injustices, and one that maintains inequality and impunity. For this reason, it generates a reaction from a local population increasingly aware of the strategies of transnational capital and its local, allied actors. Finally, from a cultural standpoint, instead of promoting the dissolution of difference in 'global homogeneity', retirement migration ultimately sparks the reinforcement and politicisation of identities, including indigenous identities.

In this way, as stated initially, international retirement migration can be an important factor in the places that it touches – not so much for its 'development' effects, but for the reactions that it can come to generate because of the way that it has developed as a part of global capitalism. In this sense, we cannot separate this migration from either the recreation of structures of inequality or the emergence of actors who fight against those structures.

Notes

1 This work has been ethnographic, based on interviews, collected documents, and above all in participant observation in the processes and political and ritual activities in these communities during the past few years.
2 Agustín del Castillo: *El periódico*, 23 March, 2009.
3 Agrarian legislation prohibits the sale of lands belonging to Agrarian Communities and *ejidos* to individuals outside those groups (Rojas 2007).
4 Agustín del Castillo: *El periódico*, 23 March, 2009.
5 Part of the 'attraction' of living in Chapala is how 'cheap' it is to live in Mexico, and immigrants recognize this. Sunil *et al.* (2007: 497) mention that 88 per cent of those surveyed said that they were in Mexico because of the low cost of living.
6 The 'community' is one form of social property recognised in Mexican agrarian legislation. As opposed to the *ejido*, it is not composed of lands granted by the state, but rather of lands 'restored' or 'recognised' as property that had historically belonged to the community (Rojas 2007).
7 PROCEDE (Ejidal Certification Program) is an instrument implemented by the Ministry of Agrarian Reform to develop the reform to Article 27 of the Constitution, which seeks to end the social property inherited from the Mexican revolution to give juridical certainty to social property and promote its privatisation.
8 Among the activities to denounce the invasion, in February 2008, a meeting in El Pandillo was organised, next door to the 'property'. At this meeting, the Assembly of *Comuneros* invited people from social movements in Guadalajara. They were met with shots and threats on this occasion as well (Moreno 2008).
9 As always, these matters are hard to prove, but in Mezcala there is talk of a $450,000 cheque given to the new authorities as a reward for their services, and that the Agrarian Inspector has also received something.
10 Manuela Camus, personal communication, 25 October 2011.
11 The 6th Declaration of the Selva Lacandona, issued by the Zapatista Army of National Liberation (EZLN) in June 2005, was a call to Mexican civil society to launch what would later be called the Other Campaign as a political alternative to the parties that were then competing in the presidential elections.

12 Don Cirilo Rojas, President of the Indigenous Coca Community of Mezcala de la Asunción. Speech given in the town plaza to introduce the book *Mezcala ¡Se querían llevar la isla!*, 12 June 2010.

13 The ethno-historic evidence (Baus de Czitromn 1982) reveals that, among the wide diversity of the inhabitants of what is now Western Mexico, the area where Mezcala is located belonged to the Coca seigniory of Poncitlán. Because of the Nahua influence and the later de-Indianisation of the zone, aspects like language were lost.

References

Archer, Christon I. (1998) 'The Indian insurgents of Mezcala Island on the Lake Chapala Front 1812–16', in S. Schroerder (ed.) *Native Resistance and the Pax Colonial in New Spain*, Lincoln, NE: University of Nebraska.

Arias, P. (2009) *Del arraigo a la diáspora: dilemas de la familia rural*, Mexico City: Porrua/UdeG.

Banks, S. P. (2004) 'Identity narratives by American and Canadian retirees in Mexico' *Journal of Cross-Cultural Gerontology*, 19: 361–81.

Bastos, S. (2010) 'Mezcala ante la globalización: renovando los amarres de la historia' in J. Cajas (ed.) *Migración, procesos productivos, identidad y estigmas sociales*, Mexico City: Universidad Autónoma del Estado de Morelos.

——(2011) 'La nueva defensa de Mezcala: un proceso de recomunalización a través de la renovación étnica', *Relaciones. Estudios de Historia y Sociedad*, 125(32), Zamora: El Colegio de Michoacán.

——(coordinator) (2012) *Mezcala: La memoria y el futuro. La defensa de la Isla en el Bicentenario*, Mexico City: Publicaciones de la Casa Chata, CIESAS.

Baus de Czitromn, C. (1982) *Tecuexes y Cocas. Dos grupos de la región Jalisco en el siglo XVI*, Mexico City: Colección científica, 112. INAH.

Blázquez, M., Cañada, E. and I. Murray (2011) 'Búnker playa-sol. Conflictos derivados de la construcción de enclaves de capital transnacional turístico español,' *El Caribe y Centroamérica*, Scripta Nova, 15(368).

Burguete, A. (2010) 'Autonomía: la emergencia de un nuevo paradigma en las luchas por la descolonización en América Latina', in M. González, A. Burguete and P. Ortiz (eds) *La autonomía a debate. Autogobierno indígena y Estado plurinacional en América Latina*, Quito: FLACSO, GTZ, IWGIA, CIESAS, UNICH.

Croucher, S. (2012) 'Privileged mobility in an age of globality,' *Societies* 2(1): 1–13.

De Ita, A. (2003) 'México: impactos del Procede en los conflictos agrarios y la concentración de la tierra,' www.landaction.org/gallery/Mon%20PaperMEXICOSpan.pdf.

Garibay, C. (2010) 'Paisajes de acumulación minera por desposesión campesina en el México actual', in *Ecología Política de la minería en México.* Centro de Investigaciones Interdisciplinaria en Ciencias y Humanidades: UNAM.

Garibay, C. and Balzaretti, A. (2009) 'Goldcorp y la reciprocidad negativa en el paisaje minero de Mezcala, Guerrero', *Desacatos. Revista de Antropología Social*, 30: 91–110.

Gobierno Municipal de Poncitlán (2006) 'Plan de Desarrollo Urbano del Centro de población de Mezcala de la Asunción', Gaceta, Información con sentido. *Órgano informativo del Gobierno Municipal de Poncitlán*, no. 2, November.

Harvey, D. (2004) 'El 'nuevo' imperialismo: acumulación por desposesión'. http://es.scribd.com/doc/16303286/Harvey-David-El-nuevo-imperialismo-Acumulacion-por-desposesion-2004 (accessed 18 October 2012).

Hernández, R. A., Sarela P. and Sierra, M. T. (2004) *El Estado y los indígenas en tiempos del PAN: Neoindigenismo, legalidad e identidades*, Porrúa, Mexico City: CIESAS

Hipólito H. A. (2012) 'Mezcala: La lucha por la defensa del Cerro del Pandillo. Historia reciente de una resistencia contra el despojo', unpublished, Universidad de Guadalajara.

Jackiewicz, E. and Crane, J. (2010) 'Destination Panama: An Examination of the Migration-Tourism-Foreign Investment Nexus', *Recreation, Society in Africa, Asia and Latin America*, 1(1): 5–29.

Janoschka, M. (2009) 'The contested spaces of lifestyle mobilities. Regime analysis as a tool to study political claims in Latin American retirement destinations', *Die Erde* 140(3): 1–20.

——(2012) 'Nuevas geografías migratorias en América Latina: Prácticas de ciudadanía en un destino de turismo residencial', *Scripta Nova XVI*, accepted for publication.

Lizárraga, O. (2008) 'La inmigración de jubilados estadounidenses en México y sus prácticas transnacionales. Estudio de caso en Mazatlán, Sinaloa y Cabo San Lucas, Baja California Sur', *Migración y desarrollo,* Segundo Semestre.

Moreno, R. (2008) 'La comunidad indígena coca de Mezcala, el sujeto de la historia en la defensa de la tierra', unpublished thesis, Universidad de Guadalajara.

MPI (Migration Policy Institute) (2006) *America's Emigrants. US Retirement Migration to Mexico and Panama*. www.migrationpolicy.org/pubs/americas_emigrants.pdf (accessed 18 October 2012).

Ochoa, Á. (1985) *Los insurgentes de Mezcala*, Zamora: El Colegio de Michoacán,

——(2006) *Los insurrectos de Mezcala y Marcos*, Zamora: El Colegio de Michoacán.

Rojas T. (2007) 'Las tierras comunales en México', in T. Rojas and R. Olmedo (eds) *Guía de restitución y dotación de tierras y de Reconocimiento, confirmación y titulación de bienes comunales del AGN*, Mexico City: CIESAS

Sunil, T. S., Rojas, V. and Bradley, D. E. (2007) 'United States' international retirement migration: The reasons for retiring to the environs of Lake Chapala, Mexico', *Ageing and Society,* 27(4): 489–510.

Talavera, F. (1982) *Lago de Chapala, Turismo Residencial y Campesinado.* Colección Científica n° 105 INAH. Guadalajara: Instituto Nacional de Antropología e Historia, Centro Regional de Occidente.

Truly, D. (2002) 'International retirement migration and tourism along the Lake Chapala Riviera: Developing a matrix of retirement migration behavior', *Tourism Geographies,* 4(3): 261–81.

Warman, A. (2003) *Los indios mexicanos en el umbral del milenio*, Mexico City: Fondo de Cultura Económica.

5 Lifestyle migrants in Spain

Contested realities of political participation

Michael Janoschka and Rafael Durán

Introduction

The transnational mobility undertaken by lifestyle migrants does not only have important impacts in the social, cultural, architectonical, economic and linguistic landscapes at the destinations as described in earlier chapters of this book. Additionally, it may also seriously alter different dimensions of the local political life, especially in municipalities that have higher concentrations of lifestyle migrants and in places where conflicts about land use policies and more generally, the appropriation of urban space take place (Janoschka 2009a, 2010a, 2011a; Huete and Mantecón 2012). Hence, different forms of often conflictive community involvement and political association have been reported from destinations in the Americas (Blazquez *et al.* 2011; Janoschka 2009b, 2011b, 2013; McHugh *et al.* 2002). But it is within the European Union and especially in Spain where the political participation and representation of lifestyle migrants has generalised during the last decade. The ratification and implementation of the Treaty of Maastricht did not only expand the freedom of residence and the mobility of capital and labour, but also established new forms of citizenship contesting some of the common notions of citizenship, especially the relation between specific entitlements and the nation-state as a polity (Wiener 1998). In other words, some important citizenship rights such as the possibility to vote and to stand as a candidate in municipal elections do not relate any longer exclusively to the membership of the citizen to a specific nation-state (Day and Shaw 2002), but include the possibility to participate politically in places different from one's nationality. This means that lifestyle migrants and other mobile citizens residing anywhere in the European Union can participate actively in local elections (both as voters and candidates) and thus express their demands within the formal arena of local politics – an aspect that is impossible in other destinations outside the European Union. As described by Janoschka (2008), lifestyle migrants often count on powerful tools, know-how and resources to transform their demands into political mobilisation and organisation, and they may take leadership within local politics, i.e. through formal representation in local parliaments and other forms of participation.

These circumstances open a fascinating field of research about the consequences that lifestyle migration has for the local political sphere, both from a conceptual perspective (e.g. addressing citizenship studies and the meaning of European citizenship) and an empirical viewpoint (e.g. observing the transformation of local governance regimes in migration societies). Given the fact that Spain is the most important European destination for lifestyle migrants, the political participation observed here can be considered prototypical for wider areas of the European Union. At the same time it characterises an important 'social laboratory' for a theoretically focused research approach regarding the outcome of the European political integration, the dispositions of free movement as a living example of the embodiment of a new transnational world (Favell and Recchi 2009) and the ways European citizens living in a country different from their nationality make use of their citizenship rights, participate actively and are represented formally in local politics. These aspects will be discussed subsequently, concerning the contested realities that develop when European lifestyle migrants residing in Spain put into practice their right to participate in the local government.

With regard to this, it is important to bear in mind that different forms of political mobilisation often canalise the complaints about deficiencies in the provision of public services in order to object to local development strategies. New political formations, protest organisations and even grassroots movements evolved among lifestyle migrants, and they possess resources (i.e. time and networks) to adopt winning strategies (Janoschka 2009). In many villages and towns, the vote of lifestyle migrants and of other migrants entitled to vote is decisive for the outcome of local elections (Durán 2011). As a consequence, lifestyle migrants have founded parties in dozens of municipalities during the last decade, and foreign councillors are now a common part of the political stage in many coastal towns and villages throughout Spain. In other words, EU foreigners have seriously challenged the dominant discourses, the composition and the path dependencies of local politics (Janoschka 2011b). However, such participation is at the same time a contested and conflictive reality of the practice of European citizenship that relates to important questions within mainstream migration studies, among others of how local political regimes integrate and permit (typically ethnic) minorities to participate in politics (Bird *et al.* 2011; Maxwell 2012; Bermudez 2010; Øostergaard-Nielsen 2011). But the case of political participation and representation of lifestyle migrants develops this debate further: in many municipalities lifestyle migrants constitute between two-thirds and four-fifths of the population, and in such cases the debates should not relate any longer to the integration of 'minorities' but consider the creation of new political and social relations to live together in such postmodern, multinational and multicultural societies. In this regard, it is surprising that the contested realities of political participation of lifestyle migrants have been addressed only in a few publications so far (Collard 2010; Ferbrache 2011; Janoschka 2010b; Durán 2005, 2011).

In order to approach this gap, we structure our arguments presented here as follows: after a short presentation of the research methodologies applied in the empirical studies regarding the political geographies of lifestyle migration to Spain in the framework of the research projects EURO_CITI[1] and MIRES,[2] we will present and discuss some of the key results. In both projects, special attention was paid to different forms of local political participation and representation in Spanish coastal municipalities in which predominantly elderly European lifestyle migrants reside. The empirical debate carried out will give us a panorama about three key issues that are pursued here: (i) quantifying and analysing the electoral turnout of lifestyle migrants in local elections in Spain; (ii) analysing the political representation of lifestyle migrants after the different local elections in Spain; and (iii) characterising and interpreting the role that foreign candidates and foreign voters have in different local political constellations. In a final step, the results of this research will then be interpreted against a conceptual frame that considers the political participation of lifestyle migrants in Spain as a practice of European citizenship.

Political participation and representation of lifestyle migrants in Spain: methodological considerations

This chapter is based on the exhaustive analysis of different statistical and empirical data that refer to the contested realities of political participation of European lifestyle migrants in Spain. In a first step, we approach the phenomenon through an analysis of official statistical data that are provided by the Spanish National Statistics Institute (INE), especially the population census *(Padrón Municipal)* and the electoral census for foreigners (CERE). In this regard, it is important to clarify a couple of aspects to understand the constraints and possibilities for EU foreigners to vote and stand as candidates in local elections. To begin with, the electoral law is a major constraint for foreign citizens who live in Spain, because different from Spaniards, foreigners have to state explicitly their intention to vote. They can vote and stand as a candidate only if they register on the electoral census at least four months in advance.

Apart from this, it is important to state that the official data collection about electoral participation in Spain does not differentiate aspects such as age or nationality. This means that no social scientist can be certain about the electoral turnout of foreigners. In other words, any research about the electoral participation of foreigners can only approximate the participation figures from the electoral census. In this regard, it is important to remember that data about registration should not be confused with voting output. Based on these reflections, our research recognises the need to provide additional empirical data about the scope of electoral participation by lifestyle migrants.

Bearing this in mind, in the course of the research projects EURO_CITI and MIRES a representative household survey was carried out, covering some of the mentioned gaps in research. Between April 2010 and February 2011, 720 face-to-face interviews with European lifestyle migrants were carried out in more than 50 municipalities using a questionnaire translated into English, German, French and Spanish. The distribution of the questionnaires followed a quota that aimed at reproducing the officially registered population with regard to regional proportions, nationalities, age structure and gender. In order to make the random household selection viable in organisational terms, only municipalities with a share of migrants from the EU-15 member states (plus Norway and Switzerland) of at least 15 per cent of the registered population were taken into consideration. Additionally, we explicitly avoided interviewing short- or long-term tourists – respondents only qualified for the survey if they had lived at least three months in Spain during the year previous to development of the survey. However, the research was carried out in the seven most important regional destinations of this intra-European mobility in Spain (the Autonomous Communities of Andalusia, Balearic Islands, Canary Islands, Catalonia, Murcia and Valencia) that concentrates approximately 90 per cent of the total target population (European lifestyle migrants aged at least 50 years) living in Spain.

Finally, and in addition to this survey, we also carried out a series of qualitative interviews to triangulate our data and provide more nuanced insights into the realities that elected foreign councillors experience. Such analysis is based upon 51 qualitative interviews with local councillors (of which 34 were foreigners and 17 Spaniards), focusing on political participation in their respective municipality. All interviews were recorded, transcribed and then analysed with MAXQdA software.

Electoral participation and representation in local governments: the political geographies of lifestyle migrants in Spain

As a key phenomenon within the context of European integration and a practical experience of a borderless Europe, more than 1.2 million mobile citizens from across Europe have transferred their permanent home to the coastal regions of the Mediterranean, and many more persons commute temporarily between Spain and different European countries. However, it can be considered that more than two-thirds of mobile European citizens from Central and Northern Europe are of retirement age (Rodríguez *et al.* 2010). The latest statistical data currently count more than 720,000 officially registered European foreigners who are aged above 50 years of which roughly 186,000 live in the region of Valencia and another 120,000 in Andalusia (INE 2013). Such data remind us that an important share of European lifestyle migrants consists of persons who are retired, early retired or close to reaching the retirement age who move to Spain looking for a different way of life. This aspect guided our research about political participation and representation, especially as different studies within the field of political science state an above-average political participation among older persons. With regard to the electoral mobilisation of EU-15 residents aged over 50 years, the relation can be confirmed: 35.2 per cent were registered on the electoral census for the municipal elections of 2011, a rate that is significantly higher than that of all adults from the EU-15 countries (27%). However, the numbers vary substantially across the regional scenarios, with exceptionally low registration numbers in the Canary Islands (23.0%) and the Balearic Islands (30.1%) but substantially higher numbers in the two most important residential destinations for lifestyle migrants, Valencia (36.4%) and Andalusia (37.1%).

Nevertheless, it cannot be taken for granted that these numbers are the total figure of voting turnout – it only constitutes the maximum possible figure. But even given the case that all registered persons voted, the abstention of European lifestyle migrants would have doubled general abstention in the municipal election of 2011. This is not a surprising fact: individual registration is only mandatory for foreigners, while Spaniards are automatically registered. In other words, lifestyle migrants suffer an important symbolical barrier that disincentives the realisation of the right to vote.

However, the average values presented above do not fully respond to the local political opportunity structures, and at the same time they hide a multitude of different situations in many hundreds of municipalities across the seven Spanish regions that are the subject of this study. For this, it is important to remember that countrywide there are more than 150 municipalities, especially in coastal areas of Andalusia and Valencia, where lifestyle migrants account for more than 15 per cent of the registered population. In 75 towns and villages, more than 25 per cent of the population are lifestyle migrants, and in 12 municipalities European lifestyle migrants are the majority of the population (INE 2013). These places present the specific scenarios in which innovative political responses of the potential lifestyle migrants to actively challenge the structuring of local politics are implemented and developed.

Such a statistical overview also corresponds with the data retrieved from the electoral census. Hence, bringing together statistical data from the population and the electoral census for the 10 municipalities with the highest percentage of foreign population countrywide (between 63 and 78 per cent of which 87.5 per cent can be considered lifestyle migrants, e.g. citizens from the EU-15), it can be observed that the inscription rate to CERE is significantly higher than it is countrywide (46.3 against 35.2 per cent). However, this correlation is similar if the 25 towns and villages with the highest percentage of lifestyle migrants are considered, and it is similar for all municipalities in which more than 20 per cent of the population are lifestyle migrants. In conclusion, the concentration of lifestyle migrants can be regarded as a key factor for the electoral mobilisation of this group.

Nevertheless, a closer look at electoral enrolment in each of the aforementioned 25 municipalities again offers a wide range of situations, with values that range from less than a third (i.e. Rojales, Calpe) to a maximum of 81.7 per cent in the village of Llíber. This poses the interesting question of how such variations can be explained. A further analysis of the statistical data does not relate aspects such as the size of the municipality, the geographic location of the municipality (coastal or inland) and the predominant nationality of the inhabitants (i.e. British, German, Dutch or French) as relevant factors. Accordingly, we will subsequently focus on the data provided by the representative household survey carried out in order to paint a more coherent explanation.

By contrasting the electoral census with the survey data and given the statistical representativeness of the survey, we can state the surprising fact that a vast majority (nearly 90 per cent) of the registered voters made use of their right to vote. In other words, 32.7 per cent of the respondents of the survey stated that they had voted in the last municipal elections. Our findings demonstrate that, in general terms, women are more likely to vote than men, and Britons and Germans are more likely to vote than other nationalities, but in both cases the differences are not statistically significant. But beyond this, some of the complementary data gathered in the survey give us some indications for further analytical and interpretative steps. For instance, a significant positive correlation between voting behaviour and the time that a person spends in Spain during the year exists: 39.8 per cent of the permanent residents voted in the last elections, while only 9 per cent of the residents that live between three and six months in Spain participated in the elections. Additionally, the proportion of voters also rises significantly if the time of residence in Spain (in years) is longer: 43.6 per cent of the residents that have lived in Spain for more than five years voted, and among those who have lived in Spain for more than 15 years this reaches nearly 50 per cent. This means that long-term lifestyle migrants almost approach the average of the Spanish population (66.5 per cent).

On the other hand, a similar significant positive relation can be observed between the voting turnout and active membership in clubs and social associations (40.2 per cent). This gives us a hint that the previously observed differences between municipalities may relate to three issues, namely previous urbanisation of the municipality, the residential stability of the lifestyle migrants and the amount of social capital of the residents themselves. Additionally, there is also a strong relation between the housing situation and the likeliness of voting: 44.4 per cent of the interviewees who live in houses of more than 150 square metres say that they had voted in the last elections, whereas this reaches only 23.3 per cent of those living in housing of less than 80 square metres. This may relate to and subsume the aspects mentioned earlier, namely that long-term residents are more likely to live in bigger houses than those who live temporarily in Spain. Additionally, we found out, in similar terms, that people who show a major interest in political questions relating to (i) the European Union and (ii) the host country Spain are significantly more likely to vote in local elections – this is an interesting issue for conceptualising the situation in Spain and the practices of European citizenship in relation to personal and political interests.

Finally, there is a positive relation between the proximity to specific political ideologies, and electoral mobilisation, especially among those who consider themselves to be 'conservatives'. This issue bridges the voting output of lifestyle migrants in Spain: here, the results of the survey correspond with information gathered in qualitative interviews, namely that lifestyle migrants overproportionally vote for the conservative party (more than 50 per cent of all valid answers). Such results do not only respond to socio-economic characteristics and a rather conservative ideological profile of the population on a scale of self-identification that was carried out in the survey. It also reflects the active strategies applied by the Spanish conservative party to attract the votes of foreign residents in general. Among others, the conservative party was the first one to acknowledge the potential that the foreign vote could have for the winning ticket in local elections, and they reacted accordingly. For instance, in the province of Alicante, several dozen foreign candidates were already included on the conservative party lists for local elections in 2003, and the number has risen substantially since then. In contrast to this, the centre-left socialist party has listed fewer foreign candidates than the conservative party in all elections since the time European foreigners have been entitled to vote.

Political representation of lifestyle migrants: a typology

This relates to the other side of the political participation coin in local elections, namely the representation that lifestyle migrants have achieved in local parliaments since they were first entitled to stand as candidates in 1999. Since then, they have been allowed to vote in four electoral events, and the number of foreign councillors integrating electoral lists has been steadily rising. In similar terms, the number of elected councillors also rose substantially, exceeding by far the number of 100 after the municipal elections of May 2011. Although this might sound less than one would expect at first sight, these councillors often play an important role, given the widespread transformations that have been taking place since their active enrolment. Based on the qualitative interviews carried out with local councillors, we have developed a typology that reflects the role and the changes that have occurred in local politics after the election of foreign councillors to the local parliament. Five different scenarios can be distinguished in an ideal-type analysis, taking into consideration that the real situation is less pure and less clear-cut than the typology might suggest.

1 **Lifestyle migrants as subjects for 'vote catching':** in many municipalities, the inclusion of European lifestyle migrants on the electoral lists, especially of one of the traditional parties, responds primarily to attract the vote of the foreign electorate. This is similar to the observed strategies in other parts of the world, especially if a specific ethnic group is targeted through this inclusion (Garbaye 2004). Such participation rather stabilises than transforms the governing local regime in a scenario in which it adapts itself to the transformations that have been induced by granting numerous

European lifestyle migrants the right to vote. In this scenario, the elected foreign councillor is usually granted the role to improve communication between the government and the foreign community. This occurs, for instance, by heading a newly created office of 'intercultural communication' or for the 'attention of the European residents', creating a specific hotline for the daily problems that lifestyle migrants, usually without sufficient command of the Spanish language, have with the local administration. But beyond this strategic assignment of a specific role that takes up some of the demands from the numerous group of lifestyle migrants, foreign councillors do not participate in the strategic political networks that take decisions in the most important fields within the local government (i.e. allocation of budgets, decisions about urban planning, development of social services and local infrastructure).

2 **Lifestyle migrants as 'catalysts of modernisation':** in some of the smaller villages that have especially high percentages of lifestyle migrants and a number of enrolled foreigners that is bigger than that of the local population, electoral participation is the clue for changing or approving the local government – the participation and representation of foreigners can significantly change the majorities. In such a situation, foreign councillors are aware of their key role, and they demand control of key departments and/or the leadership in local politics. This is especially the case in relation to questions of local infrastructure and urban planning, which are usually the most controversial topics that activate the lifestyle migrant community. The following quote provides us with a better idea of this relation:

> This is not a coalition. I usually vote with the PP [the conservative party], but I can fail and vote for the opposition or be against a plan. Then I speak with the mayor and ask him, 'how did you get into power?', because before I was elected, there were four councillors of the PSOE [the socialist party], two of the PP and one of the Bloc [the regional nationalist party]. Since I have been participating with a friend, this has changed, because we visited all foreigners personally, something that had never been done before. So, where do all these votes that went to the PP come from? These are the foreigners that voted me, because they trust me. If they want to do things now that the foreigners do not want, what do you think they will vote the next time? – They would set up their own party, eight or nine hundred foreigners that can vote here and only five hundred Spaniards, it would be easy to have the majority and then the Spaniards would not command anyone or anything here.
>
> (Interview with a foreign councillor)

Additionally, the achieved representation may also modernise certain aspects within the organisation of local government, especially in smaller villages. Many of the elected councillors were previously successful professionals and/or politicians, and they bring their experience into their new roles.

3 **Lifestyle migrants as 'catalysts of cultural conflicts':** different from the previous case, the representation of lifestyle migrants in municipalities of major size includes a major complexity. For instance, there are different localities (for example, Dénia or Jávea in the province of Alicante) with 30,000 or more inhabitants of which at least a third of the possible voters are European residents. Given their active involvement, the structuring of local politics has widely transformed in recent years, and the representation of foreigners as local councillors and/or their involvement in the government has often been a key facet of these transformations. In these municipalities, local politics are much more professionalised than in villages with fewer than 5,000 inhabitants, and, additionally, the public administration is much more complex and diversified. In these cities, much of the controversial issues are directly related to the use of languages in the public sphere, a facet of specific importance in lifestyle migrant destinations in Catalonia, Valencia and the Balearic Islands, where Catalan is given pre-eminence over Spanish. The linguistic question that lies behind the use of the Catalan language gives place to diametrically different interpretations: for the local population, the use of Catalan is part of the basic achievements of democracy in Spain. Contrary to this, many lifestyle migrants consider the use in the public sphere of any language other than Spanish (with which they usually struggle) as a means to exclude them explicitly from participating in political, social and cultural questions. On different occasions and in different municipalities, this has provided scenarios of conflict and contestation that are extremely difficult to overcome, especially as common party politics and oppositional positions may intermingle with linguistic questions. This question reminds us of remarks expressed by Favell (2008) about the wide range of symbolic exclusions which complicate participation by foreigners in different European migration societies.

4 **Lifestyle migrants as 'new and independent political force':** the manifold experiences gathered since the granting of voting rights and the subsequent increase in political representation by lifestyle migrants has also produced an array of different frustrating situations, sometimes even despair among lifestyle migrants. This is especially the case in municipalities which belong to the first and third cases in this typology. In such places, the inability to change some of the key aspects that motivate lifestyle migrants to participate actively in local politics (deficiencies in local services, the problems related to the overwhelming construction boom and the consequences of the real estate bubble burst after 2007) has often been paired with cases of corruption and/or abuse of urban planning schemes. One of the key decisions that was subsequently taken by politically engaged lifestyle migrants to overcome this situation has been the founding of parties that are controlled by foreigners and primarily respond to the discontent with the way local politics have been previously operating in the corresponding municipality. Such situations may bring lifestyle migrants into power, but they

may also simultaneously exacerbate the existing conflicts between local inhabitants and the newcomers from abroad, as well as conflicts between local entrepreneurs and the public administration.

5 **Lifestyle migrants as 'integrated and integral political power':** finally, there also exists the case that a new local political philosophy has been created by counting on the political involvement and representation of lifestyle migrants. A paradigmatic case for how lifestyle migrants achieved an integral political power position in local politics is the municipality of Teulada-Moraira in the province of Alicante, one of the places with the highest percentage of foreign population countrywide. Since 1999, the first election in which foreigners were allowed to vote, a local party has developed an integral strategy to incorporate lifestyle migrants from across the European Union. Since then, Spaniards and foreigners have achieved parity in the electoral lists, and the government tasks have been distributed with regard to the professional qualifications of the elected councillors. Among others, the political representatives belonging to the lifestyle migrant community have gained important roles in local government – for instance control of the department of finance, the department of environment and holding the position of vice-mayor. In the municipality, all official information is provided in five languages, and the administration has developed effective channels for participation and civic involvement, providing an interesting model of political representation by lifestyle migrants (Janoschka 2010b). Such a model additionally adapts to changing conditions, for example European expansion – in the 2011 local elections, the governing party also included candidates from Romania and Poland on their electoral lists.

Conclusions: contested realities of political participation

Based on our empirical research, the developed typology can provide us with some additional explanations about the initially discussed differences in electoral enrolment at the municipal level and the political outcomes of political participation by lifestyle migrants. Beyond the observed differences in electoral enrolment due to certain social characteristics, especially if permanency in Spain is considered, our research provides evidence that the local political system is a key factor for electoral mobilisation – an observation which is in line with our previous research about other forms of rather radical mobilisation in concrete planning conflicts (Janoschka 2009b, 2010a). With regard to this, we have observed that the greatest electoral mobilisation takes place in three areas: first, when lifestyle migrants feel that they play a key factor for electoral output and are considered part of the local government, especially in smaller villages (type 3). Second, when they are considered an integral and integrated part of the political landscape of their municipality, enrolment is above average (type 5). However, the third case (type 4), when lifestyle migrants regard themselves as independent political forces, has so far resulted in controversy. In some municipalities, the constitution of independent foreign parties has achieved greater electoral mobilisation. Contrary to this, in other places the mobilisation has not altered. This result is in line with the findings of our survey, in which we asked lifestyle migrants about their participation and the contested relations that have been established in the course of this participation. While nearly 70 per cent consider political participation as positive for the municipality and 60 per cent agree that lifestyle migrants should be represented on the local council, opinion drastically changes when it comes to political parties for foreigners: almost two-thirds of the respondents reject parties founded by foreigners, and less than 30 per cent support the hypothetical election of a mayor from the lifestyle migrant collective. This situation is reflected in the fact that political parties constituting foreigners have been so far successful only in a reduced number of municipalities.

All this brings us toward some final conceptual reflections which link some of the initially presented debates about European citizenship with the observed empirical data about political participation and representation of lifestyle migrants in Spain. In this regard, it is important to reflect again that different authors consider lifestyle migrants and other European 'free movers' as an embodiment of a new transnational world (Favell 2009) in which citizens increasingly escape from some of the constraints of the old national systems. Indeed, our empirical debate shows that lifestyle migrants use these freedoms of the European Union, but they make a rather selective use of the granted citizenship rights. This reminds us of the argument of Lepofsky and Fraser (2003: 127), who argue that the rising flexibility in practical uses of citizenship goes hand in hand with a transformation of its theoretical conception. In this regard, postmodern or post-national citizenship includes more than just only a collection of rights, but is also a powerful discursive mechanism which articulates identities and which has shifted from a given status to being a performative act. Such an idea leads to the question discussed here of how citizenship rights may be important for claiming the right to participate actively in local politics. According to Rose (2001), citizenship is currently shifting from being a possession towards being a capacity of 'citizenship practice' (Wiener 1998). Some authors propose that the mobility of European citizens and the formal possibilities for political participation within Europe result automatically in a European civil society. But different analyses of municipal data show, for instance, that formal political participation of EU citizens abroad is extremely low (Jacobs *et al.* 2004; Strudel 2004), and our own data give a very nuanced picture of the practice of European citizenship, at least with regard to formal political participation and representation.

Favell and Recchi (2008), who conducted qualitative research on the political interests and involvement of highly mobile foreign professionals in London, Brussels and Amsterdam, concludes that these 'Eurostars' do show no more major interest in municipal voting rights granted to EU citizens than traditional labour migrants, even if they are locally socially active, possess social capital and have only minor language problems. Apparently, it is not the right to vote which encourages political participation by foreigners. It seems instead that the symbolical signs and codes which control access to local politics even keep foreigners with perfect language skills away from active interaction with the local political elites. In the words of Pierre Bourdieu, this exclusion means that the capital of cultural practices bound to the field of local politics are so restrictively controlled and monopolised by the traditional elites, that foreigners are discouraged from participating actively in political life abroad (Bourdieu 1989). Our research about the contested realities of political participation of lifestyle migrants in Spain supports these arguments in some areas – especially if the first and third cases of the developed typology are considered. However, they also show that the practical creation of a European civil society goes beyond these traditional schemes of interpretation: the villages and towns on the Mediterranean coast are intensive laboratories of globalisation, as well as of new expressions of European citizenship which has only little connections with the bureaucratic aspects of the European Union imagined in Brussels, but much more with growing together in daily practice 'from below'.

Notes

1 EURO_CITI is the acronym of the Marie Curie Intra-European-Fellowship granted in the 7th European Community Framework Programme (PIEF-GA-2008–220287) to the Centre of Human and Social Sciences of the Spanish National Research Council in Madrid. The fellowship was implemented between July 2008 and December 2010 by Michael Janoschka.

2 MIRES is an interdisciplinary research project financed by the Spanish Ministry of Science and Innovation (Plan Nacional I+D+i, CSO2008–06458-C02–01), developed under the direction of Dr Vicente Rodríguez and carried out by the Centre of Human and Social Sciences of the Spanish National Research Council and seven Spanish universities between January 2009 and June 2012.

Bibliography

Bermudez, A. (2010) 'The transnational political practices of Colombians in Spain and the United Kingdom: politics 'here' and 'there' *Ethnic and Racial Studies* 33(1): 75–91.

Bird, K., Saalfeld, T. and A. Wüst (2011) 'Ethnic diversity, political participation and representation: a theoretical framework' in Bird, K., Saalfeld, T. and A. Wüst (eds) *The Political Representation of Immigrants and Minorities. Voters, parties and parliaments in liberal democracies* Abingdon: Routledge, 1–24.

Blazquez, M., Cañada, E. and I. Murray (2011) 'Búnker playa-sol. Conflictos derivados de la construcción de enclaves de capital transnacional turístico español en El Caribe y Centroamérica' *Scripta Nova* XV (368). www.ub.edu/geocrit/sn/sn-368.htm.

Bourdieu, P. (1989) *La noblesse d'Etat: grandes écoles et esprit de corps* Paris: Editions de Minuit.

Collard, S. (2010) 'French municipal democracy: Cradle of European citizenship?' *Journal of Contemporary European Studies* 18(1): 91–116.

Day, S. and J. Shaw (2002): 'European Union electoral rights and the political participation of migrants in host polities' *International Journal of Population Geography* 8 (2): 183–99.

Durán, R. (2005) 'Implicación política de los gerontoinmigrantes comunitarios' in Echezarreta, M. (ed.) *El Lugar Europeo de Retiro. Indicadores de excelencia para administrar la gerontoinmigración de ciudadanos de la Unión Europea en municipios españoles* Granada: Comares, 63–93.

——(2011) 'Fuerza y efecto potenciales del voto de los inmigrantes. Elecciones municipales de 2007 en España' *Revista de Estudios Políticos* 152: 115–41.

Favell A. (2008) *Eurostars and Eurocities: Free Movement and Mobility in an Integrating Europe*, Malden, MA: Wiley.

Favell, A. and E. Recchi (2009) 'Pioneers of European integration: an introduction' in Recchi, E. and A. Favell (eds) *Pioneers of European Integration: Citizenship and Mobility in the EU*, Cheltenham: Edward Elgar Publishing, 1–24.

Ferbrache, F. (2011) 'British immigrants in France: Issues and debates in a broadening research field' *Geography Compass* 5 (10): 737–49.

Garbaye, R. (2004) 'Ethnic minority local councillors in French and British cities: Social determinants and political opportunity structures' in R. Penninx *et al.* (eds) *Citizenship in European cities. Immigrants, local politics and integration politics* Aldershot: Ashgate, 39–56.

Huete, R. and A. Mantecón (2012) 'La participación política de los residentes británicos y alemanes en España: el caso de San Miguel de Salinas, Alicante', in *Revista de Geografía Norte Grande* 51: 81–93.

INE (Instituto Nacional de Estadísticas) (2013) *Estadística del Padrón Continuo a 1 de enero de 2012*. www.ine.es.

Jacobs, D., Phalet, K. and M. Swyngedouw (2004) 'Associational membership and political involvement among ethnic minority groups in Brussels' *Journal of Ethnic and Migration Studies* 30 (3): 543–59.

Janoschka, M. (2008) 'Identity politics as an expression of European citizenship practice: Participation of transnational migrants in local political conflicts', in R. Anghel *et al.* (eds) *The Making of World Society: Perspectives from Transnational Research*, Bielefeld: transcript, 133–52.

——(2009a) *Konstruktion europäischer Identitäten in räumlich-politischen Konflikten* Stuttgart: Steiner-Verlag.

——(2009b) 'The contested spaces of lifestyle mobilities: Regime analysis as a tool to study political claims in Latin American retirement destinations', *Die Erde* 140(3): 251–74.

——(2010a) 'Between mobility and mobilization – lifestyle migration and the practice of European identity in political struggles', *The Sociological Review* 58 (Issue Supplement 2): 270–90.

——(2010b) 'Prácticas de Ciudadanía Europea. El uso estratégico de las identidades en la participación política de los inmigrantes comunitarios' *ARBOR – Ciencia, Pensamiento, Cultura* 186(744): 705–19.

——(2011a) 'Habitus and radical reflexivity: a conceptual approach to study political articulations of lifestyle- and tourism-related mobilities', *Journal of Policy Research in Tourism, Leisure and Events* 3(3): 224–36.

——(2011b) 'Imaginarios del turismo residencial en Costa Rica. Negociaciones de pertenencia y apropiación simbólica de espacios y lugares: una relación conflictiva', in T. Mazón, R. Huete and A. Mantecón (eds) *Construir una nueva vida. Los espacios del turismo y la migración residencial* Santander: Milrazones, 81–102.

——(2013) 'Nuevas geografías migratorias en América Latina: prácticas de ciudadanía en un destino de turismo residencial.' *Scripta Nova: revista electrónica de geografía y ciencias sociales* 17(439). Online available: http://www.ub.edu/geocrit/sn/sn-439.htm

Lepofsky, J. and J. Fraser (2003) 'Building community citizens: Claiming the right to place-making in the city,' *Urban Studies* 40(1): 127–42.

Maxwell, R. (2012) *Ethnic Minority Migrants in Britain and France. Integration Trade-Offs* Cambridge: Cambridge University Press.

McHugh, K., Gober, P., and D. Borough (2002) 'Sun city wars: Chapter 3', *Urban Geography* 23: 627–48.

Øostergaard-Nielsen, E. (2011) 'Codevelopment and citizenship: the nexus between policies on local migrant incorporation and migrant transnational practices in Spain' *Ethnic and Racial Studies* 34(1): 20–39.

Rodríguez, V., Lardiés, R. and P. Rodríguez (2010) 'Migration and the registration of European pensioners in Spain' *ARI* 20/2010: 1–8. www.realinstitutoelcano.org.

Rose, J. (2001) 'Contexts of interpretation: Assessing immigrant reception in Richmond, Canada' *The Canadian Geographer* 45(4): 474–93.

Strudel, S. (2004) 'La participation des Portugais aux élections européennes et municipales en France' *Cahiers de l'Urmis* 9: 69–76.

Wiener, A. (1998) *European Citizenship Practice: Building Institutions of a Non-State*, Oxford and Boulder, CO: Westview Press.

Part II

Conceptual perspectives on lifestyle migration and residential tourism

6 Lifestyle migrants, the linguistic landscape and the politics of place

Kate Torkington

Introduction

This chapter takes a critical approach to the discursive construction of a privileged form of place-identity in the linguistic landscape of a particular lifestyle migrant destination in Portugal. 'Place-identity' is taken here to mean the potentially multiple dialectical relationships between the identities of places and the social identities of those who inhabit and use them, as constructed in and through discourse. The term 'discourse' is used in its broadest sense, as a multi-modal social practice which therefore encompasses other semiotic systems besides language, such as visual images (Kress and van Leeuwen 1996). By taking a socio-cognitive approach to discourse (van Dijk 2008, 2009), this means that collective identities (as well as certain identities of places) are understood as being shared socio-cognitive representations which are established and negotiated via discursive practices (Koller 2008a,b). Finally, the 'critical' part of doing critical discourse analysis (CDA) involves not merely identifying and describing the structures and strategies of discourse that may establish identities, but also interpreting and explaining them in relation to the broader socio-political contexts in which they are embedded (Wodak 2008; Wodak and Meyer 2009). In this way, an analysis of the discursive construction of collective place-identities inevitably leads to issues related to spatial power relations, since it involves exploring the ways in which different collective identities are discursively positioned in relation to places.

Lifestyle migrants (as a collective social group) are positioned in many destinations as 'desirable' migrants, particularly in places that are heavily dependent on tourism. In many destinations, including Portugal, the term 'residential tourism' is often used in the media and in official planning documents to describe the phenomenon of lifestyle migration, meaning that it is simply construed as an extension of tourism and therefore generally considered to be economically beneficial (Mazón *et al.* 2009; Mantecón 2010; Nudrali and O'Reilly 2009). This clearly helps in the construction of privileged place-identities for lifestyle migrants. It also reinforces hegemonic discourses on the legitimacy (or otherwise) of certain types of migration; discourses that are generally based on economic arguments (Mazón *et al.*

2009; Mantecón 2010) but which may also have ethnic underpinnings: affluent, northern European migrants might be positioned differently from affluent migrants from other parts of the world, for instance. The question for discourse analysts is exactly *how* such discourses are established and reproduced to the extent that they eventually become 'common sense' worldviews – or ideologies, in other words (Billig *et al.* 1988; van Dijk 1998). This is, of course, an enormous task, and the scope of discourse analytical work is invariably limited to the close examination of a relatively small number of texts[1] which are viewed as being representative in some way of the social world (Meyer 2001), with detailed attention being paid to the context(s) in which discursive practices are embedded (Wodak and Meyer 2009).

The micro-politics of place: collective identities and modes of belonging

The specific discursive practices to be examined in this chapter are real estate advertising practices in a particular lifestyle migration destination. The aim is to show how these practices impact on the micro-politics of place. The notion of politics of place can of course be understood and empirically studied in a multitude of ways. In the context of lifestyle migration, Janoschka (2008), for example, gives an account of the ways in which senior northern European migrants in Spain integrate themselves and exercise leadership via local politics, from informal involvement in social movements and grassroots activism to formal representation in local government. Croucher (2009) explores political transnationalism practices of US citizens living in Mexico. However, the focus of this chapter is how versions of place are (re)produced and negotiated through discourse that constructs identities for both places and people. Following Modan (2007), this approach explores the way in which 'legitimate' (and, conversely, marginalised/excluded) collective identities are discursively shaped in relation to places. Not only does this inevitably have a strong impact on individual modes of belonging (or not) in places, but also the micro-level ways in which collective place-identities are constructed undoubtedly have material and socio-economic implications for the ways in which places develop and change, therefore impacting on the more macro-level of politics of place.

The idea of places being nodes linked into networks of flows of movement (of people, objects, ideas) is fundamental to a contemporary understanding of both place-identity and the politics of place. According to Massey (1993: 67), places emerge from 'a particular constellation of relations, articulated together at a particular locus'. Thus, places (and their identities) are never fixed 'products', but are best seen as dynamic processes, constantly under (re)construction by the interaction of human agency, social structures and social practices. As Massey (2004: 1) notes, 'if we make space through interactions at all levels, from the (so-called) local to the (so-called) global, then those spatial identities … must be forged in this relational way too'. This fits well with Amin's (2004) case for a 'relational' understanding of the politics of place, based on both the spatial juxtaposition of difference and the effects of connectivity across relational spaces.

The concept of power geometries (Massey 1993, 1999) encapsulates the ways in which different social groups are positioned in different ways in relation to the flows and interconnections that characterise both the globalised world and local places. The positionings that forge these power geometries are, to some extent, located in the discursive practices that simultaneously shape and are shaped by collective social identities and the identities of places, as other geographers including Harvey (1996) and Amin (2004) have noted. Despite (or perhaps because of) escalating mobilities and the sense of diminishing spatial barriers in the contemporary world, place-identities clearly remain important. Place attachments feed into both individual and collective modes of belonging, which are central to the concept of identity (Jones and Krzyżanowski 2008). Yet the attachments to places that contribute to a contemporary sense of belonging are likely to be very different in the highly mobile late modern world to what they were in the past (Savage *et al.* 2005). For example, being 'born and bred' in a place no longer seems to be a fundamental prerequisite to belonging (or at least not always, and not for everyone). Nowadays, place attachments can arise when a *chosen* place of residence is perceived as valuable due to its congruence with one's lifestyle, life-story and life politics (Giddens 1991, 1994), with one's repertoire of 'ideal' possible selves (Markus and Nurius 1986) and its connections to other significant places. In other words, contemporary modes of place-related belonging are often *elective* and *relational* (Savage *et al.* 2005), in that they are actively constructed through social practices in a process that articulates spatial attachments, social positionings and networked relationships. This seems to be a particularly fruitful way of looking at modes of belonging in relation to lifestyle migrants.

Importantly, to achieve a sense of elective belonging one must 'feel comfortable' in a place. As Savage *et al.* (2005) note, this feeling can be related to the interplay of Bourdieu's concepts of habitus, capital and fields (that is, interconnecting spaces of social and spatial positions, e.g. places of work, leisure, residence, etc.). However, feeling comfortable in a place is also related to the discursive construction of 'legitimate' modes of belonging. Without the safety-net provided by the perceived ability to stake a 'legitimate' claim to being in a place, one is bound to remain in many senses an outsider, whatever one's affective relationship towards that place might be. In order to understand how individual claims to 'legitimate' belonging are achieved, a good starting point is to explore how social groups are positioned by discursive practices in the public sphere. Such discursive practices are inevitably ideological in nature,[2] and as such have a strong impact on the politics of place.

In short, what this chapter aims to address is how lifestyle migrants are collectively positioned in the discursive construction of a particular place – the so-called 'Golden Triangle' in the Algarve. The specific focus is on the *in situ* discursive practices of the real estate sector: the billboards advertising

land and properties for sale which line the roadsides of this area. Such practices contribute to the structuring of the 'linguistic landscape', i.e. the publically displayed or 'emplaced' discourse that is an integral part of many contemporary landscapes (see below). This type of positioning in public spaces feeds into the socio-cognitive representations which underlie collective identities and thus makes subject positions available for individual lifestyle migrants to take up if they so wish, for example to help to reinforce individual modes of elective belonging in the destination place. On the other hand, the socio-cognitive representations which seem to legitimise the claims to belonging of certain social groups might also be seen as weakening or negating the claims of other groups, thus reinforcing unequal spatial relations. As Trudeau (2006) has argued, landscapes provide visual representations of what/who belongs in places, by codifying membership. Whatever (or whoever) does not belong may be materially excluded, or simply not represented. In terms of the linguistic landscape, this can mean that the languages that represent certain migrant groups are highly visible, while others may be completely absent.

Setting the scene: constructing the 'Golden Triangle'

The Algarve, in southern Portugal, has become a well-established tourism and lifestyle migration destination for northern Europeans[3] over the past decades. My research site is the so-called 'Golden Triangle', which roughly corresponds to the *freguesia*[4] of Almancil in the central Algarve. Until the 1970s, the major economic activity of this area was small-scale agriculture, with some shellfish cultivation and salt extraction in the tidal lagoon area of what is now part of the Ria Formosa Natural Park. However, with the arrival of tourism, the area underwent huge changes and the hitherto small village of Almancil developed into a town.[5] The website of the *Junta da Freguesia*[6] describes this change as follows (author's translation):

> Until a few decades ago, the town was just a small collection of low, white-washed houses with a communal well in the main square. Over recent years, economic development has turned the town into a significant residential centre, with modern housing infrastructures, commerce and tourism support services.

Despite being a support centre for the upmarket residential tourism and golf developments along the coastline, the town of Almancil itself has very little to recommend it to tourists. It has no seaside (being some kilometres from the coast), no historic monuments, no picturesque streets and very little in the way of nightlife or other forms of entertainment. Most tourists seem to do little more in Almancil than pass through on their way to the coast, perhaps visiting one of the numerous real estate agencies which have flooded the town.[7]

However, although the coastal area is becoming increasingly known as a destination for northern European (particularly British and Irish) second home owners and lifestyle migrants, in the town itself there are many other migrant communities including those of African origin (from the former Portuguese colonies, especially Cape Verde and Guinea-Bissau) and, more recently, migrants from eastern European countries (especially Romania and the Ukraine), attracted by the employment opportunities offered by the construction and service industries in the area. These new social groups of incoming migrants have helped to repopulate a town which lost many of its former inhabitants through outward migration during the twentieth century.

The Almancil area is thus a place where communities of different geographic, ethnic and social origins live side by side. According to figures from the Portuguese Immigration and Border Services,[8] 3,906 foreigners were registered as living in Almancil in 2005, accounting for more than one-third of the total population. Around 25 per cent of pupils in state schools in Almancil are of foreign origin, with around 30 different nationalities represented, the largest groups being Cape Verdean, Romanian and Ukrainian (Cardoso Sousa 2007). The relative poverty of some segments of the population is reflected in the fact that that over one-quarter of state school pupils receive financial help from the Social Support in Schools Services,[9] which is much higher than the national average (ibid.).

While the majority of migrants from Africa and Eastern Europe live in rented accommodation in the town, the immediate surrounding area, in contrast, is marked by upmarket resorts and privately owned villas, including the well-known golf and beach resorts of Vale do Lobo and Quinta do Lago. The predominantly northern European property developers and estate agents who have constructed and sold such housing since the late 1970s coined the 'Golden Triangle' name for the Almancil area, since land and property prices rose rapidly to become among the highest per square metre in Portugal. The area has therefore become increasingly populated by wealthy lifestyle migrants: in 2005, 1,143 northern European residents were registered as living in the *freguesia*,[10] while the private, fee-paying International School São Lourenço had over 200 northern European students enrolled (mostly of British nationality), indicating that families with young children are settling in the area. Nowadays, a browse through the real estate websites dealing with this area reveals that there is no shortage of 'luxury' properties costing anything up to several million euros.

It is worth considering how the 'Golden Triangle' name has become part of the place-identity of the area. Place naming is one of the most basic ways that places are given identity. As the geographer Yi-Fu Tuan (1991: 688) remarked, 'naming is power – the creative power to call something into being'. The connotations of the adjective 'golden' call into being a place associated with wealth, luxury and privilege, even mythical tales of transformative magic. Furthermore, the 'triangle' designation suggests clearly defined spatial boundaries and as such may reinforce a sense of exclusivity and elitism for those privileged enough to live within those boundaries. However, as Cresswell (2004: 98) notes, the act of naming locates places in wider cultural narratives. The cultural narrative in question here is clearly one that belongs to the northern Europeans residing in this area, since the name appears to be restricted to the English language.

Place branding is an influential means of shaping, disseminating and reinforcing particular socio-cognitive representations of place and, equally, the collective identities of those who inhabit it. As a kind of branding measure, the 'Golden Triangle' name positions the place as being at once a desirable and an exclusive residential location. Although we might therefore extrapolate that this positions its residents as privileged, there are many different social groups living in the area, not all sharing the same levels of economic and symbolic capital. It is likely that many local residents are not even aware of the 'Golden Triangle' name, and, even if they are, do not share the same privileged place-identity as their northern European neighbours. We next turn to the question of how socio-cognitive representations of place become associated with specific social groups by exploring the linguistic landscape of the Golden Triangle area and how it serves to position lifestyle migrants in a distinctive way.

The linguistic landscape

The linguistic landscape[11] comprises the texts that are potentially visible to anyone who is in or passing through a geographical area, e.g. the texts on signs in city streets, shopping centres, airports and a whole host of other public spaces. Although the linguistic landscape constitutes a major part of the scenery in which public social life takes place (Ben-Rafael 2009), it is such a taken-for-granted part of our everyday experience that its importance as a social practice is often overlooked. Yet the signs that make up this feature of the landscape are in some way symbolic markers of (collective) identity and social status, operating within semiotic systems of social positioning and power relationships through which struggles for hegemony among social groups can be traced (Scollon and Scollon 2003). Social actors shape the linguistic landscape through discursive practices in specific spaces. They also respond to it and construct their own identities in interaction with the collective identities represented in it (Ben-Rafael 2009; Scollon and Scollon 2003; Trumper-Hecht 2009). However, the texts that comprise the linguistic landscape are not only social-semiotic resources for meaning-making (van Leeuwen 2005) but also, crucially, they are material elements of a place. These texts are physically located in the landscape of the very place they help to discursively construct. Discourse practices thus contribute to place-making at several levels, including the material, the territorial, the functional and the symbolic.

One of the most obvious aspects of the linguistic landscape is language choice. Such choices may be made in accordance with state language policies (in officially bilingual or multilingual regions). On the other hand, they may be based on an informational function or they may have a more symbolic function. One assumption that we can fairly safely make is that language choice in the linguistic landscape is never arbitrary. It might be, for instance, that as a 'global' language, English is perceived as being more modern and prestigious than local languages, particularly when these local languages are spoken by very few people in the world beyond the regional or national borders (e.g. Ben-Rafael *et al.* 2006; Cenoz and Gorter 2006). This may well be the case in Portugal, since Portuguese is spoken by few Europeans. Therefore, a prevalence of signs in English marks a 'tourist space' and can thus be interpreted as serving both informational *and* symbolic functions, since there is a need to communicate with tourists via a *lingua franca* as well as to promote the image of the place as tourist-friendly and cosmopolitan. This doubtless accounts for the salience of English on many of the signs in the 'Golden Triangle': signs outside shops, menu boards outside restaurants and cafés, public information boards on the beaches, fly-posters advertising entertainment and events are but a few examples of the many tourist-oriented aspects of the linguistic landscape that make ample use of English. In this respect, the place is probably no different from many other tourist destinations around the world.

However, the most striking aspect of the landscape as one drives around the area outside the town of Almancil is the predominance of roadside billboards advertising land and property sales/development. As the salient language of these billboards is English, this contributes to a representation of the area as being literally 'up for sale' to English-speaking buyers. Clearly, this aspect of the linguistic landscape goes beyond an appeal to consumption in terms of tourist practices.

Real estate advertising: constructing privileged place-identities through language choice

There are around 15 kilometres of roads running south from the town of Almancil through the countryside and connecting the coastal resorts. Over a period of two years, I collected data by photographing roadside billboards in the area. Although the linguistic landscape is dynamic in that it can potentially change overnight, in order to provide a 'snapshot' of this aspect of the Golden Triangle, I covered all the stretches of road one day in 2010, noting the contents of the billboards. Of the 106 counted, just over half were for local real estate. As noted above, the first impression one gets from these billboards is that English is the dominant language choice. To verify this, a sample of 40 photographed real estate billboards were analysed, categorising the signs according to both language choice and information arrangement. As only two languages are used in the sample (Portuguese and English), the texts were first categorised as monolingual or bilingual. Almost half the sample displayed monolingual texts in English only. None of the texts used Portuguese only, and 22 were bilingual. Of these bilingual texts, almost two-thirds were found to be 'fragmentary' (Reh 2004) in terms of the translation. That is to say, one language dominates as only part of the text is reproduced in the other language. In all cases, the dominant language was English.

However, it is not only through quantity of text that English dominates on these billboards. The arrangement of the bilingual information can be either balanced or unbalanced. A graphically 'balanced' arrangement indicates that the producer aimed to give equal prominence to both languages, whereas 'unbalanced' means that there is a marked difference in the graphics and/or spatial positioning of the texts, with one language being more salient. In the composition of a semiotic space such as a billboard, the various elements of the sign are balanced on the basis of their 'visual weight' (van Leeuwen 2005: 198), which derives from their perceptual salience (i.e. the degree to which each element attracts the viewer's attention). This salience can be achieved in terms of font size, positioning (e.g. which language is positioned above the other), use of colour, etc. Salience creates a hierarchy of importance among the elements of a sign, marking some as more worthy of attention than others (Kress and van Leeuwen 1996). The fact that English clearly dominates in terms of salience is underscored by the fact that just three of the billboards analysed were found to have both duplicate texts (in Portuguese and English) *and* graphic balance between both languages.

The salience of the English language in the billboards analysed gives a clear message about the relative importance and status given to the language – and those who speak it – by the producers of the signs. It seems to be the assumption of the producers of these texts that it is primarily those belonging to an in-group of English-speakers who have the economic power to consider buying property in this area and therefore there is little point in advertising in Portuguese, let alone other languages which are spoken in the area. Indeed, where Portuguese is used, it often seems to have been added as an afterthought; perhaps a token nod to the fact that this 'Golden Triangle' is at least *geographically* located in Portugal. Figure 6.1 is an illustration of this unbalanced positioning. The huge gold lettering of the English text is seemingly 'translated' into Portuguese at the bottom of the advertisement in small lettering, using a plain white colour. In the box on the right, along with the resort logo, is the English-only text '*Exclusive living since 1962*'.

In this way, the use of English is a marker of social allegiance, or 'solidarity, group identity and ideology' (Hodge and Kress 1988: 82), implying that the producers of the signs position themselves as members of this in-group. In fact, many of the estate agents appear, by their names at least, to be of English-speaking origin (e.g. *John Hammond*; *Michael Hickey*; *Newlyn*). Other company names employ English words, thereby also presenting an English-speaking company image (e.g. *Prime Properties*; *Exclusive Estates*; *Charm Properties*). The real estate agency *Quinta Properties* takes this a step further, by advertising its services on huge billboards throughout the Golden Triangle with images of two blonde women with strikingly northern European complexions. The straplines (in English) consist of polysemic puns such as '*Best Sellers*' (Figure 6.2) and '*Special Agents*'.

From this simple analysis, it is clear that English dominates in this aspect of the linguistic landscape, despite the fact that municipal regulations do not in fact allow for this. In Portugal, Municipal Councils draw up their own sets

Figure 6.1 Real estate billboard near Almancil

of regulations defining the criteria for granting licences for any kind of *in situ* advertising or publicity emanating from commercial activity. The regulations for the area under study[12] only permit bilingual or multilingual signs in some very limited circumstances, and do not allow monolingual signs in languages other than Portuguese at all.[13] The numerous examples of signs on which English is the most salient or the only language suggest a flagrant disregard for the local regulations. On the other hand, it also seems that the local council, by allowing these texts to remain in place, often for many months, is putting the perceived economic gains from encouraging 'residential tourism' higher on its political agenda than the local identity politics which are reflected through language choice in the linguistic landscape.

'Exclusivity Awaits You': discursive strategies for constructing privileged place-identities

The use of English, then, seems to be positioning English-speaking (potential) property buyers as part of an 'elite' in-group which seemingly includes the producers of the signs themselves (the sellers). Although 'elite' status is often discussed in the social sciences as a structural social category, based on economic wealth, political power and so on, it can also be conceived of as an ideological and aspirational subject position (Thurlow and Jaworski 2010). From this perspective, it is semiotically achieved (or at least attempted) and

Figure 6.2 Real estate billboard near Almancil

enacted through social practices, including discourse (ibid.). Through the repetition and routinisation of discursive practices such as the processes of symbolic differentiation (Rampton 2003) (including, in this case, through the foregrounding of English rather than the local language), elite identities are constructed, reproduced and reinforced through a social-semiotic process of *stylisation* (Thurlow and Jaworski 2006). Such identities are thus 'hegemonic and normative ideals … in relation to which many people, regardless of wealth or power, position themselves or are persuaded by others to position themselves' (Thurlow and Jaworski 2010: 189). Thus, while it may be fairly consensual in the literature to define lifestyle migrants as relatively 'privileged' in socio-economic terms (Benson and O'Reilly 2009), it can also be argued that in many destination places lifestyle migrants are positioned as having 'elite' status through discursive identity constructions.

However, language choice in itself is not enough to stylise elite identities. The discursive strategies used to construct identities are also of paramount importance. Promoters of lifestyle migration destinations must do their best to create representations of place that either explicitly or implicitly afford a certain type of lifestyle that they consider to be attractive to potential migrants, and at the same time differentiate the place from other possible destinations. Unsurprisingly, then, local place is often discursively constructed as being a fundamental factor in an imagined lifestyle. One way of differentiating resort areas is to make the resort name itself the 'essence' of the brand, that is, to ensure that the brand name automatically conjures up a socio-cognitive representation of place that is consistent with the sought-after lifestyle of the targeted consumer segment. As such, brand managers appeal to consumers' values and self-images and, ultimately, to the powerful discourses which have shaped those values (Morgan and Pritchard 1998). This, then, is the ideological aspect of place branding; an attempt to fix the meaning of a place as singular, bounded, and ultimately defined through counterposition against the Other who remains outside (Massey 1994).

One of the recurrent lexical themes in the Golden Triangle real estate advertising practices is that of 'exclusivity'. The lexeme 'exclusive' and its derivatives appear numerous times on the billboards in my sample. In one strapline, which proclaims '*Exclusivity Awaits You*', the nominalisation means that 'exclusivity' becomes something almost tangible and synonymous with the place itself. Texts such as these are clearly designed to activate socio-cognitive representations of the place as a symbolically bounded space. The very concept of 'exclusivity' implies both inclusion (membership of a privileged in-group) and exclusion (of both people and places that are on the 'outside').

Further examples of discursive strategies that are effectively stylising an elitist place-identity include ample use of hyperbolic evaluative words such as 'prestigious', 'superb', 'exceptional' and, of course, 'luxury' and its derivatives. The lexical choices to describe the 'properties' on sale ('villa', 'apartment', 'townhouse', 'manor house') all have lifestyle connotative meanings arising from social attitudes that are established through discourse (Myers 1994). Some slogans suggest the meshing of economic capital with other forms of symbolic capital (e.g. '*Taking property investment to the level of a fine art*') or reiterate the symbolic space of 'exclusivity' in which economic investment can take place ('*Welcome to a world of exclusive real estate investment opportunities*'). Others emphasise a combination of economic and affective investment – that is, the nexus of an imagined lifestyle and creating a home ('*Live like a king*'; '*Homes for true luxury living*'; '*Dream homes are only a few steps away*').

The semiotics of 'glocal' place-identity

The discursive strategies identified here are certainly not unique; they are easily recognisable as drawing on global advertising discourses, and may well be present in a range of other lifestyle migration/residential tourism destinations throughout the world. On the other hand, real estate advertisers need to create a sense of local emplacedness so as to differentiate from other places. In the billboards under study, this local emplacedness is achieved through devices such as aerial shots of the location, maps and written instructions on how to reach the location, local toponyms and telephone numbers with local dialling codes. In combination with the global discursive strategies, including the predominance of English, this works to construct a kind of 'glocal' place-identity. This privileged, glocal identity is reiterated through the texts of these billboards in conjunction with the images employed

In Figure 6.3, readers are urged to 'live the difference'. Like much advertising discourse, the connotations of this strapline are perhaps intentionally ambiguous, leaving the receiver of the message to work out what the 'difference' is and how it should be 'lived'. However, the images of a leisure-based lifestyle, besides being intertextual references from typical tourism

Figure 6.3 Real estate billboard near Almancil

promotional media, also activate connotative cultural schemata that suggest the difference is based on socio-economic status. These types of 'lifestyle' images are persistent in this genre of advertising: luxurious 'villas', swathes of verdant green golf courses, beaches at sunset. The people displayed are generally engaged in the types of activities associated with these leisured-lifestyle signifiers – playing golf, relaxing by the pool, strolling hand-in-hand through gentle surf. These are all 'global' images in that they have apparently 'placeless' (Relph 1976) settings which could be one of any number of tourist destinations around the world. Machin (2004) notes that the culture of branding has caused a shift from 'photography as witness' to 'photography as a symbolic system'. Products (including branded tourism destinations) are graphically represented through their meanings and values rather than through the products themselves. Therefore, we find more and more generic images, of the type found in image banks, in all fields of the media. The curious thing about the images on these billboards is that although they have the 'feel' of generic images, they mostly *do* denote the product itself – i.e. they are genuine images of particular villas for sale, specific local resort developments, golf courses or beaches. As already noted, it is the meshing of these global discourse strategies with a sense of local emplacedness that lends a 'glocal' feel to the place – something that is increasingly common in branding practices (Koller 2007), even when it is becoming harder to differentiate semiotically among countless 'local' places around the globe, particularly purpose-built lifestyle migration destinations (Torkington 2012).

Conclusions

One of the most striking features of the specific linguistic landscape described here is the dominance of the English language. On the one hand, it may be argued that this language choice reflects the importance of English in a globalised business world that is underpinned by economic concepts such as markets, production and consumption (Cenoz and Gorter 2009). By using English as a means of communication, real estate businesses are simply aiming to increase sales in an area that is, after all, an established tourism destination where English is the *lingua franca*. In that case, the language choice has to be seen as a functional part of the linguistic landscape. However, a more critical approach reveals that there is more going on here.

First, within the political economy of language, some languages emerge as having the kind of symbolic value that produces a 'profit of distinction' (Bourdieu 1981) in social exchanges which reflects the power of social groups they index (Gal 1989). Second, language choice in the public sphere not only *reflects* the power of groups, but also plays an active role in constructing collective identities and, ultimately, social divisions among groups (Gal and Irvine 1995). In the case under study, language choice in the local landscape, combined with various discursive strategies, reinforces the construction of a stylised, elitist place-identity based on privilege, difference and 'exclusivity'.

Thus, the linguistic landscape functions as a kind of interface between place, identity and local power relations. As part of the process of place-making – which, according to Harvey (1996) results from the complex dialectical interplay of different 'moments', including both the material and the imaginary construction and experiencing of places; social relations; institutionalised power and discursive activity – the texts reinforce an ideology that positions those who can stake a claim to the place through economic investment and property ownership as 'legitimate' migrants with the corresponding 'right' to make a home in the place. In other words, the power geometries of the place are, in part, constructed through the geosemiotics (Scollon and Scollon 2003) of the linguistic landscape. The identity of the so-called 'Golden Triangle' is being consistently reproduced as a place where affluent, English-speaking people have their homes, thus creating an enclavic sense of place with mapped-out boundaries (albeit symbolic rather than material) which seem to define who 'belongs' in this place.

Ultimately, such practices in many parts of the world reinforce the notion that lifestyle migration is embedded in 'consumption spaces' which are often characterised as 'enclosed and separated from wider social spheres, centred around leisure, consuming and simulation, regulated by disciplinary technologies of surveillance [and] gatekeeping' (Mansvelt 2005: 59). The purpose-built resorts that are typical of many lifestyle migration or 'residential-tourism' destinations (see, for example, Janoschka (2011) on Costa Rica; McWatters (2009) on Boquete in Mexico; Nudrali and Tamer (2011) on Turkey) are constant reminders that not only is consumption spatially located, but also that places may be produced through consumption and are themselves consumed.

However, it is important to remember that it is not only the material aspect of a place that shapes and is shaped by consumption practices (including those related to lifestyle migration, in particular the sale and purchase of land and property). The consumption of place also shapes and is shaped by dominant representations of places. Thus, such practices are reinforcing an available collective subject position for lifestyle migrants. For these 'outsiders' who may have no real sense of physical, cultural or ancestral ties with the place they have chosen as home, feelings of elective belonging are induced which are simultaneously both integrating (through in-group membership) and exclusionary, since a 'frontier' of difference is constructed leading to a powerful and distinctive sense of place-identity.

This type of empirical investigation into how discourses surrounding lifestyle migrant place-identities are constructed in the public sphere can help an understanding of how the subject positions that are made available to different 'types' of migrants impact on their own constructions of migrant identities, and, ultimately, their contribution to the politics of place. For northern European lifestyle migrants in this area of Portugal, the *in situ* construction of a privileged collective place-identity may help to explain some of the social practices of this group, for example the general apathy towards learning the local language and the overall lack of integration into the 'local' society. It is of course important to note that their lack of integration is a form of collective self-marginalisation; the majority seem content to remain on the edges of the 'local' society and make their own 'place in the sun'. This positioning might therefore be said to have overtones of (neo)colonialist discourse.

Clearly, linguistic boundaries contribute to powerful socio-cognitive representations of different modes and degrees of belonging in places. As Thurlow and Jaworski (2010: 210) note, 'the way people view and represent linguistic differences map onto their understanding, classification and evaluation of social actors, events and activities which they find significant, and to the formulation of their preferred worldviews'. While a highly visible language legitimises the claims to belonging of one group, conversely language *exclusion* may weaken the claims of other groups. It is certainly evident that the languages of eastern European migrant groups are almost entirely absent in the linguistic landscape of the Almancil area. Other forms of discursive positioning in the public sphere also contribute to the overall collective place-identities of different migrant groups. Thus, on the one hand, northern Europeans who buy property in the Algarve are generally referred to as 'residential-tourists', who, by dint of their 'tourist' status are deemed to contribute to the socio-economic progress of the country. On the other hand, migrant groups from eastern European countries fall under the label 'immigrant' – a term which evokes a far more problematic underlying social representation.

In sum, the hegemonic positioning of lifestyle migrants as economically 'beneficial' to the local area means that the privileged status accorded to them is rarely contested, and in fact rarely discussed in discourse emanating from the 'host' society. While this appears, on the surface at least, to indicate an unproblematic and even mutually beneficial relationship between lifestyle migrants in the Algarve and their hosts, as Benson and O'Reilly (2009) note, this does not mean that such relationships are necessarily symmetrical, since shifts in power and capital tend to consolidate differences among the various social groups who are, in one way or another, stakeholders in the place.

Notes

1 Texts can be defined as concrete instantiations of discourse, including written documents, bounded utterances, and multi-modal units such as public signs.

2 Since I take a socio-cognitive approach to discourse analysis, I understand ideologies to be networks of socio-cognitive representations that are deployed (typically through discourse) by different social groups to make sense of the social world and to regulate social practices (cf. van Dijk 1998).

3 From a Portuguese perspective, 'northern Europeans' include the British, Irish, Germans, Dutch and Scandinavians, which are the most representative national groups of lifestyle migrants in the Algarve.

4 A *freguesia* is the smallest geographical administrative division in Portugal.

5 It gained official status as a *Vila* (town) in 1988, as result of its development in demographic and infra-structural terms brought about by the tourism industry.

6 www.jf-almancil.pt/index.php (accessed 1 October 2010).

7 The online Directory of Businesses in Portugal (*Directório de Empresas Portuguesas*, available at www.infoempresas.com.pt (accessed 27 February 2011) cites a staggering 334 businesses in Almancil under 'real estate activities'.
8 *Serviços de Estrangeiros e Fronteiras* (SEF).
9 *Serviços de Acção Social Escolar.*
10 Source: SEF.
11 The first studies of the linguistic landscape are attributed to Spolsky and Cooper (1991) and Landry and Bourhis (1997). More recently, two edited collections (Gorter 2006; Shohamy and Gorter 2009) have expanded and developed this area of research.
12 *Regulamento da Actividade Publicitária na Área do Município de Loulé* de 6 de Janeiro de 2005.
13 See Torkington (2009) for further discussion of this.

References

Amin, A. (2004) 'Regions unbound: Towards a new politics of place', *Geografiska Annaler: Series B, Human Geography*, 86(1): 33–44.

Ben-Rafael, E. (2009) 'The study of linguistic landscapes', in E. Shohamy and D. Gorter (eds) *Linguistic Landscape: Expanding the Scenery*, London: Routledge, 40–54.

Ben-Rafael, E., Shohamy, E., Hasan Amara, M. and Trumper-Hecht, N. (2006) 'Linguistic Landscape as symbolic construction of the public space: The case of Israel', in D. Gorter (ed.), *Linguistic Landscape: A New Approach to Multilingualism*, Clevedon: Multilingual Matters,7–31.

Benson, M., and O'Reilly, K. (2009) 'Migration and the search for a better way of life: A critical exploration of lifestyle migration,' *The Sociological Review*, 57(4): 608–25.

Billig, M., Condor, S., Edwards, D., Gane, M., Middleton, D. and Radley, A. (1988) *Ideological Dilemmas: A Social Psychology of Everyday Thinking*, London: Sage.

Bourdieu, P. (1981) *Language and Symbolic Power* (trans. Raymond G. and Adamson, M.), Cambridge: Polity Press.

Cardoso Sousa, F. (2007) *Almancil e as novas oportunidades de negócio: um estudo sobre o passado, o presente e o futuro de Almancil, sob o ponto de vista dos residentes*, Loulé: Associação Empresarial de Almancil.

Cenoz, J. and Gorter, D. (2006) 'Linguistic landscape and minority languages', in D. Gorter (ed.) *Linguistic Landscape: A New Approach to Multilingualism,* Clevedon: Multilingual Matters, 67–81.

——(2009) 'Language economy and linguistic landscape', in E. Shohamy and D. Gorter (eds) *Linguistic Landscape: Expanding the Scenery*, London: Routledge, 55–69.

Cresswell, T. (2004) *Place: A Short Introduction*, Malden, MA: Blackwell Publishing.

Croucher, S. (2009) 'Migrants of privilege: The political transnationalism of Americans in Mexico', *Identities: Global Studies in Culture and Power*, 16 (4): 463–91.

Gal, S. (1989) 'Language and the political economy', *Annual Review of Anthropology*, 18: 345–67.

Gal, S. and Irvine, J. (1995) 'The boundaries of languages and disciplines: How ideologies construct differences', *Social Research*, 62: 967–1001.

Giddens, A. (1991) *Modernity and Self-Identity: Self and Society in the Late Modern Age*, Cambridge: Polity Press.

——(1994) *Beyond Left and Right: The Future of Radical Politics*, Cambridge: Polity Press.

Gorter, D. (ed.) (2006) *Linguistic Landscape: A New Approach to Multilingualism*, Clevedon: Multilingual Matters.

Harvey, D. (1996) *Justice, Nature and the Geography of Difference*. Cambridge MA: Blackwell.

Hodge, R. and Kress, G. (1988) *Social Semiotics*. Cambridge: Polity Press.

Janoschka, M. (2008) 'Identity politics as an expression of European citizenship practice: Participation of transnational migrants in local political conflicts', in R. Anghell, E. Gerharz, G. Rescher and M. Salzbrunn (eds) *The Making of World Society. Perspectives from Transnational Research*, Bielefeld: Transcript, 133–52.

——(2011) 'Imaginarios del turismo residencial en Costa Rica. Negociaciones de pertenencia y apropiación simbólica de espacios y lugares: una relación conflictiva' in T. Mazón, R. Huete and A. Mantecón (eds) *Construir una nueva vida: Los espacios del turismo y la migración residencial*, Santander: Milrazones, 81–102.

Jones, P. and Krzyżanowski, M. (2008) 'Identity, belonging and migration: Beyond constructing 'Others'', in G. Delanty, R. Wodak and P. Jones (eds) *Identity, Belonging and Migration*. Liverpool: Liverpool University Press, 38–54.

Koller, V. (2007) '"The World's Local Bank": Glocalisation as a strategy in corporate branding discourse', *Social Semiotics*, 17(1): 111–29.

——(2008a) 'Corporate brands as socio-cognitive representations', in G. Kristiansen and R. Dirven (eds), *Cognitive Sociolinguistics: Language Variation, Cultural Models, Social Systems*, Berlin: Mouton de Gruyter, 389–418.

——(2008b) '"The world in one city": Semiotic and cognitive aspects of city branding' *Journal of Language and Politics*, 7(3): 431–50.

Kress, G., and van Leeuwen, T. (1996) *Reading Images: The Language of Visual Design*, London: Routledge.

Landry, R., and Bourhis, R. Y. (1997) 'Linguistic landscape and ethnolinguistic vitality: An empirical study'. *Journal of Language and Social Psychology*, 16: 23–49.

Machin, D. (2004). 'Building the world's visual language: The increasing global importance of image banks in corporate media', *Visual Communication*, 3(3): 316–36.

McWatters, M. (2009). *Residential Tourism: (De)constructing Paradise*, Bristol: Channel View Publications.

Mansvelt, J. (2005). *Geographies of Consumption*. London: Sage.

Mantecón, A. (2010) 'Tourist modernization and social legitimation in Spain', *International Journal of Tourism Research*, 12: 617–26.

Markus, H. and Nurius, P. (1986) 'Possible selves', *American Psychologist*, 41(9): 954–69.

Massey, D. (1993) 'Power-geometry and a progressive sense of place', in J. Bird, B. Curtis, T. Putman, G. Robertson and L. Tickner (eds) *Mapping the Future*, London: Routledge, 59–69.

——(1994) *Space, Place and Gender*. Cambridge: Polity Press.

——(1999) 'Imagining globalization: Power geometries of time-space,', in A. Brah, M. J. Hickman and M. Mac Ghaill (eds) *Global Futures: Migration, Environment and Globalization*, Basingstoke: Macmillan, 27–44.

——(2004) 'Geographies of responsibility.' *Geografiska Annaler*, 86 B(1): 5–18

Mazón T., Huete R., Mantecón A. and Jorge, E. (2009) 'Legitimación y crisis en la urbanización de las regiones turísticas mediterráneas', in T. Mazón, R. Huete and A. Mantecón (eds) *Turismo, Urbanización y Estilos de Vida. Las Nuevas Formas de Movilidad Residencial*, Barcelona: Icaria, 399–412.

Meyer, M. (2001) 'Between theory, method and politics: Positioning of the approaches to CDA', in R. Wodak and M. Meyer (eds) *Methods of Critical Discourse Analysis,* London: Sage, 14–31.

Modan, G.G. (2007), *Turf Wars: Discourse, Diversity and the Politics of Place,* Maldon, MA: Blackwell.

Morgan, N. and Pritchard, A. (1998) *Tourism Promotion and Power: Creating Images, Creating Identities*, Chichester: John Wiley & Sons.

Myers, G. (1994) *Words in Ads*, London: Edward Arnold.

Nudrali, O. and O'Reilly, K. (2009) 'Taking the risk: The British in Didim, Turkey,' in M. Benson and K. O'Reilly (eds) *Lifestyle Migration: Expectations, Aspirations and Experiences*, Farnham: Ashgate, 137–52.

Nudrali, F. Ö. and Tamer, N. G. (2011) 'La búsqueda de la buena vida en un entorno cambiante: El caso de Didim, Turquía', in T. Mazón, R. Huete and A. Mantecón (eds) *Construir una nueva vida: Los espacios del turismo y la migración residencial*, Santander: Milrazones, 155–77.

Rampton, B. (2003) 'Hegemony, social class and stylization', *Pragmatics*, 13(1): 49–83.

Reh, M. (2004) 'Multilingual writing: A reader-oriented typology', *International Journal of the Sociology of Language,* 170: 1–41.

Relph, E. (1976) *Place and Placelessness*, London: Pion

Savage, M., Bagnall, G., and Longhurst, B. (2005) *Globalization and Belonging*, London: Sage.

Scollon, R. and Scollon, S. W. (2003) *Discourses in Place: Language in the Material World*, London: Routledge.

Shohamy, E. and Gorter, D. (eds) (2009) *Linguistic Landscape: Expanding the Scenery*, New York: Routledge.

Spolsky, B. and Cooper, R. (1991) *The Languages of Jerusalem*, Oxford: Clarendon Press.

Thurlow, C. and Jaworski, A. (2006) 'The alchemy of the upwardly mobile: Symbolic capital and the stylization of elites in frequent-flyer programmes', *Discourse and Society*, 17: 99–135.

——(2010) 'Silence is golden: The 'anti-communicational' linguascaping of super-elite mobility', in A. Jaworski and C. Thurlow (eds) *Semiotic Landscapes: Language, Image, Space*, London: Continuum.

Torkington, K. (2009) 'Exploring the linguistic landscape: The case of the 'Golden Triangle' in the Algarve, Portugal', *Papers from the Lancaster University Post-graduate Conference in Linguistics and Language Teaching*, Vol. 3.

——(2012) 'Place and lifestyle migration: the discursive construction of 'glocal' place-identity'. *Mobilities*, 7(1): 71–92.

Trudeau, D. (2006) 'Politics of belonging in the construction of landscapes: Place-making, boundary drawing and exclusion', *Cultural Geographies*, 13: 421–43.

Trumper-Hecht, N. (2009) 'Constructing national identity in mixed cities in Israel: Arabic on signs in the public space of Upper Nazareth', in E. Shohamy and D. Gorter (eds) *Linguistic Landscape: Expanding the Scenery*, London: Routledge, 238–52.

Tuan, Y.-F. (1991) 'Language and the making of place: A narrative-descriptive approach', *Annals of the Association of American Geographers*, 81(4): 684–96.

van Dijk, T. A. (1998) *Ideology: A Multidisciplinary Approach*, London: Sage

——(2008) *Discourse and Context: A Sociocognitive Approach*, Cambridge: Cambridge University Press.

——(2009) 'Critical discourse studies: A sociocognitive approach', in R. Wodak and M. Meyer (eds) *Methods of Critical Discourse Analysis,* London: Sage, 62–87.

van Leeuwen, T. (2005) *Introducing Social Semiotics*, Abingdon: Routledge.

Wodak, R. (2008) 'Discourse studies: Important concepts and terms', in R. Wodak and M. Krzyżanowski (eds) *Qualitative Discourse Analysis in the Social Sciences*, Basingstoke: Palgrave Macmillan, 1–29.

Wodak, R., and Meyer, M. (2009) 'Critical discourse analysis: History, agenda, theory', in R. Wodak and M. Meyer (eds) *Methods of Critical Discourse Analysis*, London: Sage, 1–34.

7 Utopian lifestyle migrants in Pucón, Chile

Innovating social life and challenging capitalism

Hugo Marcelo Zunino, Rodrigo Hidalgo Dattwyler and Ieva Zebryte

Introduction and conceptual issues

The literature on lifestyle migration places attention on mobile individuals that migrate to different places in search of a more fulfilling way of life, especially in contrast to the one left behind. Migration for these individuals is often an anti-modern, escapist, self-realisation project, a search for the intangible 'good life' (Benson and O'Reilly 1990). The emergence of 'mobile nomads' (D'Andrea 2007) not only constitutes the expression of a society that has dramatically reduced the barriers hampering the movement of individuals, commodities and ideas, it also signals a number of societal tensions and dissatisfactions which influence how individuals feel about their own existence. For Harvey (1992), the postmodern condition characterised by increasing an acceleration in the turnover of capital (via credit, electronic and plastic money, etc.) and an acceleration in consumption leads to deeper questions of identity for individuals living under this regime of accumulation, which explains that the search for identity many times means the revival of 'basic institutions' such as 'family' and 'community'. The search for identity through lifestyle migration is a complex phenomenon that triggers processes at a variety of spatial scales. The receiving community and the incomers will eventually engage in disputes over meaning, while each actor attempts to advance particularistic ends through the deployment of a range of spatial and cultural strategies. In addition, new forms of appropriation of space will emerge as groups of individuals, via material or symbolic appropriation, attempt to control its production and reproduction. These two outcomes will necessarily imply the rearticulation of power relations as actors acquire a differential capacity to exert control over other actors. In short, lifestyle migration is not a neutral process; it is deeply political, given that actors are capable of constructing meanings, engaging in disputes over meaning, and rearticulating the basis to exert power. So the question here is to what extent lifestyle migrants can challenge – discursively and practically – the way of life and customs prevalent in our late-capitalist society. Although many researchers emphasise that practices carried out by the incoming populations are subject to surveillance and commodification, we claim that they do retain the capacity to affect more general social structures of society. From our understanding, some central questions to assess this capacity are the following: How does the migration process unfold on the empirical level? What meanings are put forward? What practices are deployed to appropriate space materially and symbolically? Our approach first puts analytical attention on conflict over settlement, signalling that 'the social' gets concrete expression primarily through a system of written and unwritten rules that defines the channels open to exert power (Zunino 2006). However, this does not necessarily mean the capacity to trigger social changes is extinguished in the absence of struggles; there are always possibilities to change the value system of late capitalism society from below, from the local, from that sphere where dreams and projects attain concrete material expression.

Taking the case of the City of Pucón (Chile), this work is aimed at analysing the capacity of a particular group of lifestyle migrants – those who seek to construct a utopian being in the world – of changing social rules structuring late capitalist society. Pucón is a tourist destination located in southern Chile. It is endowed with a variety of natural amenities including a lake, rivers, a volcano, and pristine forests. In the summer, this city attracts thousands of tourists from all over the world, mostly from Europe and North America. In summer, in the small but carefully organised city centre, the local government (the Municipality of Pucón) and the powerful local chamber of commerce organise a variety of activities (festivals, concerts, marathons and other cultural events) aimed at fostering the business climate and displaying a representation of Pucón constructed in the minds of businessmen and public decision-makers eager to present an idea that exalts consumerism and hedonism. In the middle of winter, the population drops from nearly 50,000 to 20,000; streets and shops are quiet, except some stores frequented by the 'locals'. The locals are a heterogeneous group consisting of 'the Puconinos' (people raised in Pucón) and the 'afuerinos' (migrants, public officials, retirees, businessmen). Underlying the 'visible Pucón', we can witness, if we look carefully, a 'hidden Pucón' that gets expression in a number of cultural practices that take place mainly in the homes of *afuerinos* located primarily in condominiums and subdivisions near the city centre (the wealthier ones) and in rural areas distant from the core of social activity (the impoverished ones). Practices performed by incomers include shamanic rituals, oriental medicine, meditation and handcrafting; temples, organic shops, retreat and alternative medicine houses constitute the material representation of this way of life. Since these sites are sparsely located and no ostentation is made, it is difficult for visitors to witness or gain access to this world. Those who practice this way of life are Chilean and foreign migrants that have settled in the area in the last 10 years, forming a more or less compact group that can be identified by the way they greet each other (belonging entitles you to be treated as a 'sister' or 'brother'), how they talk (usually calm individuals looking directly into your eyes), how they dress (generally a 1960s neo-hippie style), and where they get together. Who are they? Why did they migrate? What are they looking for? To what extent has this group been able to transform the social rules framing their interaction? Do they represent a challenge to capitalism? In what sense?

Lifestyle migrations and the struggle over meaning

In Latin America, most researchers have deployed the framework proposed by amenity migration literature to make sense of the migration of people to tourist destinations (Otero *et al.* 2006; Hidalgo *et al.* 2009; González *et al.* 2009; Hidalgo and Zunino 2011). For most of these researchers, the spaces where amenity migration unfolds will inevitably undergo gradual transformation into spaces of capitalistic production and consumption. The depredation will exhaust their environmental resources, undermine the local culture, and create new burdens for local governance (see, for example, González *et al.* 2009; Gossnell and Abrams 2009). Although we do not challenge this finding at the general level, if we consider the struggles over meaning that the reallocation unleashes, the analytical drive moves from abstract urban processes to concrete manifestations of the human condition and how social life becomes structured. Examining this complexity, Madison (2006) articulates the notion of 'existential migration', which makes reference to individuals who choose to leave their homeland in order to become foreigners in a new culture, revealing consistently deep themes and motivations related to the construction of their own identity. Rather than migrating in search of employment, career advancement or overall improved economic conditions, these voluntary migrants are seeking greater possibilities for self-actualisation and exploring foreign cultures in order to grasp issues of home and belonging in the world generally (see Madison 2006: 238–39). Although Madison's work provides useful insights on migration and its ontology of home, we must also consider that existential migration (Zunino and Hidalgo 2010) is related dialectically to the postmodern human condition and struggles over meaning. In the midst of the increasing anxiety and dissatisfaction in the capitalistic world, individuals seek shelter in new cultures and strive to reinvent themselves and reconstruct the basis of their being in the world, yet this is not a mere outcome of society; it is a key ingredient in our contemporary state of affairs.[1]

Some researchers have noted the aforementioned existential motives driving migration but have largely ignored the complexities and the potential ramification of the process or have downplayed the capacity of migrants to create a new lifestyle and eventually challenge capitalism on concrete grounds. Korpela (2009) claims, for example, that despite the anti-materialist discourse, the Westerners' stay in Varanasi (India) is mainly a question of economic rationality and privilege, a matter of taking advantage of the capitalist order of things where they can earn money in the West and then spend it in India. The 'Indiascape' is then a part of global economic inequalities, and although migrants criticise consumerism, at the same time they utilise the capitalist world order to their own benefit. In his case study of 'hippie' practices in Ibiza, Spain, D'Andrea (2007) recognises that even though there are places where people resist commodification, the situation must be considered in the context of capitalist predation, emphasising the capacity and reach of business interests to control social practices and make individuals amenable to control via economic logic. In his work, the hippie culture is largely depicted as caught up in drugs, hedonism and superficiality.

Taking retirees' migration to the Costa Blanca (Alicante, Spain) and using a theoretical framework inspired by Bourdieu's notion of habitus, Janoschka (2011a) analyses political participation in the destination of lifestyle mobility migrants and discusses the possibilities for transforming and reinventing habitus dispositions – which also entails changing the power configurations at play in a given location. He argues that mobility can provoke a rapid shock-like transformation that triggers critical attitudes that require new interpretations and incorporations of the social world (critical reflexivity). In the empirical example, he portrays how political movements were able to change a social field within given political power relations, in this way establishing a much needed link between mobility, meaning-making practices and social change. When they move to a distant location, lifestyle migrants carry on the seed of social change; this seed is endowed with desires, dreams and plans. In the destination and in co-presence with other migrants, individuals will construct specific attachment to places, and projects will eventually achieve concrete material expression. They are not beings endowed only with existential needs, nor spiritual migrants devoid of any capacity to deeply affect structures of society, nor bohemian drug users searching for instant pleasures and gratification. Instead, lifestyle migrants carry on more or less developed *life projects*. Indeed, based on pre-mobility reflexivity, they usually arrive at the destination with ideas of how to live the rest of their existence. As Giddens' (1984) theory of structuration suggests, individuals are in a dialectical relationship with the structural features, which enables and constrains human action. This is why contemporary migrants write their dreams in the settings defined by postmodern late capitalist society. Projects, then, emerge in the midst of daily routine practices conducted in given structural settings and, therefore, projects are endowed with a *sense of reality* that is strong enough to push individuals to migrate, radically affecting the ways they make sense of the world. Then, migrants carry on utopias, defined as broad life projects that emerge in the midst of the structure-agency dialectics.

In this context, we will use the expression 'utopian lifestyle migrants' (ULMs) to refer to individuals who pursued a project emerging from a reflective attitude towards life and society before migration took place. Migration of ULMs is therefore an intentional project and the outcomes are impossible to anticipate, as they depend on the opportunities and constraints they will face and the tactics and strategies deployed to advance given ends. Of course, there are many discourses framing projects and there is no necessary unity within them.

However, as suggested by Benson and O'Reilly (2009), migration for lifestyle migrants (and ULMs) is commonly an anti-modern, escapist, self-realisation project. In recalling this work, we will examine the projects of recent utopian lifestyle migrants to the City of Pucón, Chile. This will lead us to consider their customs, goals, dreams and the difficulties encountered at the destination. Afterwards, we will discuss the issue of power and examine the opportunities open to ULMs to practically challenge the way of life and customs prevalent in our late capitalist society.

Utopian lifestyle migrants in the city of Pucón, Chile

Studies carried out by the authors in 2007 and 2008 (Zunino and Hidalgo 2010) corroborate that many migrants are taking Pucón as a destination to live and realise their utopias. In general, these individuals and families pursue a project aimed at living in harmony with nature and enacting lifestyles that are different from those suggested by modernity. These aims are worked out through practices such as alternative healing methods, religious groups based on some versions of Buddhism, biodynamic agriculture, and Waldorf-oriented teaching methods. All these practices are related to a more or less articulated eco-centric discourse. The methodological approach for collecting the experience of utopian lifestyle migrants was diachronic and synchronic, based on the analysis of primary data (interviews with representative social actors). The first phase involved working with a utopian amenity migrant, with whom there was already a mutual trust. With the help of this assistant, a sample of utopian amenity migrants was selected, according to the disposition of the migrants to participate in the study, the time available and the necessary economy that should be given to any investigation. Thus, we used an intentional sampling, which also considered the acceptance of voluntary and confidential participation in this research as criteria (Mejía 2000). Regarding sample characteristics, most interviewees were in the developmental stage of young adulthood (25–40 years), while other informants were in the stage of middle adulthood (40–60 years). Most of them (95 per cent) had completed high school; 25 per cent of the sample had attended postgraduate programmes at prestigious national and international universities.

Spiritual improvement, self-realisation, searching for a better life, escaping the fear of the same situation, and the inspiration provided by landscape amenities were some of the main motivations for migrating. María elaborates on why she migrated:

> Certainly, this is a very, very different world. I think that all this capitalist world and all that, it is only interesting for some people … . In some way this place has something that make people from Santiago come in. I think that many people come out of curiosity for the entire mystique that you can find here.

Alexander put the emphasis on the spiritual dimension as a factor that motivated him to change:

> I have the spiritual clarity about what I want, and when I came here everything was put together. Honestly, without the intention of removing the merit of the beauty, the incredible community and the place, I feel it is a personal process that makes me feel at home. It is important to say that in here there is an awesome community. … I was not interested in going against the stream.

Regarding what migrants are looking for, amenities play an essential role in the decision to migrate. However, the deepest reasons are related to finding a path that allows them a better life and an existence in communion with the spirit, beauty and 'strength' of the place, creating an obvious contrast with what they left behind. Also, this is related to living a 'slow life', a possibility of building an alternative life and a 'quiet life'. Most utopian lifestyle migrants changed their living places to start a new life project and live in mystical communion with nature.

Marcelo, a commercial engineer, talks about his searching for a way that connects him spiritually with the place:

> It was like I wanted to live and not accept the traditional role … and commercial engineering was an excellent tool to ask myself about the economic system and getting to know it. … I have lived in many places; I wanted to live a simple life, learn how to grow crops. I also worked as a carpenter. I worked very hard. I occasionally worked as a commercial engineer, administrating a place, organizing things … and from the hotel to there, I stayed in the forest. You can also do things for the community in here. There was spiritual practice. Since I was at school, I started seeking something; I started doing yoga and experienced Zen meditation, a lot of things to tell the truth, but always doing more and more meditation, opening my mind to all of this.

The narration often showed an anti-modern and escapist project, where the most pressing issue was self-realisation and the search for a more meaningful way of life. Most of the stories include reference to the desire to escape from situations like monotony, daily routine, individualism, materialism and consumerism. Many individuals depicted migration in terms of a path from lifestyles they presumed to be negative towards a meaningful and full life. The expression 'going back to the basics', understood as ongoing simplicity and originality, was commonly used.

Territory, culture and social change

Since the very establishment of human communities, the use of territory has been an inevitable source of tension among social actors who seek to obtain various kinds of benefits. In contemporary social geography, attention has been centred, for some time, on elucidating how individuals and organisations possessing particular territorial interests employ a range of strategies to organise space and produce a landscape adequate to satisfy certain demands. A constructivist approach to the notion of space enables us to consider the power relations among actors involved in the process of territorial development (see Jacobs 1992; Healey 1997, 1999; Huxley 2007; Zukin 1991; Zunino 2006). What are the options open for challenging the capitalistic production and reproduction of space? Are there any options in the first place?

A number of authors have noted that the capitalist system has been 'naturalised' by the dominant discourse, mystified and converted into an 'entity' invulnerable to political action (see Fairclough 2000; Prozorov 2004), making social change on any scale seem impossible or unrealistic. Taking up these ideas, Escobar (2000, 2005) argues that the reappropriation of place converted into territory constitutes the basis for any alternative, in the sense that common people can construct more human worlds, whether in their environmental, social or economic dimensions (also see Bramwell and Meyer 2007; Gupta and Ferguson 1997).

The notion of territoriality is central for understanding the cultural and political relevance of the ULMs. Territoriality is understood as the appropriation of a delimited space, connecting nature and human beings. Following Giménez (1996, 2001), it is useful to distinguish between utilitarian and symbolic appropriation. Utilitarian appropriation – dominant in our current culture – gives territory a material meaning, and space is understood as a commodity accompanied by an exchange value. The ULMs' territory is also endowed with symbolic and cultural meanings: it is a place where a history is inscribed (even though it has a short duration), it has directions or orientations that are deemed sacred by some traditions (North, South, East and West represent stages of the life-path of individuals) and it inspires collective representation of varying types. This symbolic appropriation of place goes hand in hand with the construction of identities, which represents an incentive for the formation of local networks which can act strategically when the right opportunities emerge to make certain meanings prevail (see Dewsbyry and Cloke 2009). Struggles and negotiations over meaning are, then, pivotal in understanding how space becomes politicised (also see Janoschka 2011b).

To evaluate the capacity for change, it is essential to theorise power and how it may eventually be exercised to stimulate processes of socio-cultural change in local territories. Following the best known theorist of power (Michel Foucault 1980, 1992, 1995), power does not constitute 'a thing' which is possessed, but rather it is something that only acquires reality insofar as it is exercised through the employment of tactics and strategies. It is through the exercise of power that discourses of reality emerge. An essential aspect of power is that it operates or circulates on different scales in non-deterministic forms (also see Clegg 1987; Zunino 2006). This means that the general structural scenario does not impose a determined 'architecture of power'; the structural factors acting at general levels do not result in a simple, mechanical 'condensation' of power relations. Based on Foucault's work, Clegg (1989) coined the notions 'agency' and 'structural' sides of power. The structural side of power is understood as a set of general, existing, socio-economic conditions that define the authority, or command capacity, of each actor. By the agency side of power, Clegg means the capacity retained by agents to act politically in given local settings.

For Foucault (1995), power exercised at the local level within the most mundane and immediate sphere of life has historically been minimised. The power of social macro-structures has effectively been given too much importance, with an almost obsessive emphasis on the capitalist structure of production and consumption. For Foucault, power has a 'capillary' character: to sustain a particular form of domination in space and through time, this must be reproduced in the local sphere. At the moment in which local actors cease to behave in accordance with the rules which prevail at the general level, a 'systemic fault' occurs and it is precisely at this space–time juncture that possibilities for gradual or sudden social change open up. It may therefore be affirmed that each revolution begins with local centres of resistance, clusters of resistance points which can gradually filter upwards to affect macro-structural levels. It is in this context that the ULMs have the capacity – as structural agents – to 'construct reality' through direct political action aimed at reinforcing the meanings they carry on and which define their group identity. Yet in Pucón, material and symbolic appropriation tend to coexist, as no significant conflicts have emerged.

Does this mean that there are no options? Capitalistic values reign unchallenged? Is not the passivity of this community involved in the unchallenged reproduction of the system? If we recall the case of Ibiza, Spain, portrayed by D'Andrea (2007), migrants there appear mostly as capitalist puppets controlled by a steady and almost unchallenged banalisation and commodification of social life. Although one can agree that the lack of political commitment and participation is a problem, the utopian migrants do challenge capitalist values at the most immediate level: in daily life, where concrete cultural practices unfold. This symbolic aspect of change remains unnoticed for many researchers as they place attention on struggles over meaning that unfolds within the formal political organisation. Like any social process, daily life occurs in the midst of the dialectic relationship between structure and agency: by performing in a certain way, social actors can not only recreate the system but also change it, via concrete practices. We will draw upon two practices to make this point.

From a critical standpoint, schooling can be thought of as a mechanism to domesticate the human spirit as it enforces certain values and worldviews that become naturalised: the child is taught how he/she must behave, what is right and wrong, and an official history is told. Lessons are packed in convenient packages that can be delivered rapidly in a broad area. There are, indeed, strong forces – the market and the government, for example – which, to a large extent, set the rules in education, making substantial changes very difficult. Most of the lifestyle migrants, however, take their children to a local Waldorf-oriented school, whose director, not surprisingly, is actually a ULM. This schooling method draws on an idea of education more as an art than as a technique. For Nobel (1998), teaching should be something more than merely a mechanical distribution of isolated facts, if teaching is to have life and meaning for students and teachers, and also if the continuously increasing quantity of information and facts is to promote life rather than death in the future. Through practices that combine science and art, it is claimed that Waldorf education allows personalised attention to children and forming human beings more aware and ready to grasp their one identity (see Nobel 1998: 151).

Similarly, many ULMs engage in the practice of permaculture, defined by Mannen *et al.* (2012) as focused on creating consciously designed landscapes which mimic the patterns and relations found in nature, while yielding an abundance of food, fibre and energy for the provision of local needs. These eco-friendly practices are also linked to promoting 'local food' initiatives which 'shorten the links' between producer and consumer through a diverse collaboration of many social sectors (small farmers, agronomic experts, retailers, and several different consumer sectors). Following Starr (2010: 480), several researchers have emphasised the possibility of consumption as a site equally important to production for achieving such social goals like sustainability and have shown how politics now touches everyday life, where activities (like food production and consumption) become politicised and those who are politically marginalised find some capacity and reach to express their politics. This movement can be considered under the tenants of the newer social movement theory in action (Starr 2010: 482) that claims that social change happens less as a result of confrontations and more because of gradual shifts in beliefs and values, signalling the importance of cultural innovations and meaning-making practices. The search for identity – at the core of the perspective of social movements – carries great potential for innovation and transformation, which is why alternative lifestyles should not be considered marginal but as an appropriate reaction to new forms of control.

Conclusions

Attempting to materially or symbolically appropriate territory entails putting forward a set of ideas, values and beliefs that are inscribed in a specific territoriality that emerges from social and cultural practices performed in daily life. This situation can lead to struggles over meaning within the formal political apparatus, opening up avenues of social change as individuals and groups of individuals exert power at strategic nodes. This is the way resistance and the possibility of change has been studied in instrumentally oriented and conflict-driven literature. The new social movement proponents instead place attention on how meaning-making practices open the way for cultural and social innovations to gradually 'stick' in society and transform the value-system of the dominant capitalist society. The cultural innovations brought about by ULMs constitute deliverable efforts to work through existing channels and make their values prevail on the most immediate scale: where projects achieve concrete expression, the sphere of daily routines. Both Waldorf-oriented teaching methods and permaculture initiatives constitute examples of means through which specific values are recreated, allowing their ideals to achieve material expression and preventing consumerism from penetrating their constructed reality. In our view, the ULMs portrayed in this study represent one defence against the interests of the dominant society, working with the arms offered by the very system itself. If they act strategically when envisioning any gap or opportunity that opens up, they could eventually be effective in bringing changes at more general and permanent levels. This entails making their action and social practice deeply political, as suggested by the literature on new social movements. Notwithstanding that ULMs are trapped in the local, living in a utopian dream world, we cannot ignore the revolutionary potential they hold.

This study opens up a research agenda aimed at disclosing the particularities of lifestyle migrants in other areas of Chile and the world, deepening our understanding of this phenomenon via ethnographic work of longer duration. This will allow us to advance analytical categories and concepts which better capture the particularity of lifestyle migration. Research projects already under way are attempting to inquire more deeply into the ULMs' way of life, aspirations, and potential to affect deeper structures of society.

Acknowledgement

This text is in part an outcome of the FONDECYT 1100588 project. We thank CONICYT-Chile for funding investigation and giving it the necessary continuity. The authors would like to express their gratitude to the research assistants, with a special mention to Camila Del Río for her work in the coordination and transcription of the material collected in the interviews.

Note

1 In a similar vein, D'Andrea (2007) claims that new forms of subjectivity and identity are being developed in dialectic interplay with major global processes.

References

Benson, M. and O'Reilly, K. (2009) 'Migration and the search for a better way of life: a critical exploration of lifestyle migration', *The Sociological review*, 57(4): 608–25.

Bramwell, B. and Meyer, D. (2007) 'Power and tourism development in transition', *Annals of Tourism Research*, 34: 766–68.

Clegg, S. (1989) *Frameworks of Power*, London: Sage.

D'Andrea, A. (2006) 'Neo-nomadism: a theory of post-identitarian mobility in the global age', *Mobilities*, 1(1): 95–119.

——(2007) 'Deciphering the space and scale of global nomadism', in S. Sassen (ed.) *Deciphering the Global: Its Scales, Spaces and Subjects*, London: Routledge, 201–20.

——(2011) 'Methodological challenges and innovations in mobilities research', *Mobilities*, 6(2): 149–60.

Dewsbyry, J. and Cloke, P. (2009) 'Spiritual landscape: existence, performance and immanence', *Social & Cultural Geography*, 10: 695–711.

Escobar, A. (2000) '¿El lugar de la naturaleza y la naturaleza del lugar: globalización o postdesarrollo?' in Lader, E. (ed.), *La colonialidad del saber: eurocentrismo y ciencias sociales,* Buenos Aires: Clacso.

——(2005) 'El 'postdesarrollo' como concepto y práctica social,' in Mato, D. (ed.) *Políticas de economía, ambiente y sociedad en tiempos de globalización*, Caracas: Universidad Central de Venezuela.

Fairclough, N. (2000) 'Representaciones del cambio en el discurso neoliberal' *Cuaderno de relaciones laborales*, 16: 13–35.

Foucault, M. (1980) 'Power and Strategies', in Gordon, C. (ed.), *Power/Knowledge: Selected Interviews and Other Writings*, New York: Pathenon.

——(1992) *La microfísica del poder*, Madrid: La Piqueta.

——(1995) *Discipline and Punish: The Birth of the Prison*, New York: Vintage.

Giddens, A. (1984) *The Constitution of Society: Outline of the Theory of Structuration*. Cambridge: Polity Press.

Giménez, G. (1996) 'Territorio y cultura' *Estudios sobre la culturas contemporáneas*, ii: 9–30.

González R. Otero, A., Nakayama, I. and Marioni, S. (2009) 'Las movilidades del turismo y las migraciones de amenidad: problemáticas y contradicciones en el desarrollo de centros turísticos de montaña,' *Revista de Geografía Norte Grande*, 44: 75–92.

Gosnell, H. and Abraham, S. (2010) 'Amenity migration: diverse conceptualizations of drivers, socioeconomic dimensions, and emerging challenges', *Geojournal*, 23: 34–67.

Gupta, A. and Ferguson, J. (1997) 'Beyond 'culture': space, identity and the politics of difference,' in Gupta, A. and Ferguson, J. (eds) *Culture, Power, Place: Explorations in Critical Anthropology*, London: Duke University Press.

Harvey, D. (1989) *The Condition of Postmodernity: An Enquiry into the Origins of Cultural Change*, London: Basil Blackwell.

Healey, P. (1997) *Collaborative Planning: Shaping Places in Fragmented Societies*, London: Macmillan.

Hidalgo, R., Borsdorf, A. and Plaza, F. (2009) 'Parcelas de agrado alrededor de Santiago y Valparaíso ¿Migración por amenidad a la chilena?' *Revista de Geografía Norte Grande*, 44: 75–92

Hidalgo, R. and Zunino, H.M. (2011) 'Negocios inmobiliarios en centros turísticos de montaña y nuevos modos de vida: el papel de los migrantes de amenidad en la comuna de Pucón, IX región de la Araucanía, Chile', *Estudios y perspectivas en turismo*, 23: 45–64.

Jacobs, J. (1992) *The Death and Life of Great American Cities*, New York: Random House.

Janoschka, M. (2011a) 'Habitus and radical reffiexivity: a conceptual approach to study political articulations of lifestyle- and tourism-related mobilities', *Journal of Policy Research in Tourism, Leisure & Events*, 3(3): 224–36.

——(2011b) 'Imaginarios del turismo residencial en Costa Rica. Negociaciones de pertenencia y apropiación simbólica de espacios y lugares: una relación conflictiva,' in T. Mazón, R. Huete and A. Mantecón (eds) *Construir una Nueva Vida. Los Espacios del Turismo y la Migración Residencial*, Milrazones, Costa Rica: Santander.

Korpela, M. (2010a) 'Living happily ever after or ending up in another crises? Bohemian lifestyle migrants in Varanasi, India', Proceedings, Maynooth: The EASA conference.

——(2010b) 'Me, myself and I: Western lifestyle migrants in search of themselves in Varanasi, India', *Recreation and Society in Africa, Asia & Latin America*, 1(1): 53–73.

Madison, G. (2006) 'Existential migration. Conceptualising out of the experiential depths of choosing to leave "home"', *Existential Analysis*, 17(2): 238–60.

Mannen D., Hinton, S., Kuijper T. and Porter, P. (2012) 'Sustainable organizing: A multiparadigm perspective of organizational development and permaculture gardening', *Journal of Leadership & Organizational Studies*, 14(6): 769–91.

Nobel, A. (1998) 'On art, science, education and the human factor', *Journal of Human Values*, 4: 149–54

Otrero, A., Nakayama, I. and Marioni, S. (2006), 'Amenity migration in the Patagonian mountain community of San Martín de Los Andes, Neuquén, Argentina' in Moss, L. (ed.) *The Amenity Migrants: Seeking and Sustaining Mountains and their Cultures*, Wallingford: Wallingford Press. 2006.

Prozorov, S. (2004) 'Three theses on 'governance' and the political', *Journal of International Relations and Development*, 23: 267–93.

Starr, A. (2010) 'Local food: A social movement?' *Cultural Studies → Critical Methodologies*, 10(6): 479–90.

Waldren, J. (1996) *Insiders and Outsiders: Paradise and Reality in Mallorca*, Providence, RI: Berghahn Books.

Zukin, S. (1991) *Landscapes of Power*, Los Angeles: University of California Press.

Zunino, H. M. (2006) 'Power relations in urban decision-making: neo-liberalism, "techno-politicians" and "authoritarian redevelopment" in Santiago, Chile', *Urban Studies*, 43, 1825–46.

Zunino, H.M. and Hidalgo, R. (2009) 'Spatial and socioeconomic effects of social housing policies implemented in Chile: the case of Valparaíso', *Urban Geography*, 30, 514–42.

Zunino, H. and Hidalgo, R. (2010), 'En busca de una utopía verde: migrantes de amenidad en la comuna de pucón, IX Región de la Araucanía, Chile', *Scripta Nova. Revista electrónica de geografía y ciencias sociales*, 14(331). Electronic edition.

8 Quest migrants

French people in Morocco searching for 'elsewhereness'

Catherine Therrien

Introduction

In the writings about contemporary migrations, research presenting Morocco as a country of emigration and France as a country of immigration seems to envisage mobility exclusively from the South to the North. Even if it cannot be compared to the migratory flow of Moroccans to France, a migration from the North to the South exists, too. Indeed Morocco is a destination appreciated by many Europeans and especially by the French. The opportunity to have an experience offering a change of scene without feeling out of their element is the main reason why French people are attracted to Morocco. Morocco is an Arabic–French-speaking country, a few hours flight from France, with a nice climate and political stability. It therefore fulfils a desire for 'nearby exoticism' by providing French people with an experience of differences within reassuring colonial reference marks. The French can freely move between France and Morocco, easily build their migration project during their different stays and even leave France without a definite project. It is possible for them to settle in Morocco with the only objective to search for a better quality of life. Indeed, the migration channels of some French people reflect the views of some writings about lifestyle migrations: the key motivation for those migrations has been the search for something intangible, encapsulated in the phrase 'quality of life' (O'Reilly 2007).

Nevertheless, as my interest in the French living in Morocco increased during a three-year cross-country study of transnationalism funded by the European Commission,[1] I found the existing migration categories do not reflect the trajectories of some migrants interviewed during our fieldwork. Although the 'lifestyle migrants' category seems to be the most relevant one to categorise them, yet some differences in migration trajectories exist between them and British retirees settled in Spain (Gustafson 2008; Casado-Díaz 2006; Rodríguez 2001), Quebecers settled in Florida (Tremblay and O'Reilly 2004) or French people settled in Marrakech (Petermann this volume; Bousta 2007), for example. That is what led me to create the particular category of 'quest migrants', which allows us to deal with the specific trajectory of these migrants.

This chapter, based on data collected through the above-mentioned European research consortium, proposes to clarify this innovative concept of quest migrants, arguing it can encompass the migration trajectories motivated by lifestyle rather than economic factors (McIntyre 2011; O'Reilly and Benson 2009) as well as the quest for well-being (spiritual or existential). By relating the concept of quest migrants to other migrant categories which were created to explore similar trajectories, I will first show its capability to encompass these different categories and to nuance the category of lifestyle migration. Next I will give some contextual elements concerning the French presence, I will indicate the methodology used to collect the data, and I will describe the different migration trajectories of the French interviewed. Then I will explain how my analysis led me to create and propose the new and original category of 'quest migrants'.

Quest migrant: an all-encompassing category

If some other migrant categories have been developed to throw light on similar phenomena, the quest migrant category has the advantage of being fully inclusive, which is not the case of the other categories. The *mobile lifestyle migrants with Bohemian aspirations* (Korpela 2009) met in Varanasi, the *global nomads* D'Andrea (2007) followed between Spain and India, the *utopian lifestyle migrants* discovered in Pucón (Chile) by Hidalgo *et al.* (this volume), the *seek refuges* depicted by Hoey (2009) in rural Northern Michigan, the *spiritual migrants* established in the Canadian Rockies highlighted by Locke (2006) and the *spiritual* and *hedonistic-expressive expatriates* interviewed by Giguère (2010) in Rishikesh and Goa (India) can all be defined as quest migrants. In contrast, the French quest migrants I met in Morocco are not all committed to a spiritual quest or bohemian ideal (Benson and O'Reilly 2009). As I will argue in this chapter, this category also helps refine the lifestyle migrant category by introducing a significant distinction: if lifestyle migration can be defined as an escape *from* somewhere and something, while simultaneously an escape *to* self-fulfilment (Benson and O'Reilly 2009), a distinction has to be made between the different meanings given by migrants to this self-fulfilment: are they looking to *live* better or to *feel* better? As we will see later on, the specificity of quest migrants' narratives can be found in a common search for well-being made possible through a quest for 'elsewhereness'.

Some contextual items concerning the French presence in Morocco

In the present context, when Moroccan emigration to Europe is drawing the attention of media and the academic world, it seems necessary to recall that Morocco was a country of immigration in the early twentieth century. From 1912 to 1956, the centre of Morocco was under French protectorate, and the north and south under Spanish protectorate. In that colonial era, a lot of

Europeans (particularly French and Spanish) started to migrate to Morocco. The settlement of French people in Morocco grew steadily during the whole colonial period. In 1955, the year before Morocco gained its independence, it was the reverse: departures started to outweigh arrivals. When Morocco became independent, more and more Moroccans were appointed to the administration, which urged a good many French people to leave. In the 1960s, departures slowed down (Cassaigne 1964), but in the early 1970s they again gained momentum when more and more agricultural lands became Moroccan (which put an end to the last remnants of the colonial period) and Arabic became the language used for teaching in schools.

Since the end of the protectorate, relations between France and Morocco have been based on cultural, scientific and technical cooperation (Picod-Kinany 2010). Various bilateral agreements were signed between the two countries in such domains as development, tourism, the tax system and laws concerning the family. It is also worth mentioning that France is the first customer and the first supplier of Morocco and ranks first industrially and commercially, with more than 1,000 French firms and 520 subsidiaries presently in Morocco (Picod-Kinany 2010). All these historical, economic and political reasons explain why the French presence in Morocco is still fairly important today. According to the website of the French Embassy in Morocco, over 42,000 French people reside in Morocco,[2] mostly in Casablanca and Rabat. It is the most important foreign presence, followed by the Spanish. And yet very few researchers in social sciences focus on this contemporary French presence.

It is rather easy to summarise the contemporary works on French migration. In Germany, Petermann and Escher (this volume) revealed the neocolonial paradise of French migrants in Marrakech. In France, Picod-Kinany (2010) in her PhD thesis in sociology dealt with European migration to Morocco, and more particularly French migrants. In Morocco, Bousta (2007) made a connection between tourism and migration in the case of residential tourists settled in Marrakech, and the work of Mohamed Berriane (2010) focuses on the new migratory dynamics and specifically, in recent years, on the European migration to Morocco. Our study within the framework of the European research project dealing with transnational links in the Franco-Moroccan space (Virkama *et al.* 2012) has contributed to an exploratory description of various courses of migration taken by the French in Morocco. In my PhD thesis in anthropology (Therrien 2012, 2009) I studied the migration and identity trajectory of foreigners in mixed couples living in Morocco; 10 out of 31 couples in the sample were Franco-Moroccan. As far as we know, it is the only research tackling French contemporary migration to Morocco.

Research methodology

For the initial European research consortium on transnationalism we (the Moroccan team) did semi-structured interviews in different cities (Fez,

Meknes, Rabat, Casablanca, Mrirt, El Hajeb, Temara and Karia Ba Mohamed) with 60 French persons[3] and 21 Moroccan returnees. A year later (in 2010), we collected the life stories of 21 of them during a second phase of the research. My personal reflection about quest migrants emerged at the end of this research. The analysis of the collected interviews from a new viewpoint has made it possible to create this new category of quest migrants. I selected 10 out of the 60 French interviewees (five men and five women) corresponding to the category of quest migrants. We had only mentioned them in the research report for the consortium (Therrien and Harrami 2010), so I went more deeply into the biographical analysis to grasp the reasons why I had created such a category. To what extent and how were the quest migrants different from the others? What were the points these various migrants had in common whose motivations first looked so diverse? These are some of the questions which structure this chapter.

I would like to emphasise the importance of the narrative approach which gave rise to this new concept of quest migrants. The narrative approach 'is now seen as one of the fundamental ways in which humans organize their understanding of the world' (Cortazzi 2001: 1). Life stories give the possibility to grasp the meaning each person gives to his or her course of life while a close relationship is created between the researcher and the interviewee. Without that trusting relationship and the freedom of expression made possible by the narrative approach, I could not have had access to some essential biographical elements whose analysis gave birth to the concept of quest migrants.

The migration trajectories of French people

For the majority of French interviewees, the departure for Morocco had been stimulated by a professional challenge, either with an expatriate contract,[4] a local job or a plan to create a business. Morocco offers a lot of financial and fiscal advantages to foreign investors, which enables them to create a company at low cost with limited expenses. Work conditions and regulations which are not as restrictive and stressful as they are in France attract businessmen too. For some young French people, their mobility to Morocco was connected with a training period and consequently regarded as an experience likely to give them a professional opportunity to fit into the international job-market. We therefore met some of them who, after a training period, were working in local or international organisations. The Mediterranean climate, the gap between the standards of living in France and Morocco and the fiscal advantages offered to foreign senior citizens are the main motivations for retired French people, as they know they can afford a comfortable way of life in Morocco. However, it is important to be careful about the category of retired people because the collected empirical data confirm what O'Reilly (2007) noted in her study on the British in Spain, where many of those officially retired people were working or engaged in informal labour activities. Marriage was also a ground for migration in some cases. Some French people had followed their French spouse for the duration of their contract as expatriates. The fact of being in a mixed couple had also been a stimulus for many of them to go and live with their spouse in Morocco. Some trajectories can be considered as following the history of family migration. We met some people born in Morocco of French migrants, who had grown up in Morocco, then had lived in France for some time as adults, and then returned to Morocco.

To feel better, not to live better

A characteristic of all the migration trajectories followed by these French people can be summed up in the search for a better quality of life and/or a strong desire for 'elsewhere'. If in their stories the quest for a better life goes with a kind of weariness due to the social, economic and political climate in France, 'elsewhere' refers to a desire to live an experience out of their element (synonymous with adventure and exoticism for some, and with 'otherness' and/or a possibility to live in another way for others). What makes the peculiarity of quest migrants is precisely the combination of these various elements. If for most French people settled in Morocco the motivation for migration mixes the search for a better quality of life with the desire for an exotic change of scene, the migration trajectory of quest migrants would rather sound like a quest for 'otherness' and/or a possibility to exist differently. In their case, the improvement of their quality of life is not the motivation for their migration, but it follows from their quest for 'elsewhereness'.[5] Their priority is not to settle in an environment likely to allow them 'to live better', but to live an experience expected to make them 'feel better'.

Unlike the majority of the French migrants interviewed, quest migrants do not assess this better quality of life according to the climate, the acquisition of social capital or a better standard of living. They appreciate their life in Morocco because it corresponds to the meaning given to their migration, which is the pursuit of a quest. Moreover it is important to specify that over half of the quest migrants were living in Morocco in modest conditions and some had a professional and economic situation relatively more stable and comfortable in France than in Morocco. They were ready to live 'worse' in order to feel 'better'.

Some parallels between quest migrants, and travellers' trajectories

In her thesis about Western expatriates settled in India, Nadia Giguère (2010) identified the main motivations for departure mentioned in travel literature. The Canadian anthropologist rightly stresses that travellers' motivations (personal quest, search for differences and desire to transform one's identity) are not dealt with in the writings about migration which focus on social motives and collective efforts to achieve a migration project rather than on migrants' motives and individual trajectories. This thesis allowed me to draw parallels between the quest migrants' trajectories and those of travellers.

A migration trajectory stimulated by an inner quest

The first parallel we can draw is because both migrants and travellers pursue a quest. The analysis of the quest migrants' narratives shows that their accounts were structured around an idea of an inner quest.

> I was in a kind of quest … not spiritual, but … I was somehow in search of something else, in quest for the Orient on different levels: philosophic, human, political and artistic.
>
> (Benjamin)[6]

Beyond his plan to improve his interpretation of Arabic music, Benjamin wanted to escape in order to live a life that did not suit him any more. The narrative of Elizabeth also reveals that, beyond her project of a 'salon de thé', Elizabeth pursued the dream to live in a colonial house, symbolically related for her to the quest for a family identity:

> In fact, the choice of the house … it was to give life again to what I imagined about my grandparents. I ensured the continuation of the family … which I didn't know in France, since I have no true roots as my mother was of mixed origin. My biological father is not my father … . My biological father was mixed, too, as his mother was born in Pondichéry … I am the pure product of French colonies. … When you have mixed origins, you have no sense of belonging. You are neither eastern, nor western, and anyway, even when you wish for a perfect integration, it is not possible. Or at least it is rather exceptional. And you are always in search of your origin. So that's that, that's right. It is the reconciliation between myself and the past.
>
> (Elizabeth)

The search for her origin and the desire for a symbolic reconciliation with the colonial past of her grandparents (both on her father's and her mother's side) express the quest for identity of this particular French woman who feels *no sense of belonging*.

The idea of a quest also appears in the choice of a narrative vocabulary which gives them the possibility to represent the immaterial aspect of their migration trajectory and which reflects the feeling of an inner call they had to follow. These quest migrants mention 'a call', 'progress', 'chance', 'destiny' or 'intuition'. In some cases the stories look like initiation rites. For example, Benjamin begins the story of his departure as follows:

> I don't even remember which day I left. At one point I had to go. Anyway I was already in a kind of void, travelling, socially disconnected. So, at one point, after a beer or something else, well, I had to go. … I think I went to Bure as an activist against burying nuclear waste, then I

> went to the Drôme to play eastern music, I found myself in the Cevennes for a fortnight, bathing naked in the Tarnon, then in a medieval village with a shaman, then I walked on the road to Compostelle, and after that I found myself in Fez. It was a sort of initiatory transition.
>
> (Benjamin)

Sara, who spent over 10 years travelling round the world before settling in Morocco, regards destiny and intuition as the driving force of her mobility:

> I was predestined to travel whatever might happen, it's what I wanted, and nothing else. My mother knew that quite well, so she never tried to keep me back, she said: anyway I could not stop you. I go where I feel I have to be. It's very simple. When I feel I have completed all that I had in one place, another place calls me automatically, it's out of my control, it's like that. It's my feeling. I finish what I was doing, and I start something else.
>
> (Sara)

Aïcha, a French Muslim convert and member of a Sufi fraternity located in France, explains her departure to Morocco as part of her spiritual progression:

> I always say that, in fact, I follow my master. Wherever he goes, I follow him. … In a way I was prepared for that, for a spiritual life. Since I was a child, I used to speak to God. … Man proposes and God disposes. We can propose, we can say I will be this, I will be that, but … it's God who decides.
>
> (Aïcha)

She came to Morocco with some members of her fraternity during the Festival of World Sacred music in Fez, and then she met a man and settled in Morocco.

> I met a man … that's it, a man from Fez, and then … we got married. We can say that things are made concrete through marriage. Because in a way, I feel my life is in Morocco more than in France.
>
> (Aïcha)

Unlike spiritual expatriates (Giguère 2010) who were attracted by the myth of India and pursued a quest for a spiritual experience (an inner transformation), Aïcha was a Muslim convert and member of a Sufi fraternity before going to Morocco. She decided to live in Morocco several months per year,[7] because settling in Morocco and getting married allows her to feel closer to God in her everyday life. Her quest does not mean a search for an inner space but a desire to fulfil herself as a Muslim every day.

These three narratives present migration as the answer to an inner call: 'I had to go, I follow my master, another place called me.' By following such a road, they were guided from one place to another which led them to Morocco, mostly in search of a kind of 'elsewhereness' which seemed to be required for the pursuit of their quest.

Elsewhereness as a central element of the quest

When we analyse the common elements in these different quests, we can see all of them are rooted in a kind of elsewhereness. This elsewhereness, indispensable for the quest, allows them to be in harmony with an inner call. For the vast majority of these migrants it meets their desire for 'otherness' and their need to exist in another way. Although they did not come to Morocco by chance (all these migrants mentioned some ties established with the country before settling), it is important to point out that it is not Morocco alone but elsewhereness that offered them the possibility to live their quest.

An experience of 'otherness'

Although a predisposition to mobility seems to be relatively common in the trajectory of the French individuals we met in Morocco (Therrien and Harrami 2010), quest migrants' specificity is actually to be found in their motivation for an 'elsewhere'. Just like travellers, what they search for is not a comfortable life in different scenery – as desired by a lot of French people we met in Morocco – but an experience of otherness. By looking back on their migration trajectory, several of them explained it by their keen eagerness for cultural differences and intersubjective encounters. Through otherness what these quest migrants seek is also to be confronted with themselves:

> Maybe I wished to discover something else. To raise questions about myself too, about religion as I said before, a sort of introspection. When you are elsewhere, it is easier to see yourself.
>
> (Aurélien)

The 'Other' as a reflection of oneself seems indispensable for the quest. As in the case of travellers, to keep their distance from their usual reference marks makes it possible for them to be in contact with other people, but also with their own selves. This desire to question themselves in contact with cultural differences is probably not to be separated from an attraction to some forms of spirituality evoking a kind of otherness. Nathalie did yoga, Sara had become a Buddhist, Benjamin, Aïcha and Aurélien had found their way to Sufism (two were members of a fraternity, and two were Muslim converts). For Father Etienne, a Franciscan priest, otherness was integrated in his project to announce peace. By sharing his daily life with Muslims, he was confronted with his own religion and led to discover that 'the relation of believers to religion is the same for everyone'.

Other signs of this desire for otherness appear in the language and places of residence of these migrants. Unlike the large majority of French people who do not speak, or hardly speak, dialectal Arabic and think it is of no use to them, nearly all the quest migrants really want to have a good command of that language. I realised during the fieldwork that the quest migrants of Fez knew each other because they had attended the same dialectal Arabic lessons given by one of them. The fact that six of them lived in medinas and Benjamin had built an adobe house in a small village was related, in the narratives, to their wish to meet local people. Unlike the migrants Giguère (2010) met in India, who define themselves as expatriates and live in touristic border-zones, the quest migrants dissociated themselves from 'the yellow number plates',[8] that category which, for them and for Moroccans, refers to individuals 'living in a bubble', in reference to the title of Fechter's (2007) article. When they stand out from expatriates, 'those French people in SUVs who don't give a damn, want to get money and ask themselves if they will have the possibility to go to New York or Madrid next year' (Benjamin), what these migrants emphasise is their different relations with the 'others'. They are not in Morocco for money, status or adventure. Most of them really experienced genuine encounters with local people. Benjamin could speak dialectal Arabic, and some of his best friends were members of the Sufi fraternity he had joined as a musician; Elizabeth had been elected at the local elections in her area; Father Etienne's religious community was located within modest surroundings where he was in permanent contact with Moroccans; Aurélien and Nathalie were in a mixed couple and had close relations with their in-laws; Sara was continuously visiting far-away rural communities in order to find hosting families for her enterprise of responsible tourism; Aïcha felt more comfortable in the practising Muslim community. The desire for a genuine encounter with local people is clearly one of the major points distinguishing quest migrants from other French lifestyle migrants, who, as I noticed through my observations,[9] are in a social configuration of keeping to themselves.

A distance to exist in a different way

As it is related in travel literature, the impression of distance when one is far away from his/her familiar references offers a possibility for an identity transformation. The quest migrants declare that their migration to Morocco allowed them 'to start afresh on new bases, to start a new life, at last to be acknowledged, to give a meaning to daily life, to explore a new style of being'. In their point of view, 'elsewhereness' gives them the possibility to exist differently. They explain their feeling of well-being through this identity transformation. Benjamin's narrative is a good example:

> To live with Moroccans enables you to escape from your own culture in a certain way. It allows you to get out of those particular circles operating around you when you are with people of your own culture. You enter into another culture so you can build yourself again … I have quite frankly

> found a place where I feel better … and moreover with the possibility to re-create myself, to consider myself, to exist in a new and different way.
>
> (Benjamin)

His immersion in Morocco has transformed him, even in his body language. It is striking to see that when he speaks to a Moroccan all his body is transformed, his hands start dancing, he becomes very expressive, whereas, when he speaks to a French person, he drops his hands and his body language becomes more discrete. If Benjamin says he feels better in Morocco, it is because elsewhereness (i.e. Morocco when we met him, but it could be anywhere, except in France) enabled him to start afresh to build his life on new bases, with a new way of seeing himself, and so feeling as if he had rebuilt his identity.

A closer analysis of the life stories shows that elsewhereness allows quest migrants to distance themselves and be transformed, giving them a sense of improved well-being. For Guillaume, his project in Morocco brings him 'an inner peace, a balance, some reasons for getting up in the morning, acting, doing things in a positive way'. Benjamin talks about a 'blossoming experience, relief and relaxation'. Elizabeth is 'reconciled with herself', Aïcha tells of her 'true reason for living', Sara mentions her 'inner development' and for Sandra and Aurélien it was 'a new start'. This search for improved well-being can certainly be related to a sense of weariness before their migration, as mentioned in several interviews.

> I came to Morocco for very personal reasons. A kind of weariness with life which was not necessarily linked to France, it was rather a problem with myself. I needed to go away, far away, alone, to progress in myself, in my life, in my choices, to find out who I am.
>
> (Guillaume)

Sandra, who had lost her father and her husband in a car crash and had no more contact with her son after a conflict, explains her migration to Morocco as a means to escape from painful memories:

> We cannot forget our pain, we cannot forget our life, or the past, but with a certain distance, even if we miss different things, it is less difficult, less heavy to bear. It's a new start … a little less difficult.
>
> (Sandra)

An analysis of the collected data shows that quest migrants and travellers have common interests: a personal quest (which in the case of the quest migrants refers to a quest for well-being), a desire to experience cultural 'otherness' and a need to transform one's identity. However, their trajectories are different on some points. While travellers come back home at the end of their journeys, quest migrants have no plan to return and, in addition, they have considerably modified their representations of home.

Absence of plans to return and uncertainty about a definitive settlement

It is striking to see that only one of the 10 quest migrants had moved to Morocco with the intention to return to France, which is not the case of French expatriates and trainees since their stay in Morocco is a temporary step in their trajectory. It is easy to see the connection between their weariness with life in France and the absence of plans to return. Sandra, who escaped her painful past, as already mentioned, had absolutely no intention of going back to France. Nathalie went to Morocco to live with the man she loves but she says she would have made the decision to live outwith France even if she had not met him. In France she felt she had not found her place.

> I was living a life that did not suit me; that did not correspond to me. That's why I made a big bet on my departure for Morocco where I could achieve something both personal and professional.
>
> (Nathalie)

France did not suit Benjamin, Guillaume or Sara, who all felt a gap between their way of living and thinking and some cultural references shared by most French people:

> Professionally I cannot manage. I cannot find my place. I love my country, my relatives and my friends are over there, I like the language, I like the culture, I like all that. But I could not live there the whole year, no. I am much closer to all that is … the Indian mentality, or let's say eastern mentality, not eastern … all that is Hinduism, Buddhism, and so on, and in France, the way of thinking, working, living.
>
> (Sara)

So the absence of plans to return is intrinsically related to the motivation for their departure: breaking off social and family networks, professional difficulty to find their place, cultural incompatibility. It is relevant to mention that life stories reveal that most quest migrants, just like other French migrants interviewed for our research, had gone through a hardship some time before their migration: divorce or separation, expropriation, redundancy, economic difficulties, bereavement, etc. As pointed out by Hoey (2009), lifestyle migrants seemingly relocate at turning points in their lives. For a majority of quest migrants a return to France did not make sense because they did not feel they had really left France. As they were free to travel and maintained transnational ties (Glick-Schiller *et al.* 1996) with France and create new attachment bonds in Morocco, several considered they had two homes. Just like some other contemporary migrants, quest migrants felt as if they had several homes. Nevertheless, the absence of an idea of return is not due only to their desire to escape a life that no longer suited them, to their transnational lifestyle and to the possibility to have a pluri-local home (Lucas and Purkayastha 2007), but also to their identity transformation related to their experience of elsewhereness. If the quest migrants did not wish to return to France, it is because their experiences of mobility and migration had considerably transformed their representations of home.

A feeling of home connected with well-being

First of all, their feeling of home, in accordance with their inner quest, was linked to something immaterial (spiritual or existential). This feeling of home was connected with the impression of being in accordance with their inner project:

> It's an inner feeling which is difficult to describe. It is not a place, it is not a period. Rather such moments of life that at a certain moment, if you are where you must be, you feel at home.
>
> (Sara)

> I consider my homeland is more inside me. … There is a saying by Saint Augustin you probably know: My God, I searched for you outside for a long time and I did not see you. Then one day I came back home and you were waiting for me. … Our homeland is the same for every man whether he is Muslim, Christian, or atheist. It is not here. If there is a passage, it is here, not just Morocco, but the whole earth. I deeply feel I am in God's hand.
>
> (Etienne)

If all of them told me they felt at home in Morocco it is because their representations of home were connected with that sense of personal fulfilment they said they had encountered through their migration.

> I had not definitely decided to settle in Morocco for ever. I knew I wanted to stay for a long time, but the gradual sense of home came by steps. As your network of friends grows larger, as your house is being built, as your professional situation gets more steady and stable, after some time you look back and you say: 'It is here where I want to be.' All that I have built as a man, I have built it here. That journey which was likely to last one year turned out to be a complete course of life.
>
> (Benjamin)

When Benjamin states all that he has built in his life as a man was built in Morocco, in fact he does not really mean his professional life, as he had left a stable job as director of a music school and a comfortable life in France. What he has built or rebuilt in Morocco gives him a feeling of home in this country, and this is his own identity, a more suitable identity, which gives him a positive social image. Some of them also associated their feeling of home with France, but rather in terms of memories and emotional ties. Even though they defined themselves as French (Virkama *et al.* 2012) these quest migrants did not connect their home to a national territory. It should be mentioned that some of them had a stronger feeling of home in Morocco than in France.

> In France, it is me who found myself differently. In France, in fact, I did not feel … at home. I have never felt at home in France, I think. My experiences of life in other countries made me deeply realize that in my heritage, in my past lives, I must have got a sense of things that was much more eastern than western.
>
> (Guillaume)

Aïcha, who had strong ties with France through her fraternity, felt more at home in Morocco because she could more easily and completely practise her faith in a Muslim environment.

> Why do I feel more at home here than in France? Well, listen, it is true that when you are in a Muslim country, maybe you can feel fulfilled much more easily, you see. When you are in France, it is more difficult for a Muslim. … I mean a French Muslim convert … in fact Islam is misunderstood most of the time. … Whereas here, you really live it.
>
> (Aïcha)

It is important to point out that, if they had no plans to return to France, they had no plans to settle definitively in Morocco. At the time of our meeting, they all told me they felt good living in Morocco (for some, better than living in France). They might one day want to leave, but they would not return to France. As pointed out by Korpela (2009: 22): 'The ideal location is always somewhere far away from one's country of origin.' As I mentioned before, it is not Morocco in itself, but 'elsewhereness' that offered them the possibility to live their quest. For them, to give up that 'elsewhereness' would mean giving up the essence of their quest.

These representations of home connected with a strong desire of 'elsewhereness' is confirmed by the answers quest migrants gave me about the place of an imagined funeral. Since some did not feel at home in France and some felt they had several homes, it is not surprising that it was far from evident for them to consider being buried in France. Cremation was more often mentioned than burial because it may take place anywhere and in more the one place:

> In Morocco, in France … in another place, if in the next 10 years I live a very strong experience in another country, it might be there, I don't mind.
>
> (Benjamin)

> It's not a definite place. For that too, it's a question of feeling. A place where I'll feel well.
>
> (Aurélien)

What is meaningful concerning their answers about the imagined burial place is again this persistence of elsewhereness. The excerpts from interviews show that the nomadic aspect is intrinsic to the quest migrants' life. However, such mobility is not a specific feature limited to quest migrants. It has been underlined that the course of life of several French migrants interviewed was often a set of experiments with mobility. The specific characteristic of quest migrants, has to be found in the sense they give to this elsewhereness, which refers to a feeling of well-being.

Conclusion

Since the existing migration categories do not reflect the trajectories of some French migrants interviewed during a study on transnationalism carried out in several different countries, the analysis of their narratives led me to create a particular category, the 'quest migrants'. In this chapter, I have claimed that the specificity of these migrants' narratives is to link the improvement in their quality of life with their quest for well-being and not, unlike the majority of the other French lifestyle migrants I met, in accordance with a better standard of living, a new lifestyle or an exotic change of scenery. Comparing their trajectories with those of travellers allowed me to point out that their nomadic way of life is connected to a personal quest, not so much for living but for *feeling* better, rooted in a kind of elsewhereness where they can live in accordance with their inner call (their quest) and, essentially, exist differently. However, I also argue that some significant differences exist between the trajectory of travellers and those of quest migrants: though travellers return home after their experience of otherness, for the French quest migrants a return to France is not even considered. First, because they connect their feeling of well-being with their experience of elsewhereness, and second, because their experience of otherness has considerably transformed their identity and therefore their representations of home. In conclusion, the quest migrant category, thanks to its inclusive and all-encompassing quality and the fine shading it contributes to lifestyle migration studies, can shed new light on the field of lifestyle migrations.

Notes

1 Transnationalisation, Migration and Transformation: Multi-Level Analysis of Migrant Transnationalism' (TRANS-NET), a three-year cross-country study of transnationalism funded by the European Commission 7th Framework Research Programme in Socio-Economic Sciences and Humanities.

2 It is important to specify that this is an approximate number. Our fieldwork shows that French lifestyle migrants are not necessarily registered at the Consulate, which was the case of several quest migrants interviewed.

3 In this text the word 'French' refers to people of French origin. The Moroccan migrants who have adopted French nationality and the French natives of Moroccan origin (second generation) are not included in that category. As concerns Moroccan authorities, anyone on Moroccan territory who has Moroccan nationality (even the binationals) is considered Moroccan.
4 French administration considers expatriates are all the French living abroad, whereas in Morocco, expatriation corresponds to a particular status: They are people working for France in Morocco (teachers, diplomats, people working for French cultural services or enterprises, etc.) with an expatriate limited contract. Most of them had applied for a position in other countries, but they were sent to Morocco. Many French teachers have a resident or local contract. They are not expatriates and do not get comparable pay and benefits as such.
5 Whereas the word 'elsewhere' is used as a noun referring to an actual place, the neologism 'elsewhereness' is rather an abstract notion which makes it possible to approach the different motives for migration in the case of lifestyle migrants in general and that of quest migrants in particular.
6 All the extracts of interviews have been translated from French into English.
7 Aïcha is still officially residing in France where she gets an RMI benefit (income support), which allows her to live as a painter. She lives in Morocco with a tourist status for several months a year.
8 The number plates of foreign diplomats' cars on the Moroccan territory are yellow.
9 Canadian, I have been living in Morocco since 2001.

References

Benson, M. and O'Reilly, K. (2009) 'Migration and the search for a better way of life: A critical exploration of lifestyle migration', *The Sociological Review*, 57(4): 608–25.

Berriane, Mohamed (2010) 'L'immigration vers Fès. Le sens des nouvelles dynamiques du système migratoire euro-africain.' Conference paper, *African Migrations Workshop. The contribution of African Research to Migration Theory.* Sénégal, 16–19 November.

Bousta, R. (2007) 'From tourism to new forms of migration: Europeans in Marrakesh' in C. Geoffroy, and R. Sibley (eds) *Going Abroad: Travel, Tourism and Migration. Cross-cultural Perspectives on Mobility.* Newcastle upon Tyne: Cambridge Scholars, 158–67.

Casado-Díaz, M.Á. (2006) 'Retiring to Spain: An analysis of difference among North European nationals', *Journal of Ethnic and Migration Studies*, 32(8): 1321–39.

Cassaigne, J. (1964) 'La situation des Français au Maroc depuis l'indépendance (1956–64)' Paris: Centre d'étude des relations internationales, Éditions Maghrébines.

Cortazzi, M. (2001) 'Narrative analysis in ethnography', in Atkinson, P., Coffey, A., S. Delamont, J. Lofland and L. Lofland (eds) *Handbook of Ethnography,* London: Sage, 384–94.

D'Andrea A. (2007) *Global Nomads: Techno and New Age as Transnational Countercultures in Ibiza and Goa*, London: Routledge.

Fechter, A.M. (2007). 'Living in a bubble: Expatriates' transnational spaces', in A. Vered (ed.) *Going First Class? New Approaches to Privileged Travel and Movement*, Oxford: Berghahn, 33–53.

Giguère, N. (2010). *De l'aller retour au point de non retour. Étude comparative de l'expérience interculturelle des expatriés occidentaux en Inde*, unpublished thesis, University of Montreal. https://papyrus.bib.umontreal.ca/jspui/bitstream/1866/4348/2/Nadia_Giguere_2009_these.pdf (accessed 10 October 2012).

Glick-Schiller, N., Basch, L. and Szanton-Blanc, C. (1996) 'Transnationalism: A new analytic framework for understanding migration', in N. Glick-Schiller, L. Basch, and C. Szanton-Blanc (eds) *Towards a Transnational Perspective on Migration*. New York: Academy of Sciences, 1–24.

Gustafon, P. (2008) 'Transnationalism in retirement migration: The case of North European retirees in Spain', *Ethnic and Racial Studies*, 31(3): 451–75.

Hoey, B.A. (2009) 'Pursuing the good life: American narratives of travel and a search for refuge', in M. Benson and K. O'Reilly (eds) *Lifestyle Migration: Expectations, Aspirations and Experiences*, Aldershot: Ashgate, 15–30.

Korpela, M. (2009) 'When a trip to adulthood becomes a lifestyle: Western lifestyle migrants in Varanasi', in M. Benson and K. O'Reilly (eds) *Lifestyle Migration: Expectations, Aspirations and Experiences*. Aldershot: Ashgate, 15–30.

Locke, H. (2006) 'The spiritual dimension of moving to the mountains', in L. Moss (ed.) *The Amenity Migrants: Seeking and Sustaining Mountains and Their Cultures*. Oxford and Cambridge: CABI International: 26–33.

Lucas, S. and Purkayastha, B. (2007) '"Where is home?" here and there: Transnational experiences of home among Canadian migrants in the United States', *GeoJournal* 68: 243–51.

McIntyre, N. (2011) Mobilities, lifestyle and imagined worlds: Towards understanding conflicts in paradise. Conference paper, *2nd International Workshop on Lifestyle Migration and Residential Tourism*, Madrid, 23–25 March.

O'Reilly, K. (2007) *The Rural Idyll, Residential Tourism, and the Spirit of Lifestyle Migration*, in Conference Proceedings of Thinking through Tourism. London: ASA.

O'Reilly, K. and Benson, M. (2009) 'A new life? Expectations, aspirations, and experiences of lifestyle migration', in M. Benson and K. O'Reilly (eds) *Lifestyle Migration: Expectations, Aspirations and Experiences*. Aldershot: Ashgate, 1–51.

Picod-Kinany, A. (2010) 'L'émigration européenne. Le cas des Français au Maroc', Saarbrücken: Éditions Universitaires Européennes.

Rodríguez, V. (2001) 'Tourism as a recruiting post for retirement migration', *Tourism Geographies*, 3(1): 52–63.

Therrien, C. (2009) *Des repères à la construction d'un chez-soi. Trajectoires de mixité conjugale au Maroc*, unpublished theis, University of Montreal. https://papyrus.bib.umontreal.ca/jspui/bitstream/1866/4048/4/Therrien_Catherine_2009_These.pdf (accessed 19 October 2012).

Therrien, C. (2012) 'Trajectories of mixed couples in Morocco: A meaningful discursive space for mixedness,' *Revista de Sociologia*, 91(1): 129–50.

Therrien, C. and Harrami, N. (2010) *Country report of the Moroccan team*. TRANSNET research project. www.uta.fi/projektit/transnet/dissemination.php.

Tremblay, R. and O'Reilly, K. (2004) 'La mise en tourisme des communautés transnationales: le cas des Britanniques en Espagne et Québécois en Floride', *Tourism Review* 59: 20–23.

Virkama, A., Therrien, C., Harrami, N. and Kadri, A. (2012) 'Franco-Moroccan transnational space: Continuity and transformations' in P. Pitkänen, A. Içduygu and D. Sert (eds) *Migration and Transformation: Multi-Level Analysis of Migrant Transnationalism*, International Perspectives on Migration, 3, 108–68.

Website

Ambassade de France (Maroc): www.ambafrance-ma.org/presence-francaise/index.cfm.

9 Second home expansion in Portugal

Spatial features and impacts

Maria de Nazaré Oliveira Roca, Zoran Roca, José Antonio Oliviera and Luís Costa

Introduction

Recent land use and landscape changes in Portugal have largely been incited by the expansion of second homes. The importance of the second home expansion has been recorded by the last three Population and Housing Censuses: in the inter-census 1991–2001 and 2001–11 periods, the number of second homes increased 40 per cent and 23 per cent, while the number of first home dwellings grew only 16 per cent and 13 per cent, respectively. In 2011, 1,133,166 second homes represented 19 per cent of all dwellings. The second home phenomenon has indeed become a remarkable new spatial occupation and population mobility feature evident in diverse parts of the country. They can be found not only in the highly urbanised and dynamic littoral but also in the aged and stagnating rural interior, as well as in areas with attractive natural and cultural landscapes and other amenities. Like in other Southern European countries, the share of second homes in the housing stock has been greater than in other parts of Europe.[1]

Prior to the 2008 crisis that affected the construction sector, the expansion of second homes may be explained by a wide range of factors, such as (i) the still strong bonds to the place of origin, mostly rural, among the first and second generation of internal migrants and among Portuguese emigrants who spend weekends and/or their vacation in their former permanent residences, or built second homes while they were already abroad; (ii) the general improvement in income level and, consequently, the adoption of consumption patterns where the second home is supposed to serve recreation and leisure needs, as well as an additional long-term safe investment in the context of the behaviour of the Portuguese real estate market; (iii) the nationwide expansion of a modern road network and the generalised use of private automobiles; (iv) the increasing attractiveness of Portuguese landscapes reflected in the growing number of foreigners, mostly retirees, who spend a significant part of the year in Portugal. Development policy agendas aimed at socio-economic sectors and territorial dynamics have increasingly attributed importance to second homes as an integral part of the Portuguese tourism industry. However, the spatial impacts of second homes on the territories of their expansion have been perceived in different ways from diverse government policy perspectives. For instance, second home tourism is considered one of the top-ten priorities explicitly called for promotion by the National Strategy for Tourism Development, while the National Programme for Spatial Planning recommends controlling its expansion because of the effects it can have on the management and sustainability of land use and landscapes. However, the feasibility, if not credibility, of such policy statements is questionable given that they have not been grounded on any solid scientific interpretation of this phenomenon. Apart from a few local field studies about some specific rural and coastal resort areas that were carried out in the 1980s, 1990s and 2000s, no in-depth research on second home tourism *per se*, or in broader terms, has ever been undertaken at regional and national levels. In fact, the growing omnipresence of second homes and the inherent environmental, economic, cultural and other aspects of land use conflicts and/or synergies are nowadays frequent discussion topics among policy- and opinion-makers, especially in the mass media, but this phenomenon has not yet become part of the research agenda in Portugal.

In this chapter, for the first time, a spatial typology of second homes in Portugal is presented and discussed. It was produced as part of a national research project,[2] so far the only comprehensive research endeavour that has explicitly dealt with the issue of second home expansion and its impact on territorial development at the national and regional levels. In view of the lack of any previous research in Portugal, the specific objectives of such typology were to provide, first, a classification of territories according to second homes expansion, and, second, a description of major features of this phenomenon and its impacts in each spatial type.

Conceptual–methodological framework

Spatial distribution patterns and, particularly, spatial typologies have been a rare subject in second home research (Pettersson 1999). Decades ago, Coppock (1977) identified the rural–urban fringe, holiday resorts and the scattered populated rural countryside as locations for second homes. Other important studies are the following: Barke (1991) on the spatial distribution of second homes in Spain in the 1970s and 1980s; Deffner *et al.* (2002) on a spatial typology based on the proportion of empty dwellings in the Greek municipalities of the Evoikos Coastal Area; Shellito and Pijanowski (2003) on the spatial distribution of seasonal homes in the upper Great Lakes region; Gallent *et al.* (2003) on the changing geography of second homes in rural Wales; Colás and Cabrerizo (2004), who used multiple logistic regression to identify the factors behind the spatial distribution of second home owners in Spain; Visser (2004) on a typology of regions according to the use of second homes in South Africa; Marjavaara and Müller (2007) on attractive second home landscapes in Sweden. A common feature of most of these research contributions on spatial distribution and typologies is that they are mostly based only on one or two indicators.

The lack of more numerous and comprehensive spatial typologies in the literature is probably because second homes research has been conducted mostly in countries where this phenomenon is spatially concentrated and/or place-specific (Gallent *et al.* 2003; Müller *et al.* 2004). Spatial typologies have been lacking even in Southern Europe, where second homes expansion is evidenced across entire countries. Any research on second homes, especially when spatial patterns and typologies are to be determined, is confronted with the lack of consensus about the definition of second home. This is because of the complexity of their origins, frequency of occupancy and purpose of use. As Coppock (1977: 11) stated, 'the dynamic character of the second home, particularly the changing relationship between the first and second home ... makes identification and measurement difficult'. This situation is mirrored in the multiplicity of terms in the literature, such as 'second homes', 'vacation homes', 'seasonal homes', 'weekend homes', 'cottages', 'recreational homes', among others, and researchers have to rely on definitions set by the available data sources. In this chapter, the following definition of second homes by the Portuguese National Institute of Statistics is adopted: classical family dwelling of seasonal or secondary occupancy where no family member lives permanently.

The Portuguese Population and Housing Censuses include the following three variables related to second homes at the county level: total number of second home dwellings; year of construction of the building in which the second home dwelling is located; and number of second home dwellings per building. However, given that only data on the number of second home dwellings from the last census, held in 2011, have been available to date, the typology was produced on the basis of the information contained in the 1991 and 2001 censuses. Using the above three variables, five indicators were built as outlined hereunder.

- Share of second home dwellings in the total number of dwellings in 2001 – an indicator of the frequency of occurrence of second homes. It has been widely used to determine the intensity and pressure of second home expansion on land (Di *et al.* 2001, in the USA; Casado-Díaz 2004, in Spain).
- Rate of change in the number of second home dwellings between 1991 and 2001 – an indicator of their expansion. It was also used, for example, by Müller (2002) in Sweden and Casado-Díaz (2004) in Spain.
- Share of second home dwellings in mainly residential buildings constructed between 1991 and 2001 in the total number of second home dwellings in 2001 – an indicator of the importance of newly built second homes. It can express the intensity of second homes owned by urbanites with no previous bonds to the place where second homes are located.
- Share of second home dwellings in mainly residential buildings with one dwelling in the total number of second home dwellings in 2001 – an indicator of the importance of individual second homes, more commonly present in rural areas.
- Share of second home dwellings in mainly residential buildings with 10 or more dwellings in the total number of second home dwellings in 2001 – an indicator of the importance of second homes in multi-storey buildings. In

Portugal, and also Spain (Aledo and Mazón 2004), second homes in multi-storey buildings are a common feature of metropolitan suburbs and vacation resorts.

In an attempt to perceive if there were significant changes in the spatial types of second homes during the 2000s, the first two indicators – share of and rate of change of second homes – were analysed using data from the 2011 census. The typology covered all 278 counties of continental Portugal, i.e. without the ultra-peripheral archipelagos of Azores and Madeira.

The county was chosen as the spatial unit of analysis for the following reasons: variations in the values of the indicators among counties are significant; the county is the basic administrative unit of local government; Spatial Master Plans are designed and implemented at this level; and, the results of this analysis could serve as baseline framework for local land use and development planning. The choice of the county as the unit of analysis also prevents generalisations that would hide a considerable concentration of second homes in a few amenity-rich places within a region, as pointed out by Casado-Días (2004) for Spain, Deffner *et al.* (2002) for Greece and Gallent *et al.* (2002) for England.

Cluster analysis was the statistical set of techniques chosen to build a multicriterial typology of Portuguese counties according to the features and dynamics of second home expansion. Besides geographical information systems (Coccossis and Constantoglou 2005; Marjavaara and Müller 2007) and the neural network model (Shellito and Pijanowski 2003), cluster analyses have been quite frequently used to produce multicriterial typologies in spatial planning research, especially in the areas of regional development and tourism (Leatherman and Marcouiller 1996; Paquette and Domon 2003; Schuckert *et al.* 2007). Ward's hierarchical agglomeration method was chosen as preferable on the basis of the cartographic analysis of the five indicators mentioned above, and on the basis of numerous studies that concluded that this method is indeed one of the best overall performers (Rencher 2002). Ultimately, combining the use of the coefficients of the agglomeration schedule representing the squared Euclidian distance and the differences between these coefficients, these criteria and the empirical knowledge on the subject (Milligan and Cooper 1985), six clusters were selected. They are identified as shown in Figure 9.1, described and discussed below.

Findings

The peri-urban fringe

This cluster comprises 86 counties in the peri-urban fringes of Lisbon and Porto and of coastal and interior regional and sub-regional urban centres such as Braga, Aveiro, Viseu, Coimbra, Évora and Faro. It is characterised by a relatively weak presence of second homes (18.8 per cent),[3] but with a rate of

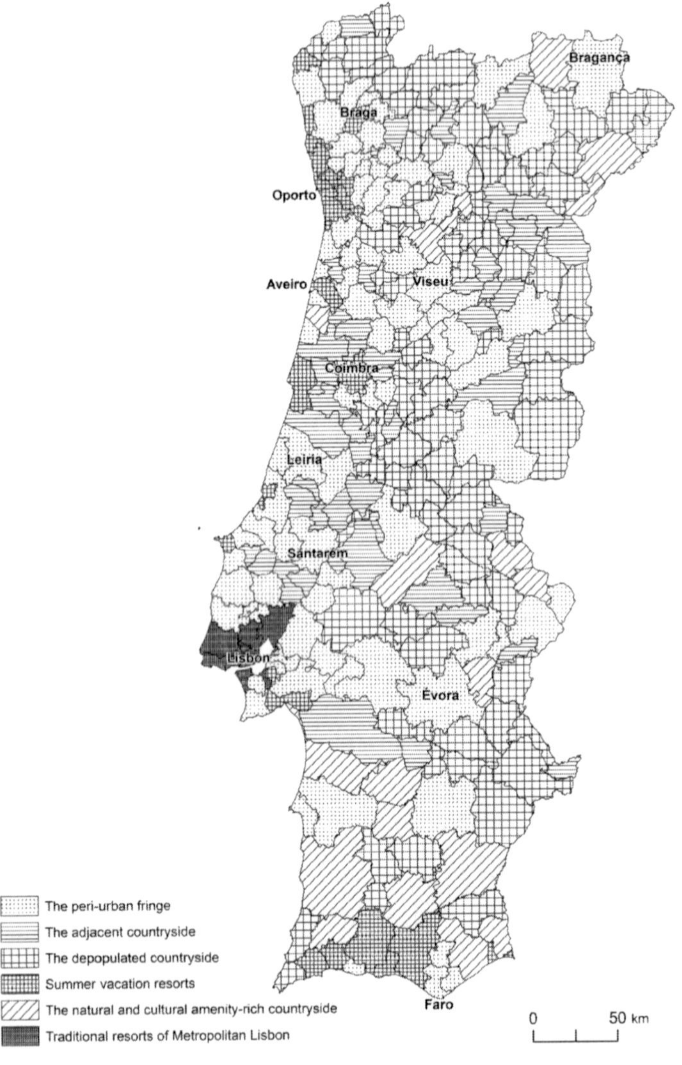

Figure 9.1 Types of counties according to characteristics of second home expansion

increase (41.2 per cent) above the national average (40 per cent) and a strong presence (28.7 per cent) of newly built second homes.

Peri-urban areas were identified in many studies as a major consumption space for second homes. Within weekend commuting distance of large urban centres, Jansson (1994) identifies the 'weekend leisure space', Halseth and Rosenberg (1995) the 'rural-recreational countryside' and Lundgren (1974) the 'recreational hinterlands'. In Sweden, Müller (2002) shows that many urbanites choose the outskirts of the metropolitan areas for their second homes. The same holds for the Netherlands (Dijst *et al.* 2005). Also in Spain, Casado-Díaz (2004) highlights that almost two-thirds of all tourist journeys are made by second home owners to places in the peri-urban fringe.

In Portugal, second homes are dispersed in the peri-urban space. In recent years, however, they have tended to be more concentrated because most of the Municipal Master Plans which regulate urban land use including second housing became effective in the 1990s, and these areas have become developers' favourite locations for the establishment of gated communities. Owing to better transport accessibility in the rural–urban fringe, many second homes that belong to employed people have become their first homes and it is likely that this process will continue. They are also bought with the intention of becoming first homes after their owners retire. The combination of these two trends will eventually transform parts of the rural–urban fringe into suburbs. Such trends were also registered in the Madrid Metropolitan Region (Valenzuela 2003).

There are also second homes in Portugal that are, in fact, alternative residences for economically active owners who share their time between the 'first' and 'second' home. In this case, the dwelling is not only used for recreational purposes, but also as a workplace because of ever-better transport accessibility, more flexible work relations and increased use of information and communication technologies. Ultimately, second home users will become part-time residents in the city and in the countryside (Ericsson 2006).

The adjacent countryside

In this cluster, the proportion of second homes (22.1 per cent) is above the national average (20 per cent). They are predominantly single homes (89 per cent) and register the weakest growth (14.8 per cent). Most of the 52 counties are contiguous to peri-urban areas of Lisbon or of regional or sub-regional urban centres on the coast and in the interior such as Bragança, Leiria and Santarém. In the countryside, adjacent to the rural–urban fringe, a considerable number of second homes are owned mostly by former residents that migrated to Lisbon or to regional and sub-regional centres or abroad. Most recently, over the 1990s, due to the relatively fast growth of these cities, there was a growing demand for cheap first housing that was met in the nearby countryside by converting second homes into first homes or by building first home dwellings. Such a trend was facilitated by improvements in road infrastructures, which led to the expansion of the commuting area not only in Lisbon but also in regional and sub-regional centres. Eventually, these rural areas will become peri-urban due to the rapid expansion of the suburban zones of those cities, as was pointed out above. A similar process was also registered in Greece (Andriotis 2006) and Spain (Aledo and Mazón 2004).

The depopulated countryside

This cluster is marked by the largest share of second homes (31.2 per cent), mainly in one-dwelling buildings (92.7 per cent), and by a rate of increase (48 per cent) above the national average. Most of the 83 counties are depopulated rural areas, with an aged population, mainly the result of strong emigration and out-migration in previous decades. In other countries of Southern Europe, a large proportion of second homes are also located in the depopulated countryside (in Spain: Collantes and Pinilla 2004; in Greece: Deffner *et al.* 2002). Likewise, second homes appear in depopulated, peripheral areas of Northern and North-western European countries such as Ireland (Paris 2006), Wales (Davies and O'Farrell 1981), Scotland (Downing and Dower 1977) and Sweden (Aronsson 2004). However, their presence is less intense than in Southern Europe. In Portugal large, mostly younger, segments of the population of the north region and of the northern part of the centre region emigrated to North-western Europe from the early 1960s to the mid-1970s, while strong out-migration to metropolitan Lisbon characterised the southern parts of the centre region and south-eastern parts of the Alentejo region. Those migrants still maintain strong kinship bonds with their villages of origin and many have renewed their old houses, or built new ones nearby. Thus, their earlier first residences became a second home, and are mainly occupied during summer holidays or longer weekends, depending on the distance between the place of first residence and the second home. This made second housing affordable not only to higher income but also to lower income groups. Also in Spain, the high proportion of second homes in rural areas is explained as a result of early out-migration/emigration (González 2009).

The growth of second homes (48 per cent) above the national average (40 per cent) in the depopulated Portuguese countryside may indicate two quite different processes. First, in many counties, particularly in the North, the rural exodus continued in the 1990s, which contributed to the increase in the stock of second homes. Second, in the centre, Alentejo and Algarve regions, such increase is related to a growing interest among urbanites without previous links to rural areas, including foreigners, for buying and restoring old, mostly empty houses, particularly in villages with a valuable built heritage (see Sardinha this volume).[4] In Portugal, the growing interest in these territories as temporary places of residence can also be explained by the diminishing of travel time as a result of the development of road infrastructures linking the depopulated countryside in the interior to the metropolitan areas of Lisbon and Porto.

Summer vacation resorts

This cluster is characterised by the highest proportion of newly built second homes (32.3 per cent), a high percentage of second homes in multi-dwelling buildings (37 per cent) and a high rate of overall increase (64 per cent) in second homes. Most of the 26 counties are scattered along the western coast or concentrated in the western and central parts of the Algarve region. In many countries in Europe and other parts of the world, summer vacation resorts are the main destination of second home owners and other tourists, particularly in coastal and mountain areas such as those in Turkey (Tamer *et al.* 2006), Greece (Deffner *et al.* 2002), Spain (Mazón *et al.* 2010), Sweden (Müller 2004), Norway (Flognfeldt 2006), USA (Burby 1979), New Zealand (Keen and Hall 2004) and Argentina (Muñoz *et al.* 2003). To spend vacations in coastal resorts is appealing to many Portuguese and foreign tourists. The driving force behind the choice of such resorts for second home location is the desire to spend vacations on the beach, enjoying the Mediterranean climate and the unique cultural milieu (King *et al.* 1998).

The natural and cultural amenity-rich countryside

A strong presence of second homes (28 per cent) with the highest rate of increase (110 per cent) characterises this cluster. Most of the 21 counties are in rural areas with protected natural and cultural landscapes such as the natural parks of Montesinho, International Douro River, São Mamede, Guadiana River and South-western Alentejo, Vicentine Coast and Formosa Ria. This type of second home area was identified in Australia (Paris 2006), the USA (Diamond 2005), England (Paris 2006), Wales (Pyne 1973), Sweden (Müller 2004), Norway (Flognfeldt 2006) and Turkey (Tamer *et al.* 2006), among other countries.

In Portugal, the demand by nationals and, particularly, foreigners for second homes has increased considerably in the natural and cultural amenity-rich countryside, especially in the Alentejo and Algarve regions.[5] Here, second homes are often built in previous open space zones, usually Protected Natural Areas or in unique cultural landscapes. Indeed, a common trend in Southern Europe and Scandinavia is 'a turn towards a more tourist validation of the second home, which implies a greater demand for second homes in scenic areas' (Müller 2004: 249). While in the attractive cultural landscapes second home owners occupy restored old traditional country houses, in the natural amenity-rich areas they choose newly purpose-built houses, usually within gated communities or tourist resorts. This trend is also reported by Paris (2006: 8): 'Large fully-commodified second home developments … have become widespread in many European and North-American countries'.

Traditional resorts of metropolitan Lisbon

This cluster comprises the city of Lisbon and nine suburban counties of its metropolitan area. It is characterised by the lowest percentage of second homes (11.5 per cent) and a low rate of increase (16.8 per cent) and, at the same time, by the highest share of second homes in multi-dwelling buildings (48.1 per cent). The assumption that second homes are mainly located in rural areas has been challenged by authors such as Hoogendoorn and Visser (2004) and Paris (2006), who argue that second homes might well be located in metropolitan areas. The counties belonging to this cluster, with the exception of Lisbon, are traditional summer resorts. National and, particularly, foreign second home owners are concentrated mostly in the counties of Sintra and Cascais, popular tourism destinations since the nineteenth century. In recent decades, however, the growth of second homes did not follow the pace of first home expansion in the Lisbon metropolitan area due to accelerated suburbanisation. Also, probably most of second homes are not purchased for leisure and recreational purposes, but rather as a profitable investment (Paris 2006).

Second home expansion in the 2000s

The only available data from the 2011 census confirmed that, like in 2001, the highest shares of second homes in the total number of dwellings were in three spatial settings: in counties in the depopulated countryside; in counties in the natural and cultural amenity-rich countryside; and in counties with summer vacation resorts (Figures 9.2 and 9.3). In most of these types of counties, high growth rates of second homes were also registered (Figure 9.4) in the period 2001–11. Regarding the counties in the peri-urban fringe, the 2011 census showed that they continued to be characterised by a relatively low share of second homes but a high rate of their growth, particularly in the Oporto metropolitan region. It also seems that some counties that in 2001 were in the adjacent countryside, by 2011 fell within the peri-urban fringe, particularly in the case of coastal medium-sized cities such as Brangança, Leiria and Santarem, where a relatively large increase in the number of second homes was registered.

However, it has to be highlighted that the pace of growth of the second home phenomenon has decelerated significantly in all types of counties in the period 2001–11. In continental Portugal, the growth rate fell almost to half, i.e. from 40 per cent to 23 per cent. This trend is probably related to the considerable decrease in the purchasing power of the Portuguese population caused by very low growth or even stagnant GDP that was accentuated in the second half of the 2000s and was further aggravated with the 2008 world financial crisis that hit Western Europe and North America in particular. On the other hand, as a consequence of such crisis and of austerity measures imposed on Portugal by the International Monetary Fund, the European Commission and the European Central Bank in 2011, after more than a decade of falling emigration rates, from the beginning of the 2010s emigration started to increase.[6] Given that economic recovery is expected only in the medium or long run, this means that many Portuguese emigrants' first homes might become their second homes. Consequently, an increase in the rate of

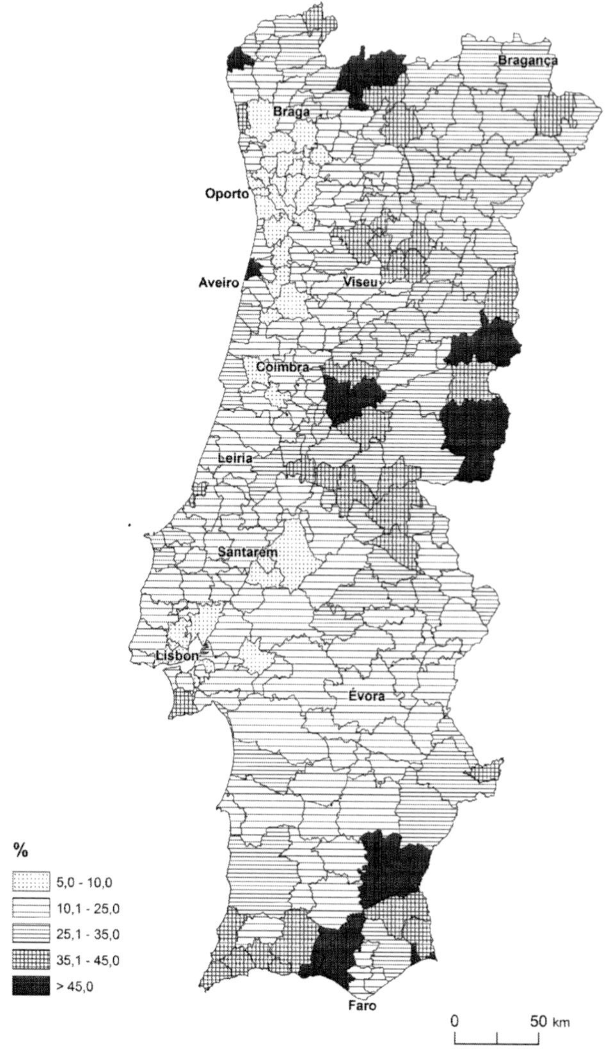

Figure 9.2 Share of second homes in the total number of dwellings, 2001

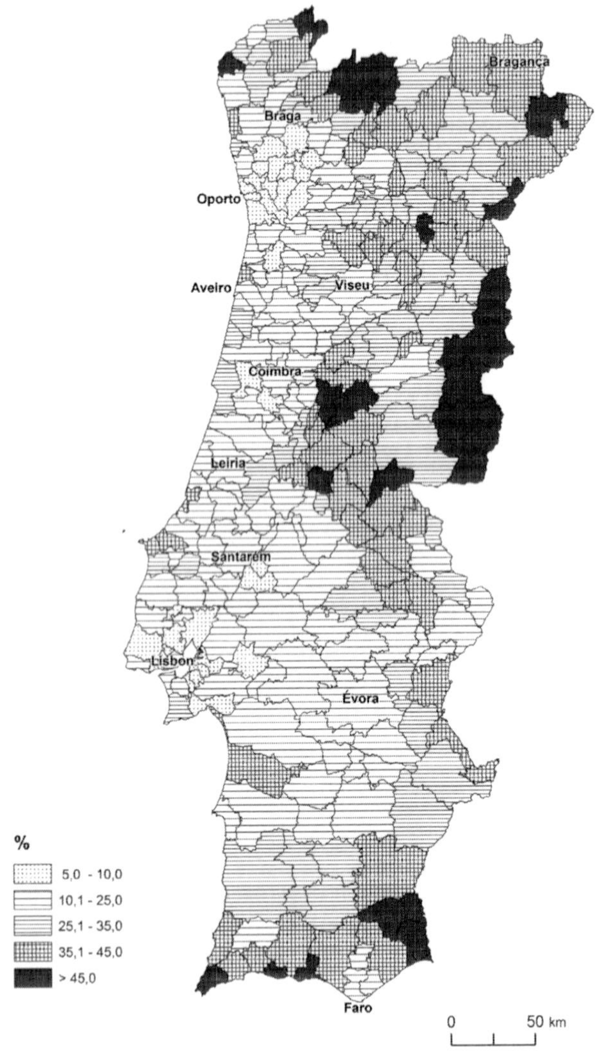

Figure 9.3 Share of second homes in the total number of dwellings, 2011

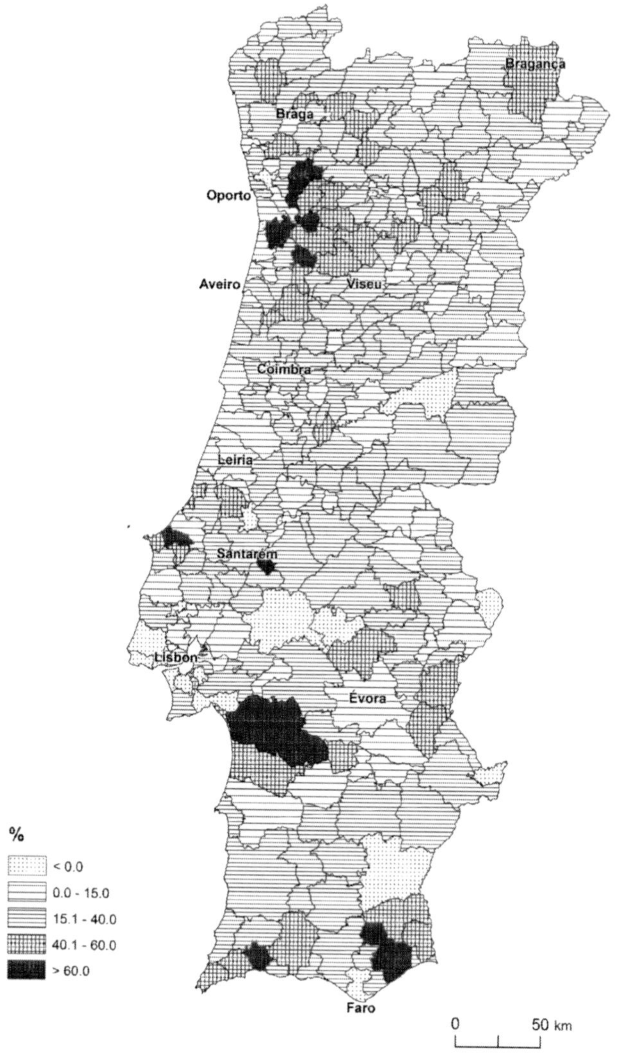

Figure 9.4 Rate of change of the number of second homes in the period 2001–11

change in the number of second homes can be expected from the 2021 census, mostly in urban and peri-urban areas of Portugal, from which most emigration originates.

According to an analysis[7] of central and local government documents, specialised media and field observation, another new feature of second home expansion was revealed in the 2000s: a significant growth of tourist resorts that offer second home housing. For instance, a search of the real estate press and internet sites of the Oeste Region (some 100 km northwest of Lisbon with an area of 2,200 km^2 corresponding only to 2.5 per cent of the continental territory of Portugal), revealed 18 resorts, with 12 of them in the planning stage. It was also found that a considerable part of the investment is foreign, as is the market for potential buyers. The real estate market dealing with tourist resorts and gated communities with second home housing has been shrinking since 2008. According to information obtained from the specialised media (e.g. interviews with developers), the beginning or further phases of their construction have been postponed until the economic recovery. However, luxurious resorts, mostly in the Oeste and in the Algarve regions, continue to be built, or their projects will be implemented in view of the fact that (i) most of the potential buyers belong to the highest income groups that are least affected by the crisis; (ii) real estate firms are looking for new consumer markets in emerging countries such as Russia, Brazil and the Arab States; and (iii) they are still considered a good alternative investment in a time of financial market uncertainties.

It has to be stressed that Portugal, unlike Spain and Ireland, did not experience a construction boom followed by a construction burst and Portuguese banks did not have to be rescued by the central government or by international financial institutions as was the case for those two countries. Thus, the emergence of 'ghost second home developments' are not a frequent feature in the Portuguese landscape. This is largely because since the 1990s, the central government has interfered in all stages of planning processes related to construction by controlling their expansion in both zones within the urban perimeters of towns and on land allocated for tourism developments. This has been accomplished mainly through monitoring and control measures incorporated in the Municipal Master Plans, including the licensing of construction in those zones.

In lieu of conclusion

The findings of the cluster analysis of the geographical settings (i.e. spatial types) of second home expansion at the county level validated the initial assertion that this phenomenon is an important land use and landscape feature in most parts of Portugal. Four quite distinct main categories of counties where the second home phenomenon has been significant have emerged: (i) counties in the rural–urban fringe; (ii) counties in the depopulated countryside; (iii) counties with summer vacation resorts; and (iv) counties in the natural and cultural amenity-rich countryside. Furthermore, second homes in older, predominantly restored, individual houses are much more frequent in depopulated areas, while newly built second homes represent an important share of their stock in peri-urban areas, as well as in vacation resorts where they are frequently in multi-storey buildings. Also, each spatial type of second home expansion corresponds to a specific type of second home owner. Out-migrants and emigrants predominate in the depopulated countryside, that is in the areas of their origin. The cultural and amenity-rich countryside mostly attracts urbanites, including foreigners, with no previous bonds to these areas, in search of the 'rural idyll'. At the same time, affluent Portuguese and foreign owners of second homes have been major consumers of space in the rural–urban fringe, vacation resorts and the natural and cultural amenity-rich countryside. Some of them have chosen to buy second homes in gated communities or tourist resorts.

Furthermore, the prevailing characteristics and dynamics of second home expansion bring about different social, economic, cultural and environmental impacts in these areas. In the peri-urban fringe, second home owners attracted by the amenities of the countryside compete for land use, making it difficult for the local population to buy land for other uses, such as agriculture or permanent housing. Second home expansion also generates an increasing demand for other urban land uses such as commerce and services, communal and road infrastructure, recreational facilities and shopping centres. Such land use changes often lead to the adulteration and, eventually, the vanishing of traditional cultural landscapes, new power relations among development stakeholders and indeed the generation of new territorial identities (Roca and Roca 2007).

The Portuguese depopulated countryside is characterised by the decreasing importance of agriculturally productive land and of the agricultural population, as well as by the emergence of recreational facilities, such as the establishment of forest reserves for hunting and the use of areas of water for leisure activities (e.g. cruising in the Douro River in the North; nautical sports in the lake of the Alqueva Dam in the Alentejo region) and spa-leisure, all for the consumption of urbanites (Ilbery and Bowler 1998). According to some authors (Pinto-Correia *et al.* 2006, Baptista 2006), these are areas where the transition from the productivist to the post-productivist countryside (Marsden *et al.* 1993), although still incipient, has been taking place most intensively. The expansion of such recreational land use is another factor attracting potential second home owners to these areas, an increasing number of whom are foreigners. However, the land use changes that were brought about can cause irreversible alterations to the traditional cultural landscape, although depopulation can contribute to the degradation of these same landscapes (e.g. increased susceptibility to forest fires, soil erosion and other natural hazards).

Furthermore, there is strong pressure on communal infrastructures and services in the depopulated areas during the summer months due to the increase in the number of residents. Supply does not always meet the demand,

and new capital investments are needed. However, such costs are likely to be worthwhile because (i) they are compensated by property tax revenues collected exclusively by local governments, (ii) they are largely covered by EU funds and (iii) they require the creation of new jobs, which can retain or even attract population, especially the young, thus contributing to the diversification of the local economic base. Hence, second home ownership may play an important role in the preservation of humanised landscapes that are at risk in such areas.

In the natural and cultural amenity-rich countryside, the construction of tourist resorts and gated communities offering second housing in previously open space zones has already started to cause significant environmental and landscape impact, such as reduction in natural landscapes, diminishing land carrying capacity and consequent environmental problems such as coastal erosion, slope impermeabilisation, decreasing quality of fresh and salt water, raised pressure on sewage systems, and increase in solid waste. In these areas, recreational and sports facilities (e.g. swimming pools, tennis courts and golf courses) are frequently built near renewed old second homes, thus radically transforming traditional landscapes. In Portugal, as in other European countries, most social, economic, cultural and environmental changes in the rural–urban fringe, amenity-rich countryside and to a lesser extent in the depopulated countryside are largely consequences of increasing rural gentrification mainly in the form of second home expansion (Woods 2005: 88), since owners belong to higher income groups than the local rural population. According to Philips (2000, 2008), gentrification involves the refurbishment or doing up of an area and an accompanying change in the social composition of this area. It implies the emergence of 'gentrified rural lifestyles' (Philips 2000: 14) reflected in social spatial complexes (Zukin 1990) such as golf courses and retail centres that 'can be seen as being simultaneous material and symbolically gentrified' (Philips 2000: 15). Thus gentrification converts such areas into potentially contested spaces. The lifestyles and economic interests of the local population and second home owners commonly diverge; thus conflict situations are indeed likely to emerge between these two groups.

One way of avoiding the disruption of the social and economic fabric of such spaces brought about by rural gentrification would be to enhance the level of place attachment among second home owners. The higher the sense of care for the site of their second home the higher the chances for owners' active preoccupation with and contribution to the implementation of local development initiatives including the valorisation of local and regional material and immaterial identity features through, for example, strengthening environmental and socio-cultural consciousness in local communities, encouraging protection of natural and cultural heritage, stimulating efficiency and effectiveness of local institutions, etc. (Oliveira *et al.* 2010). Another way of preventing spatial conflicts caused by increased rural gentrification would be to enforce the existing spatial planning instruments and, where needed, to design and implement new ones aimed at controlling second home expansion and, consequently, preventing the emergence of contested rural spaces.

Notes

1 For instance: Spain 27 per cent; France: 9 per cent; the Netherlands: 5 per cent; UK and Germany: 1 per cent (source: Casado-Díaz 2004).
2 'SEGREX – Second Home Expansion and Spatial Development Planning in Portugal', financed by the Portuguese Fund for Science and Technology, Lisbon, carried out in the period 2008–12 jointly by the e-GEO Research Centre for Geography and Regional Planning, Universidade Nova de Lisboa, and the TERCUD – Territory, Culture and Development Research Centre, Universidade Lusófona de Humanidades e Tecnologias, Lisbon.
3 In this section, the figures in parenthesis represent the mean value of an indicator in a cluster.
4 In Northern and North-western Europe, the depopulated countryside also attracts second home buyers not only because of kin bonds but also due to the large surplus of empty housing stock (Müller 2002; Aronsson 2004; Keen and Hall 2004).
5 An indication of such demand is the great number of advertisements on real estate in daily and weekly newspapers.
6 In 2011, according to estimates brought forward by the Secretary of State of the Portuguese Emigrant Communities, between 100,000 and 120,000 Portuguese left the country. The main destinations of these most recent emigrants are the former colonies of Portugal such as Brazil and Angola, i.e. countries that have been registering sizeable GDP growth rates in recent years. For instance, a press release by the State Immigration Department of the Brazilian Ministry of Justice issued information that only between December 2010 and June 2011 the Portuguese's applications for permanent visas in that country grew from 276,703 to 328,856. Source: www.ionline.pt/portugal/mais-100-mil-portugueses-emigraram-2011 (published 27 December 2011, updated 34 weeks ago). (Accessed 23 August 2012).
7 This analysis was conducted in 2010 as part of the aforementioned project SEGREX.

References

Aledo, A. and Mazón, T. (2004) 'Impact of residential tourism and the destination life cycle theory', in F.D. Pineda, C.A. Trebbia and M. Mugica (eds) *Sustainable Tourism*, Southampton: WIT Press.

Andriotis, K. (2006) 'Hosts, guests and politics: coastal resorts morphological change', *Annals of Tourism Research*, 33(4): 1079–98.

Aronsson, L. (2004) 'Place attachment of vacation residents: between tourists and permanent residents', in C.M. Hall and D.K. Müller (eds) *Tourism, Mobility and Second Homes: Between Elite Landscape and Common Ground*, Clevedon: Channel View Publications, 75–86.

Barke, M. (1991) 'The growth and changing patterns of second homes in Spain in the 1970s', *Scottish Geographical Magazine*, (107): 12–21.

Baptista, F.O. (2006) 'O rural depois da agricultura', in M.L. Fonseca (ed.) *Desenvolvimento e Território: Espaços Rurais Pós-agrícolas e Novos Lugares de Turismo e Lazer*, Lisbon: Centro de Estudos Geográficos, 85–105.

Burby, R.J. (1979) *Second Homes in North Carolina: An Analysis of Water Resources and Other Consequences of Recreational Land Development*, Raleigh: Water Resources Research Institute of the University of North Carolina.

Casado-Díaz, M.A. (2004) 'Second homes in Spain', in C.M. Hall and D.K. Müller (eds) *Tourism, Mobility and Second Homes: Between Elite Landscape and Common Ground*, Clevedon: Channel View Publications, 215–32.

Coccossis, H. and Constantoglou, M.E. (2005) 'The need for spatial typologies in tourism planning and policy making: the Greek case', in *45th Congress of the European Regional Science Association*, Amsterdam, 23–27 August. http://ideas.repec.org/p/wiw/wiwrsa/ersa05p693.html (accessed 28 June 2012).

Colás, J.L. and Cabrerizo, J. A. (2004) 'Vivienda secundaria y residencia múltiple en España: Una aproximación sociodemográfica', *Geo Crítica/Scripta Nova, Revista Electrónica de Geografia y Ciencias Sociales*, 8(178). http://www.ub.es/geocrit/sn/sn-178.htm (accessed 28 June 2012).

Collantes, F. and Pinilla, V. (2004) 'Extreme depopulation in the Spanish rural mountain areas: a case study of Aragon in the nineteenth and twentieth centuries', *Rural History*, 15: 149–66.

Coppock, J.T. (ed.) (1977) *Second Homes, Curse or Blessing*, Oxford: Pergamon Press.

Davies, R.B. and O'Farrell, P. (1981) *An Intra-Regional Locational Analysis of Second Home Ownership*, Cardiff: Dept of Town Planning, University of Wales.

Deffner, A., Sayas, J. and Panayotatos, E. (2002) *Socio-Spatial Differentiations and Second Home Settlement Development: The Case of the Evoikos Coastal Area*. www.isocarp.net/Data/case_studies/155.pdf (accessed 28 June 2012).

Di, Z.X., Mcardle, N. and Masnick, G.S. (2001) *Second Homes: What, How Many, Where and Who* [Working Paper N01–02]. Harvard: Joint Centre for Housing Studies – Harvard University. www.jchs.harvard.edu/sites/jchs.harvard.edu/files/di_n01–2.pdf (accessed 28 June 2012).

Diamond, J. (2005) *Collapse: How Societies Choose to Fail or Survive*, London: Penguin.

Dijst, M., Lanzendorf, M. and Smit, L. (2005) 'Second homes in Germany and the Netherlands: Ownership and travel impact explained', *Tijdschrift voor Economische en Sociale Geografie* 96(2): 139–52.

Ericsson, B. (2006) 'Second homes in Norway: Factors motivating for ownership and usage, with differing market perspectives and planning parameters', *Scandinavian Journal of Hospitality and Tourism*, 6.

Downing, P., and Dower, M. (1977) *Second Homes in Scotland*, Dartington: Dartington Amenity Research Trust.

Flognfeldt, T. (2006) 'Second homes, work commuting and amenity migrants in Norway's mountain areas', in E. Moss (ed.) *The Amenity Migrants: Seeking and Sustaining Mountains and Their Cultures*, Oxfordshire: CABI Publications, 232–44.

Gallent, N., Mace, A. and Tewdwr-Jones, M. (2003) 'Dispelling a myth? Second homes in Rural Wales', *Area*, 35(3): 271–84.

——(2002) *Second Homes in Rural Areas of England*, Cheltenham: The Countryside Agency.

González, J.A.G. (2009) 'El turismo de retorno: modalidad oculta del turismo residencial', in T. Mazón, R. Huerte and A. Mantecón (eds) *Turismo, Urbanización y Estilos De Vida: Las Nuevas Formas de Movilidad Residencial*, Barcelona: Icaria Editorial, 351–65.

Hall, C.M. and Müller, D.K. (2004) 'Introduction: second homes, curse or blessing? Revisited', in C.M. Hall and D.K. Müller (eds) *Tourism, Mobility and Second Homes: Between Elite Landscape and Common Ground*, Clevedon: Channel View Publications, 3–14.

Halseth, G. and Rosenberg, M.W. (1995) 'Cottagers in an urban field', *Professional Geographer* 47: 148–59.

Hoogendoorn, G. and Visser, G. (2004) 'Second homes and small-town (re)development: the case of Clarens', *Journal of Family Ecology and Consumer Sciences*, 32: 105–15.

Ilbery, B. and Bowler, I. (1998) 'From agricultural productivism to post-productivism', in B. Ilbery (ed.) *The Geography of Rural Change*, Harlow: Longman, 57–84.

Jansson, B. (1994) *Borta Bra Men Hemma Bäst: Svenskars Turistresor under Sommaren*, Umeå: Geografiska Institutionen.

Keen, D. and Hall, M. (2004) 'Second homes in New Zeeland' in C.M. Hall and D.K. Müller (eds) *Tourism, Mobility and Second Homes: Between Elite Landscape and Common Ground*, Clevedon: Channel View Publications, 174–95.

King, R., Warnes, A.M. and Williams, A.M. (1998) 'International retirement migration in Europe', *International Journal of Population Geography*, 4(2): 91–112.

Leatherman, J.C. and Marcouiller, D.W. (1996) 'Estimating tourism's share of local income from secondary data sources', *Review of Regional Studies*, 26(3): 317–40.

Lundgren, J.O.J. (1974) 'On access to recreational lands in dynamic metropolitan hinterlands', *Tourist Review*, 29: 124–31.

Marjavaara, R. and Müller, D. (2007) 'The development of second homes assessed property values in Sweden 1991–2001', *Scandinavian Journal of Hospitality and Tourism*, 7(3): 202–22.

Marsden, T., Murdoch, J., Lowe, P., Munton, R. and Flynn, A. (1993) *Constructing the Countryside*, London: UCL Press.

Mazón, T., Huete, R. and Mantecón, A. (2010) 'Il turismo residenziale in Spagna nella prospettiva sociologica,' in T. Romita (ed.) *Il Turismo Residenziale: Nuovi Stili di Vita e di Residenzialità, Governance del Territorio e Sviluppo Sostenibile del Turismo*, Milano: Editore Franco Angeli, 67–93.

Milligan, G.W. and Cooper, M.C. (1985) 'An examination of procedures for determining the number of clusters in a data set', *Psychometrika*, 50: 159–79.

Müller, D. K. (2002) 'Reinventing the countryside: German second-home owners in southern Sweden', *Current Issues in Tourism*, 5: 426–46.

Müller, D.K. (2004) 'Second homes in Sweden: patterns and issues', in C.M. Hall and D.K. Müller (eds) *Tourism, Mobility and Second Homes: Between Elite Landscape and Common Ground*, Clevedon: Channel View Publications, pp. 244–258.

Müller, D.K., Hall, C.M. and Keen, D. (2004) 'Second home tourism impact, planning and management', in C.M. Hall and D.K. Müller (eds) *Tourism, Mobility and Second Homes: Between Elite Landscape and Common Ground*, Clevedon: Channel View Publications, 15–32.

Munõz, J.M.B., Dadon, J.R., Matteucci, S.D., Morello, J.H., Baxendale, C. and Rodríguez, A. (2003) 'Preliminary basis for an integrated management program for the coastal zone of Argentina', *Coastal Management*, 31(1): 55–77.

Oliveira, J., Roca, Z. and N. Leitão (2010) 'Territorial identity and development: From topophilia to terraphilia', *Land Use Policy* 27: 801–14.

Paquette, S. and Domon, G. (2003) 'Changing ruralities, changing landscapes: exploring social recomposition using a multi-scale approach', *Journal of Rural Studies*, 19(4): 425–44.

Paris, C. (2006) 'Multiple homes, dwelling & hyper-mobility & emergent transnational second home ownership', in European Network for Housing Research, *ENHR Conference – Housing in an Expanding Europe: Theory, Policy, Participation and Implementation*, Ljubljana, 2–5 July. http://www.enhr.net/index.php (accessed 28 June 2012).

Pettersson, R. (1999) *Foreign Second Home Purchases – The Case of Northern Sweden, 1990–96*, CERUM Working Paper No. 14, Umeå: Umeå University.

Philips, M. (2000) 'Making space for rural gentrification', in *II Anglo Spanish Symposium on Rural Geography*, University of Valladolid, Spain, July 2000. www.ub.edu/geoagr/102.PDF (accessed 22 August 2012).

——(2008) 'Rural gentrification', *SciTopics*. www.scitopics.com/Rural_gentrification.html (accessed 19 August, 2012).

Pinto-Correia, T., Breman, B., Jorge, V. and Dneboska, M. (2006) *Estudo Sobre o Abandono em Portugal Continental. Análise das Dinâmicas da Ocupação do Solo, do Sector Agrícola e da Comunidade Rural. Tipologia de Áreas Rurais*, Évora: Universidade de Évora.

Pyne, C. B. (1973) *Second Homes*, Caernarvonshire: Caernarvonshire County Planning Department.

Rencher, A.C. (2002) *Methods of Multivariate Analysis*, New York: John Wiley & Sons, Inc.

Roca, Z., Roca, M.N.O. (2007) 'Affirmation of territorial identity: A development policy issue', *Land Use Policy*, 24: 434–42.

Schuckert, M., Möller, C. and Weiermair, K. (2007) 'Alpine destinations life cycles: challenges and implications', in R. Conrady and M. Buck (eds) *Trends and Issues in Global Tourism*, Heidelberg: Springer, 121–36.

Shellito, B.A. and Pijanowski, B.C. (2003) 'Using neural nets to model the spatial distribution of seasonal homes', *Cartography and Geographic Information Science*, 30(3), 281–90.

Tamer, N.G., Erdoğanaras, F. and Güzey, Ö. (2006) 'Turkey, social, economic and physical effects of second-home development based on foreign retirement migration in Turkey: Alanya and Dalyan', in International Society of City and Regional Planners, *42nd ISoCaRP CONGRESS*, Istanbul 14–18 September.

Valenzuela, R.M., (2003) 'Second homes in metropolitan areas: the Madrid Autonomous Region', *Estudios Turísticos*, 155/156: 113–57.

Visser, G. (2004) 'Second homes: reflections on an unexplored phenomenon in South Africa', in C.M. Hall and D.K. Müller (eds) *Tourism, Mobility and Second Homes: Between Elite Landscape and Common Ground*, Clevedon: Channel View Publications, 196–214.

Woods, M. (2005) *Rural Geography: Processes, Responses and Experiences in Rural Restructuring*, London: Sage Publications.

Zukin, S. (1990) 'Socio-spatial prototypes of a new organization of consumption: the role of real cultural capital', *Sociology*, 24: 37–56.

Part III

Emerging geographies of lifestyle migration and residential tourism

10 Contested realities and economic circumstances

British later-life migrants in Malaysia

Paul Green

Introduction

Increasing numbers of older migrants from high-income countries are settling or spending long periods of time in Southeast Asia, encouraged in part by governments in the region who are now incorporating international retirement or second home programmes into their development strategies. Since 2002, for example, the 'Malaysia My Second Home' (MM2H) programme has attracted over 18,000 visa applicants of various nationalities (Ministry of Tourism Malaysia 2012). Studies of international retirement migration (IRM) in the region are almost non-existent (though see Howard 2008; Ono 2008; Toyota 2006). Little understanding exists, in other words, of how and why foreign nationals from Australia, Europe and the United States are spending their later years in some of the world's most popular tourist destinations.

This chapter addresses this lack of research by focusing on the experiences of older, British migrants living in Penang, Malaysia. Specifically, I illustrate the extent to which financial and economic concerns, alongside socio-economic differences, shape the worldviews and associated lifestyle choices of British migrants living in and/or moving through Penang. As I suggest, a growing literature on lifestyle migration has yet to recognise the central role of financial concerns in shaping the everyday lives and what I term as the 'imagined futures' of migrants based in Southeast Asia. While lifestyle migrants tend to be viewed as 'relatively affluent' individuals, it is important to similarly address the significance of socio-economic differences and the extent to which 'relative affluence' represents a moveable feast of experience, based on shifting currency exchange rates and an evolving awareness of cheaper retirement destinations, for example. By addressing these concerns, this chapter highlights how and on what terms these aspects of difference map onto contested understandings of social and physical space in a migrant context.

Difference, on these terms, is filtered through the worldviews and experiences of what I term 'expatriate retirees', 'anti-expatriates' and 'marginal retirees.' As categories of analysis these terms are not used by migrants in their everyday life (Brubaker and Cooper 2000: 4). Nor is it my intention to suggest that *all* migrants conform in an absolute sense to the experiential boundaries of this conceptual framework. The depiction of expatriate retirees and anti-expatriates, as examples, nevertheless highlights the extent to which an awareness of 'other' migrants feeds into residential and lifestyle choices in Penang. The presence of 'marginal retirees', meanwhile, complicates the 'official' representation of retirement in Malaysia and a tendency within migration studies to incarcerate national subjects within specific national borders (Green 2011). While expatriate retirees may live in state of the art condominiums overlooking the Strait of Malacca, less affluent marginal retirees are literally unable to buy into the financial terms and conditions of the MM2H programme. As I suggest in this chapter, this process of exclusion contributes to an understanding of retirement migration 'in' Malaysia that needs to be located across the borders of Malaysia, Thailand and Indonesia (and beyond).

This chapter is based on ethnographic fieldwork conducted during 2011 in Penang. Research, a combination of participant observation and focused conversations, took place in migrant homes, cafés, restaurants and other relevant social spaces. The contested spatiality of migrant experience in Penang ensured a multi-sited dimension to fieldwork; research in 'expatriate enclaves' located on the coast of northern Penang was complemented by engagement with anti-expatriates and marginal retirees in particular in the urban, 'heritage' centre of Georgetown.

The economic and socio-economic dimensions to migration

Studies of transnational migration tend to focus on the flow of working migrants from the developing to the developed world (Howard 2009: 193). As Oliver (2008: 7) suggests, sociological and anthropological studies of migration specifically focus in this context on the archetypal figure of the young economic migrant. Within this particular academic and disciplinary construct (Gupta and Ferguson 1997) migration, in other words, is primarily associated with the economic motivations of individuals originating from the global south (Tsuda 2003: 85). While anthropologists traditionally developed fields of area and regional knowledge around distinct culture traits of honour-and-shame, caste hierarchy and personhood (Gupta and Ferguson 1997: 7) it can be argued that in the transnational field of migration studies, culture has been replaced or at least superordinated by the classificatory virtues of economic imperatives. Recent studies of 'Western' subjects living in Asia have only reinforced the association of migration with economic concerns, employment and specific age groups through a tendency to focus on the lives of young, working expatriates based in the region (Fechter 2007; Yeoh and Willis 2005).

A recent focus on the subjectivity, experience and consumption practices of lifestyle migrants, global nomads and international retirees (Benson and O'Reilly 2009; D'Andrea 2007; Oliver 2008) has facilitated fresh pathways of representation and enquiry within the broader field of migration studies. However, if we compare the construction of knowledge in this field to bureaucratic process (Kapferer 1995), it is clear that migrants from north and south are being internally differentiated on the basis of contrasting and hierarchialised classificatory schema. While economic migrants, it seems, prioritise a search for economic security and stability in their lives, relatively affluent lifestyle migrants and retirees have the time and financial stability to focus on privileged 'projects of the self' and a search for a better quality of life. Both examples represent a partial fiction. As Constable's (1999) study of Filipina domestic workers in Hong Kong illustrates, for example, economic migrants also engage in projects of the self and indulge in an ongoing search for a better quality of life and lifestyle.

Economic concerns and motivations are similarly relevant to the lives of lifestyle migrants. D'Andrea's (2007) research participants may forsake material concerns, such as income and career, in pursuit of an expressive lifestyle. Such lifestyles still require funding. It is no coincidence that global nomads and backpackers frequent parts of the world where there are abundant sources of casual work and/or where everyday costs are conducive to the sustainability of an expressive lifestyle project. The latter concern is reflected in the tendency of young travellers to maintain a daily budget during their time 'on the road' (D'Andrea 2007: 148). Such forms of mobility, in other words, are underwritten by, 'rational, economic decisions' made by individuals in relation to cost-of-living and/or casual employment disparities between specific locales, nation-states and regions (Tsuda 2003: 85). Clearly, the comparatively low cost of food, accommodation and other daily expenses in nation-states such as India actually creates the macro-economic framework for expressive lifestyle culture to flourish on the contemporary global stage.

Understanding both the macro- and micro-economic dimensions to movement from north to south is particularly relevant to the study of international retirement or what may best be viewed as 'later-life' migration. While studies of 'retirement migration' are constrained by their association with normative and culturally specific delimiters of retirement (typically, 60 or 65 years) the use of the term 'later-life' by Warnes and Williams (2006) provides a more flexible basis to focus on the experiences of migrants who may have taken early retirement, been forced to retire early or simply be married to older spouses. A focus on a numerical boundary of 50 years also draws attention to government policy. In terms of financial thresholds and income expectations, the MM2H programme specifically encourages over-50-year-old applicants to live and buy property in Malaysia.

Retirement, whether enforced, taken early or otherwise, brings an uncertain financial future (Howard 2008). Even 'relatively affluent' retirees cannot preempt how long they will live and for how long they will need to 'stretch' savings and investments. It is no coincidence, on these terms, that American retirees head towards Panama and Mexico and not Canada. A study by the Migration Policy Institute (2006: 51) suggests that economic considerations, in terms of costs-of-living and taxation policies, for example, represent the primary motivation for the movement of American 'seniors' to Latin

America. As the recent global economic and euro crises demonstrate there is a need to recognise the extent to which savings and investments are embedded in fragile, global finanscapes (Appadurai 1996). The fragility of finanscapes may be diluted or strengthened through migration, as investments, pensions and other forms of retirement income become susceptible to the vagaries of an ever-shifting currency exchange system. The concept of 'relative affluence', then, is itself relative and contingent on the dynamics of the global economy.

Little understanding exists of the meaning of 'relative affluence' *within* particular migrant communities. Lifestyle migrants of all ages are often and uniformly viewed as financially stable individuals. There is a need to consider how socio-economic differences, background and life history influence 'how individuals create meaning in the particular contexts in which they live' (Oliver 2008: 48). On one level, the actual availability of financial resources may pre-empt the kinds of choices migrants make in terms of purchasing or renting property or accommodation, which in turn leads to the physical segregation of migrants based on scales of affluence. Socio-economic difference can also be felt in more subtle yet pervasive terms, shaping individual negotiations and navigations of a range of localised social, cultural and physical landscapes. It is important, in other words, to recognise how 'difference' feeds into contested understandings of physical landscapes, local life and community in the quotidian arena of migrant life (Oliver 2008: 47–48).

Studies of later-life or retirement migration tend to focus on the experiences of particular national subjects *in* specific national fieldsites and spaces. On one level, this focus denies the extent to which later-life migrants are hypermobile subjects, a point reinforced by an ageist tendency in migration studies (Hazan 2009) to equate *extensive* movement with young people. At the same time, migrant experiences of belonging, dwelling and mobility may be contingent on an individual's ability to fit governmental imaginings of desirable, ageing residents in the context of retirement and other visa policies. The MM2H programme, for example, excludes over-50-year-olds of limited funds from acquiring its 10-year, renewable visas. Howard (2009: 195) similarly speaks of the precarious visa status of 'marginal' Westerners living in Thailand. While these policies affect the lives of later-life migrants living in particular national spaces, questions emerge as to how these exclusionary processes shape mobility. How might a 'marginal', later-life Westerner living in Thailand experience 'retirement' on a visa run in Malaysia? How might the visa policies of both Malaysia and Thailand shape experiences of belonging and mobility for a retiree who cannot live in one particular country for extended periods of time?

In this chapter I consider questions of macro- and micro-economic influence and socio-economic difference in the lives and contested worldviews of later-life British migrants living in or staying for short periods of time in Penang, Malaysia. I first consider the experiences of what I term as 'expatriate retirees'. Next, I discuss life in Malaysia from the perspective of what I term as 'anti-expatriate' residents. Finally, this chapter focuses on the worldviews and experiences of 'marginal' migrants: individuals who may live in Penang in cheap, hotel accommodation or regularly move across national borders as a result of their ongoing status as 'non-residents' in Southeast Asia.

Expatriate retirees

Many foreign residents, including a significant contingent of British retirees and MM2H-ers, live in the two northern enclaves of Batu Feringgi and Tanjung Bungah. Batu Feringgi is an international tourist destination, a concentrated beach strip replete with hotels, restaurants and souvenir shops. Upon leaving Batu Feringgi, in the direction of the heritage town of Georgetown, you will soon arrive at or pass through Tanjung Bungah. The sea front here is dominated by condominiums, the occasional hotel and building sites that promise to soon clutter the (sea) views of apartments situated away from the beach. Practically all residents choose to live in high rise apartments, as opposed to houses which are available in the area. For some residents, their elevated lifestyle facilitates the creation of an 'expat bubble' (Fechter 2007), a space in which boundaries of Otherness can be maintained, in light of the polluting threats of local street life, especially burglary. Car ownership, alongside routine exploration of modern shopping malls and closed, air-conditioned eateries, ensure that the bubble is maintained in public space.

Later-life residents in this area can, most certainly, be described as 'relatively affluent', even if there are degrees of difference in terms of wealth among these migrants. Some of the people I met owned property overseas and had acquired vast and luxurious apartment spaces serviced by their own, private lift or elevator in Penang. Many, if not all residents, can be described as 'expatriate retirees' who, in other words, have previously worked as expatriates in middle management or banking in Asia or built a career in the higher levels of the Hong Kong Police Force, as examples. Some of these residents choose to enrol onto the MM2H programme, while others prefer to use tourist visas and leave the country every three months in order to renew their visa. This tendency to use tourist visas ensures that little reliable statistical data exists of the actual number of retirees and later-life migrants based in Malaysia.

Despite their 'relatively affluent' status many residents are acutely aware and spoke at length about the financial benefits of living in Malaysia. Viewed through a comparative lens (Benson and O'Reilly 2009: 610) I was consistently told how much *cheaper* it was to live in Malaysia, in terms of rent and property prices and everyday costs of living. John, who was in his 50s and had worked in the Hong Kong Police Force, spoke of the highly affordable costs of health care and dental treatment. Medical bills, including consultancy fees, were ridiculous he pointed out. John spoke of the time when his visiting father had a heart attack and subsequently received treatment while in Penang. The health insurers in England, he added, could not believe the bill. Alongside the economic benefits of access to such facilities, migrants like

John are also highly impressed by the quality of the treatment and the quick and direct access available to leading consultants, whose status is enhanced in some cases by their association, in terms of training, with leading medical schools in Ireland.

The comparative project of retirement is multi-layered. Comparisons of 'here' and 'there' may incorporate yet transcend a focus on one's previous life and home. 'There' may represent one of several places in the 'national order of things' (Malkki 1992: 26) that migrants have considered in their global hunt for an economically viable life in retirement. John had considered retiring in Australia, a country he liked, but was less impressed by the fact that the Australian Tax Office treats the worldwide income of residents as national property. Malaysia, by contrast, does not tax income, including government pensions, from overseas. Nor does it impose inheritance taxes (The Expat 2011: 9). Such concerns are of great importance to some migrants, as reflected in the *Daily Telegraph's* recent depiction of Malaysia as a 'newcomer tax haven' (Henderson 2011).

Andy, another British migrant who had also built a career in the Police Force in Hong Kong, cared little for the polluted beaches in Penang. There were much better places to have a beach holiday in Asia, he argued. Yet Andy chose to live, buy and invest in property in Malaysia, as opposed to Thailand, for example, because of the former's relatively transparent property law frameworks, which are based on British law, and the fact that all documentation is or can be produced in English. With this in mind, Andy felt that his investments were, from a jural and financial perspective, in comparatively safer hands.

The future, of course, is harder to predict. Simon, in his early 60s, was worried about his health and the health of his finances. While the former undoubtedly represented an important concern, he also talked at length about the current state of his finances and investments. All of his investments were in pounds sterling. The fall of the pound relative to the Malaysian ringgit in recent years had greatly affected his income. Simon had also underestimated the persistence of the global financial crisis, which he initially estimated would last for 'just' three years. He spoke with anger of bankers still receiving increments and bonuses, the overwhelming influence of Goldman Sachs in the global economy and a potential Armageddon scenario that could emerge through the current euro crisis. Simon felt that because of these financial concerns his future, which included the issue of whether he remained in Malaysia, was somewhat uncertain. His future, on these terms, was further complicated by the financial needs of his son, who was due to graduate from university in the UK in two years with a view to potentially taking on further studies. Simon planned to reassess his plans at the point of his son's graduation, illustrating the extent to which projects of the self and future may be embedded in dependent kinship ties. I met several migrants, like Simon, with dependent children living overseas.

Some residents are sure of one aspect of their future – they will not return to their homeland or previous home because they simply cannot afford to live there. While John had considered several potential places to live and retire he was well aware that he could not afford to continue living in Hong Kong, where property was so expensive that he would have ended up living in a shoe box. When I met Nick and Fiona, a British couple in their 50s, they were both excited and nervous after exceeding their budget and buying a dream apartment with views of the Strait of Malacca. A key reason for moving to Malaysia was that they simply could not afford to continue to live and, therefore, live on a long-term, sustainable basis in England. The cost of a mortgage and everyday living costs were high enough to inspire Fiona to look at overseas living options. She came across details of the MM2H programme on the internet and the couple decided to move to Penang. This is not to suggest this couple have fitted easily into community life on Penang's northern shores. Fiona in particular felt that age had played a significant role in their inability to build a wide net of friendships with other British migrants and foreigners in Penang. In the section below, I consider further aspects of difference amongst British later-life migrants, focusing on the lives of what I term 'anti-expatriate' residents.

Anti-expatriates

British later-life migrants can also be found in other parts of Penang, typically residing in the 30-minute driving space (depending on time and traffic) between Tanjung Bungah and Georgetown. These residents *tend* to be less affluent than their compatriots on the northern shores, though they have sufficient funds to lead a comfortable lifestyle in Penang. Such migrants may self-identify as 'alternative people' (D'Andrea 2007: 2) who define themselves by what or who they are not. Sitting in a small café/bar in Georgetown one night, Simon, who was in his early 50s, suggested that he had little time for expats or tourists and clearly distanced himself from identifying with these or in fact any labels or categories of identification. While reluctant to conform to a particular notion of identity (Brubaker and Cooper 2000) Simon's rejection of labels at least set in place boundaries that defined his landscape of sociability, which excluded expatriate retirees yet included local Malaysian residents. This is an important source of difference between expatriate retirees and anti-expatriates. While the former have little inclination to connect with locals, or may speak in some cases of the difficulties of doing so, Simon's tendency to frequent a local open air food court of more than 20 hawker stalls near his home, for example, ensured regular contact and conversation with residents in the area.

'Anti-expatriates', as I label them, tend to avoid living in the midst of expats. As Paul, an ex-low ranking officer in the British Army explained, expats typically congregate in 'national' communities, building friendships with their British, French or German compatriots. Anti-expatriates tend to rent in apartment blocks, as opposed to condominiums, where there are few if any other foreign residents. Residency, like friendship, is less defined by the desirability of living in a specific residential area than simply avoiding the nationalistic, expatriate 'zone' of the northern shores. Anti-expatriates live in what they feel are 'local' residential areas. Like Simon, Paul and his German wife Meike did not own a car. Anti-expatriates are comfortable using Penang's extensive, inexpensive and often crowded bus network to navigate the social and physical landscapes of Penang.

Anti-expatriates, like expatriate retirees, talk at length of the affordability of life in Penang, which facilitates access to apartments with shared swimming pools, health and dental care and inexpensive yet delicious food. At times, it is difficult to separate a celebration of affordability from lifestyle choice. As Rob and Samantha, a couple in their early 60s explained to me, they had little inclination to eat in what they described as 'sanitised' air-conditioned eateries serving relatively expensive yet bland, westernised food. Anti-expatriates in particular buy into Penang's local reputation as the food capital of Malaysia. Endless varieties of Chinese and Malay food are available across the island from food stalls which tend to offer a specific choice of dishes, or even one specific dish, cooked on site and to order. A meal can cost as little as a US dollar. As Rob commented, it is cheaper to eat at these stalls than cook at home, but again this misses the point in some ways of why the kitchen in one's apartment is primarily a space to make tea or coffee. Anti-expatriates appreciate eating like 'the locals' in a sociable environment where a sweat-inducing combination of humidity and spicy food offers the perfect excuse to indulge in cold beer or an array of freshly squeezed fruit juices.

Like expatriate retirees, anti-expatriates may be acutely aware of the need to manage finances and plan for what is nevertheless an unpredictable future. British residents in general in Malaysia tend to have travelled widely in Southeast Asia and thanks to the recent growth of budget airlines, such as Air Asia, continue to frequently explore the region. In 2010 Paul and Meike went to Cambodia. They loved Phnom Penh and the coastal town of Sihanoukville and were astounded by how cheap Cambodia was in contrast to the costs of living in Penang. When I met this couple in 2011, they were making plans to move to Phnom Penh, a decision made at the expense of a life by the beach as a result of the medical facilities available in the capital city. Following encounters with foreigners living in Cambodia Paul and Meike were also confident of meeting warm, friendly people, commenting that it had a 'good' expat community there. The couple's decision was not made on the basis of economic concerns alone. As Paul commented, they do tend to get 'itchy feet' every few years. Their decision to move to Cambodia, however, points to a potentially growing trend as later-life migrants look for opportunities to live in cheaper surroundings amidst concerns that costs of living are on the rise in some parts of Southeast Asia.

Some anti-expatriates learn of potential future homes in the region through their encounters with backpackers in Penang. Penang continues to attract backpackers travelling overland between Thailand and Malaysia and beyond, for example. While tourists stay in international hotels in Batu Feringgi, backpackers are more at home in the space of a few streets in Georgetown where there are several cheap hostels, guesthouses, budget travel agencies and cheap eateries and bars. The area attracts anti-expatriates, who prefer the company of travellers with a supposed 'international' mindset than their compatriots in the north and have long-standing relationships with local café/bar owners. Jim, in his early 60s, liked to drink at least twice a week in the area. He enjoyed talking with people from all over the world, noting that it was important to spend time with 'young people' as they enabled Jim to feel young himself.

As I discuss below, this contact zone of anti-expatriates and backpackers is also frequented by later-life migrants living in Thailand or Indonesia and retirees visiting Penang from beyond the region for cheap dental treatment, for example. A number of later-life foreigners can also be found living in cheap hotels in the area. As I suggest below, the presence of these migrants and retirees confound any attempt to situate retirement migration 'in' Malaysia within Malaysia and the 'glossy' confines of the MM2H programme alone.

Marginal retirees

This backpacker zone, as I call it, has undergone significant changes in recent years. In 2008 inner Georgetown gained recognition as an UNESCO world heritage site. The area is becoming increasingly gentrified. A staple of the hippie trail and what Cohen (1973) referred to as drifter-tourism, this area is now home to luxury and mid-range boutique hotels, artist galleries and 'heritage' cafés nestling in traditional townhouses. Some things do not change. In the evenings, female and transgendered sex workers patrol some of the streets while established hawker stalls continue to cater to an array of local and foreign customers. A lesser known fact, particularly among expatriate retirees, is that the area is also home to a significant contingent of both highly mobile and a more settled group of later-life foreigners. Some migrants have been living in the same room, in the same, inexpensive hotel, for a number of years, relying on and renewing their tourist visa as and when necessary. Usually single and predominantly male, these latter individuals have neither the funds nor the inclination in some cases to subscribe to a state-sponsored retirement or second home programme. Like expatriate retirees, the lives of what I term as 'marginal retirees' – marginal at least in their ability to access residential status in Malaysia – can be affected by shifting currency rates. Jonathan, a British retiree in his late 60s, spoke of the huge effect on his life of a weak pound in recent years. Jonathan had limited savings and relied on a meagre state pension. A 20–25 per cent shortfall in income, he noted, had ensured that he had little funds available for alcohol or what he termed as 'food splurges' and was all too aware that he could not afford to pay for significant health care should he fall seriously ill in Malaysia.

Significant numbers of later-life foreigners live or spend significant periods of time in Southeast Asia, reliant on renewable tourist or other relevant visas that ensure they must transgress national borders every month, two months or more, in order to maintain what Howard (2008) notes as an insecure sense of residence in the region. Indeed, later-life migrants in the region are also then vulnerable to any potential changes in immigration policy and visa guidelines. Owing to its proximity, Penang attracts a lot of 'visa-runners' from Indonesia and Thailand, who typically spend a few days in Georgetown. Some migrants have been visiting Penang on these terms for several years or more and like Jonathan, above, prefer to stay in their 'usual' hotel, partly because it tends to attract supposedly like-minded, older travellers. Social networks, established over several years and inspired by age if not nationality, have developed between the residents and visa-runners staying in these hotels, where communal tables provide the space for people to catch up on and share the latest news and gossip and indulge in a hot drink or beer from the hotel fridge.

These later-life migrants may not live in Malaysia, but they typically hold a highly intimate attachment to Penang in particular. Trevor retired as an aircraft maintenance engineer at the age of 44. He had spent the last eight years of his now retired life in Java. Every six months he comes to Penang to renew his visa, usually spending a week there. A key factor in heading to Penang to do this, as opposed to another nearby destination such as Singapore, was that Trevor had established good relations with the Indonesian immigration officers based at the Consulate-General in Penang. This was important to Trevor. In his experience 'different' offices worked with different guidelines or at least interpretations of guidelines. It was also the case that after spending a lifetime working in the region, Trevor had spent a lot of his working and now retired life coming and going from a place he loved, Penang. As in the case of other 'visa-runners' Penang represents a liminal space for him to reflect on a life history and project (Bousiou 2008: 181) that includes an intimate, reflexive and ongoing relationship with cafés, bars and hotels and different, even shifting, versions of a 'past self' located in just a few streets of inner Georgetown.

The continual need to renew visas may lead some migrants to feel a sense of homelessness in their frequent movement across national borders. Mark, in his early 50s, was an orthopaedic nurse. Following a motorcycle accident he was forced to take early retirement. When I asked him where he was living he simply said, 'between Thailand and Penang'. Mark claims to have clocked 32,000 miles on his motorcycle in just two years. In some ways, Mark's motorcycle adventure is a lifestyle choice, though he admits to losing 'patience' with Malaysia after being stopped three times between the border and Penang in recent months. At the same time, he spoke of concerns over his health and did not seem to celebrate his residential location between two nation-states. He is still 'full of pins' after the accident, he told me, and struggles with arthritis. He was pessimistic about his long-term health. His choice to live on the road, amidst these health concerns, is clearly shadowed by the narrow range of visa options available to Mark in Southeast Asia. Thailand offers one-year retirement visas to over-50-year-olds and the financial criteria for applicants are more generous than those stipulated in the MM2H programme. Whether Mark chooses to apply for this visa in the future and whether he meets the annual income requirements noted in Thai immigration guidelines is another matter.

Conclusion

The official website of the MM2H programme offers a narrative and visual 'window' into an idealised national vision in which governments and affluent 'second homers' indulge in a mutually beneficial economic contract designed to meet the needs of both parties. The foreign resident buys property, a tax-free (Malaysian) automobile and offers little threat to the local employment market. In return, the MM2H resident engages with a generous national tax regime, plays golf on discounted golf courses, sits back (while always spending) and enjoys the favourable climate. In reality, this national programme is built on a 'global order of things', to extend Malkki's (1992) thesis, where retirees and later-life migrants seek a comparative national space in which the fear and insecurity of permanent unemployment can be metamorphosed into a vision of an affordable lifestyle and a potentially secure financial future. Malaysia's private health care system, while not accessible to all incomers, not least female domestic workers, male construction workers and marginal retirees, ensures that most expatriate retirees and anti-expatriates can afford to get and be ill in Malaysia.

As suggested in this chapter, there are a range of macro- and micro-economic factors that need to be placed at the forefront of analysis of the growing movement of migrants from north to south. The complexity of this process is encapsulated by the experiences and concerns of migrants in Penang, which on one level highlight the need to question and further examine what 'we' might mean by the term 'relative affluence'. For some expatriate retirees relative affluence is filtered through a global and regional understanding of affordability, property laws and taxation policies. Simon's case illustrates the extent to which expatriate retirees may be subject to the vulnerabilities of global finanscapes and currency exchange rates in ways that have implications for how and on what terms a resident can imagine building a future and sense of belonging in a particular place. There is a need to further examine how Simon's uncertain future, as an example, feeds into his ability to invest emotional and practical time and resources into his current project of the self, as it connects to transnational kinship ties, in Penang.

This chapter has also highlighted the importance of recognising 'difference' within national migrant groups and the extent to which socio-economic differences and variable income levels, in this case, feed into one's engagement with a range of social, cultural and physical landscapes in Penang and beyond. Some anti-expatriates may not be able to afford a condominium unit with a private elevator, yet their avoidance of the northern shores and an associated lifestyle also points to a mergence of economic and moral difference that in turn feed into lifestyle, relationship and residential choices. The case of marginal retirees, based in other parts of the region, or perhaps between nation-states, ultimately demonstrates the importance of engaging with migrant experiences of and in Penang on regional, global and yet national terms. While Trevor's case highlights intimate, long-standing attachments of visa-runners to inner Georgetown, there is clearly a need to further examine the impact of national immigration frameworks, as demonstrated by the experiences of Jonathan and Mark, in shaping or at least contributing to experiences of mobility, social exclusion and health problems in later life.

References

Appadurai, A. (1996) *Modernity at Large: Cultural Dimensions of Globalisation*, Minneapolis: University of Minnesota Press.

Benson, M. and O'Reilly, K. (2009) 'Migration and the search for a better way of life: a critical exploration of lifestyle migration', *Sociological Review,* 57(4): 608–25.

Bousiou, P. (2008) *The Nomads of Mykonos: Performing Liminalities in a 'Queer' Space*, New York: Berghahn.

Brubaker, R. and Cooper, F. (2000) 'Beyond "identity"', *Theory and Society*, 29: 1–47.

Cohen, E. (1973) 'Nomads from affluence: notes on the phenomenon of drifter-tourism', *International Journal of Comparative Sociology,* XIV(1–2): 89–103.

Constable, N. (1999) 'At home but not at home: Filipina narratives of ambivalent returns', *Cultural Anthropology,* 14(2): 203–28.

D'Andrea, A. (2007) *Global Nomads: Techno and New Age as Transnational Countercultures in Ibiza and Goa*, London: Routledge.

Fechter, A.-M. (2007) *Transnational lives: Expatriates in Indonesia*, Aldershot: Ashgate.

Green, P. (2011) 'The enemy within? Personhood, friendship and difference amongst Brazilian nationals living in Japan', *Journal of Ethnic and Migration Studies,* 37(3): 373–88.

Gupta, A. and Ferguson, J. (1997) *Anthropological Locations: Boundaries and Grounds of a Field Science*, Berkeley: University of California Press.

Hazan, H. (2009) 'Essential others: anthropology and the return of the old savage', *International Journal of Sociology and Social Policy,* 29(1/2): 60–72.

Henderson, L. (2011) 'Expats expand horizons in the quest to live the dream', *Daily Telegraph,* 21 April. www.telegraph.co.uk/property/expatproperty/8458265/Expats-expand-horizons-in-the-quest-to-live-the-dream.html (accessed 23 May 2012).

Howard, R. (2008) 'Western retirees in Thailand: motives, experiences, wellbeing, assimilation and future needs', *Ageing and Society,* 28: 145–63.

——(2009) 'The migration of Westerners to Thailand: an unusual flow from developed to developing world', *International Migration,* 47(2): 193–225.

Kapferer, B. (1995) 'Bureaucratic erasure: identity, resistance and violence – Aborigines and a discourse of autonomy in a North Queensland town', in D. Miller (ed.) *Worlds Apart: Modernity through the Prism of the Local*, London: Routledge.

Malkki, L. (1992) 'National geographic: The rooting of peoples and the territorialization of national identity amongst scholars and refugees', *Cultural Anthropology,* 7(1): 24–44.

Migration Policy Institute (2006) *America's Emigrants: US Retirement Migration to Mexico and Panama.* www.migrationpolicy.org/pubs/americas_emigrants.pdf (accessed 21 May 2012).

Ministry of Tourism Malaysia (2012) *Malaysia My Second Home Programme.* www.mm2h.gov.my/statistic.php (accessed 10 March 2012).

Oliver, C. (2008) *Retirement Migration: Paradoxes of Ageing*, London: Routledge.
Ono, M. (2008) 'Long-stay tourism and international retirement migration: Japanese retirees in Malaysia', *Senri Ethnological Reports,* 77: 151–62. http://ir.minpaku.ac.jp/dspace/bitstream/10502/2043/1/SER77_013.pdf (accessed 10 March 2012).
The Expat (2011) *MM2H: Malaysia my Second Home (special edition).*
Toyota, M. (2006) 'Ageing and transnational householding: Japanese retirees in Southeast Asia', *International Development Planning Review,* 28(4): 515–31.
Tsuda, T. (2003) *Strangers in the Ethnic Homeland: Japanese Brazilian Return Migration in Transnational Perspective*, New York: Columbia University Press.
Warnes A. and Williams A. (2006) 'Older migrants in Europe: a new focus for migration studies', *Journal of Ethnic and Migration Studies,* 32(8): 1257–81.
Yeoh, B.S.A. and Willis, K. (2005) 'Singaporean and British transmigrants in China and the cultural politics of "contact zones"', *Journal of Ethnic and Migration Studies,* 31(2): 269–85.

11 Russian second home owners in Eastern Finland

Involvement in the local community

Olga Lipkina and C. Michael Hall

Introduction

Transnational second home migration has become a topic of increasing academic interest (Williams and Hall 2002; Hall and Müller 2004; Gallent, Mace and Tewdwr-Jones 2005; Hall 2006, 2011; McIntyre, Williams and McHugh 2006; Paris 2011), particularly in the European context where mobility and foreign property ownership have become easier as a result of European Union policies (O'Reilly 2000, 2007; Breuer 2005; Janoschka 2010; Åkerlund 2011; Lampič and Mrak 2012). However, despite the general interest in second home tourism and mobility there are only a limited number of studies that look specifically at cross-border second home tourism. These include studies of Germans in Sweden (Müller 1999); British in France (Hoggart and Buller 1995; Puzzo 2007; Benson 2009) and in Spain (O'Reilly 2000, 2007; Casado-Díaz 2009; Janoschka 2010; Haas 2012); US citizens in Mexico (Truly 2002; Torres and Momsen 2005a, 2005b; Janoschka 2009); Hong Kong Chinese second homes in the Chinese mainland (Hui and Yu 2009); Norwegians in Sweden (Müller 2011); and Russians in Finland (Lipkina 2011, in press; Pitkänen 2011).

Cross-border second home destinations are often studied from the perspective of reasons for the destination choice, activities at the site of the cottage and impact, while life in the host society and experiences at foreign second homes are still largely neglected. Few studies illuminate the attitudes and relationships between hosts and newcomers (Müller 2002; Müller and Hall 2004), and discuss the participation of foreign second home owners in the local community (Müller 2011). Participation of transnational retirement migrants at their new place of residence has received academic attention (see O'Reilly 2007; Casado-Díaz 2009; Janoschka 2009, 2010; Haas 2012). However, there is clearly potential for differences in relationships between migrants and host communities depending on whether migrants are regarded as permanent residents or as 'permanent visitors', with the latter potentially being the case with respect to second home purchase (Hall 2011). The aim of this chapter is therefore to further the discussion on foreign second home owners' participation in the host communities, as they do not permanently reside at their second homes, but instead visit them occasionally. Russian second home ownership in Finland is used as an example.

In the context of second home ownership, community involvement does not necessarily presume participation in local level decision-making. Finnish and foreign second home owners are not permanent residents in an area and they therefore have limited formal rights of participation in local planning or community development in Finland (Nylander and Leppänen 2006). Nevertheless, second home owners do engage with local communities in various ways (Müller 1999; Hall and Müller 2004), especially retirement migrants who live permanently or for most of the time at their new place of residence (Janoschka 2009, 2010; Haas 2012). However, studies show that permanent connection with a place through a second home does not necessarily lead to social inclusion in the new society. Thus, part-time and permanent migrants potentially remain 'not within and not [without] the new place' (O'Reilly 2007: 278), and may socialise mostly with their own nationals or other foreign residents in the area (Casado-Díaz, Kaiser and Warnes 2004; Haas 2012). In the case discussed in the present chapter, Russian second home owners cannot reside permanently at their second homes due to the limitation on the total number of days permitted in Finland as defined by the visa regime (180 days per year maximum without any social services). Consequently, the discussion in the chapter is constructed around second home owners who visit their summer houses for short periods, and thus are potentially more challenged to get involved in local communities.

This chapter is constructed around participation in events and associations relating to interests, as well as interactions with neighbours. Community involvement requires knowledge about an area including existing activities, services and specialisations. The way a person orients themself within a local society shows possibilities for participation. As a result, it is extremely important to understand the activities and possible obstacles for involvement in order to appreciate the broader context of potentially contested spatialities of leisure mobility.

The use or disuse of services and space can also indicate the extent of involvement in the local community, even though the use of services by second home owners is usually viewed from the perspective of economic contribution to the local economy. Wide use of local services and products, and participation in local events and associations can indicate a deep involvement and even integration in the host society (Müller 1999). Economic networks in second home communities may also be(come) social networks. Nevertheless, in this chapter, use of services as an indication of involvement is presented along with the actual economic impact of second home owners with deeper involvement in the local community resulting in a higher economic outcome.

Russians in Finland: across the border

Finland and Russia share an uneasy historical past: Finland has been under Russian rule and they were enemies during the Second World War. The annexation of Finnish land by Russia after the Second World War created a national trauma in Finland. Thus, Finnish national identity has been constructed through portraying the Soviet Union as the 'other' (Paasi 1999). The Finnish–Russian border became a point of contact between the two neighbouring states only after the Soviet Union's collapse. Within 20 years of a relatively open border crossing, mutual visits to Russia and Finland have become a growing trend (Tilastokeskus 2011), with recent Russian transborder tourism also now including second home ownership.

Tight control of property purchases by foreigners in Finland lasted from Finnish independence from Russia in 1917 until EU accession in 1995. From 2000 there were no restrictions on second home property purchase for foreigners in Finland (except for the Åland Islands) (Hedström 2011). Despite the short period in which Russians have had the right to property ownership, they have increased the extent of annual foreign real estate purchases in Finland threefold, from 267 in 2005 to 913 in 2008 (see also Pitkänen 2011). Russians constitute the absolute majority among foreign property buyers in Finland, and account for about 70 per cent of the total annual foreign purchases according to the National Land Survey of Finland (own calculations; see also Maanmittauslaitos 2008). However, in terms of total national property purchases the phenomenon is relatively small, and only accounts for approximately 1 per cent of the total Finnish real estate market (own calculations; see also Maanmittauslaitos 2008; Brax 2010).

The growing number of Russian second home owners has been evaluated both positively and negatively by local inhabitants in Finland (Kotilainen, Piipponen and Pitkänen 2010; Lipkina and Pitkänen 2010). Fears and concerns related to Russian second home ownership has received great media coverage that is dominated by negative views of the phenomenon (Pitkänen 2011). These negative Finnish attitudes towards Russians are still affected by the historical memory (Paasi 1999; Pitkänen 2011). The controversy surrounding Russian second home ownership in Finland suggests that the topic requires further examination from the perspective of participation in the host society, as Russians represent a culturally and linguistically distant group of foreigners, as well as the possibilities and obstacles for involvement, since Russian second home ownership is not welcomed by most Finns (Pitkänen 2011). Therefore this chapter addresses the problem of participation and its possible outcomes for Russian second home owners.

Why Finland?

Within the spectrum of motives for second home ownership two major groups can be identified (see Jaakson 1986; Kaltenborn 1998; Müller 1999; Hall and Müller 2004; Van Patten and Williams 2008): motives for having a cottage and the driving factors for a destination choice. The second group of motives represents a particular interest in terms of transborder second home ownership. Four main motives for Russian second home ownership in Finland have been identified (Lipkina, in press). First, an extremely positive image of the country, which is related to perceived physical safety and economic security in Finland. Safety presumes freedom to remain at the cottage and leave it unattended for a long time without worry. Finland is also a safe investment market for Russians in contrast to their home country. Second, a positive image has been formed through good experiences with Finns and an absence of negative attitudes. Russians do not have any conflicts with members of the host society. They believe that they are treated very well and presume that they and their investments are welcomed in Finland. This has significantly contributed to the decision to buy a cottage in Finland. Third, amenity and lake landscapes are strong attractions for Russians in Finland. Russians are unable to acquire a lakeshore property in their home country. Finally, prices for real estate in Finland are lower than in Russia (Lipkina in press).

Participation and impact

Interaction with and interpretation of community are discussed within studies on community participation (Flora and Flora 1996; Umemoto 2001; Manzo and Perkins 2006). Participation is a wide term, which is understood as taking part in something, whereas community participation presumes engagement in community and its processes (Hall 2008). Manzo and Perkins (2006) identify three dimensions of community participation: cognitive, affective and behavioural. These reflect different ways of experiencing the community as a place and as a community of neighbours. The cognitive dimension implies one's sense of self through neighbouring social interactions and through neighbourhood. The affective dimension includes emotional relationship to the place (place attachment) and with local groups or neighbours (sense of community). The behavioural dimension presumes participation in community planning as well as social activities at the community level (Manzo and Perkins 2006). This ideal structure of community participation does not always work in practice and leads to different senses of community and attachment to it, including cases where people do not identify with the community and do not participate in any activities (Müller 1999; O'Reilly 2007) and may even sense feelings of alienation (Jell and Jell-Bahlsen 2003).

Obstacles for participation include language barriers, cultural differences or culturally specific norms and different values and viewpoints (Müller 1999; Umemoto 2001; Casado-Díaz 2009) that can all easily lead to alienation of new residents. Furthermore, 'This otherness is reinforced if there is a lack of other common associations or identity boundaries … with those in a given community' (Umemoto 2001: 22). Such alienation may be overcome by planning strategies, whereby community and regional planners create an atmosphere of sharing. One of the ways to do this is to encourage welcoming and valuing of cultural expression and diversity represented by newcomers as a part of community dialogue (Flora and Flora 1996; Umemoto 2001). The development of informal social networks among inhabitants is another way to support participation and community development (Flora and Flora 1996).

Involvement in the local community through service use and activities is important for the development of rural communities (Sievänen, Puota and Neuvonen 2007; Hall 2008). Thus, involvement in the local community and the economic impact of second home owners are strongly interrelated. As Manzo and Perkins (2006: 339) pointed out: 'those who are more attached to their neighborhoods are more likely to invest their time and money into the neighborhood'.

Second home owners are often considered to be a source of economic revival in rural areas due to their recurring visits (Müller 1999; Müller, Hall and Keen 2004; Sievänen *et al.* 2007; Hui and Yu 2009; Hoogendoorn and Visser 2010, 2011; Hall 2011; Hiltunen, Pitkänen, Vepsäläinen and Hall 2013). Even though their visits are rather short, rural areas can significantly benefit from second home owners' expenditures. The key factor that affects expenses at the site of a second home is the distance or separation between the primary residence and the summer cottage (Müller *et al.* 2004; Hoogendoorn and Visser, 2010, 2011; Hall 2011). The longer the distance from the permanent home, the higher are the per day expenditures at the second home location. Other aspects of the second home owners' economic impact include municipal rates and taxes and payments for utility services. Second home owners also support local businesses, such as shops, restaurants and local farms. However, local economies usually do not specialise solely in the needs of second homes (Müller *et al.* 2004; Hoogendoorn and Visser 2011) unless they are highly specialised resort communities (Hall 2011; Hiltunen *et al.* 2013). Second home purchase in rural areas can also facilitate entrepreneurship, as newcomers may lead to the establishment of new economic networks, and see possibilities for development in the area or implementing business ideas (Williams and Hall 2002; Fountain and Hall 2002; Hoogendoorn and Visser 2011).

Alongside the positive impact of second homes, some negative economic consequences for rural areas have also been identified. Among them are demands for additional services and infrastructure, displacement of local inhabitants, and localised inflation of goods and services (Müller *et al.* 2004; Janoschka 2009; Hoogendoorn and Visser 2010, 2011; Hall 2011; Paris 2011). In circumstances where the overall housing stock is constrained, the relative affluence of in-migrants along with the overall demand for second home properties may also drive up property values creating pressures on local affordable housing (Flora and Flora 1996; Hall 2011; Paris 2011) as well as on the relative allocation of central budgets to regions (Müller and Hall 2003). Participation in and interactions within the community can lead to greater involvement of newcomers in local life as well as mutual better knowledge. In the longer term, involvement may encourage social and economic investment in the community. However, language and cultural barriers can also lead to alienation of foreign newcomers, who are usually perceived negatively by locals due to fear of price hikes and xenophobia. As a result, locals usually do not recognise the economic importance of new inhabitants, and 'do not see the newcomers as an important resource for community and fail to integrate them into it' (Flora and Flora 1996: 218). Therefore, such potentially contested spatialities in the Finnish context become a significant issue both in the local setting and as part of a broader understanding of the implications of cross-border second home mobility.

Russian second home owners in the Savonlinna region of Finland

The research on Russian second home ownership discussed in this chapter has been undertaken in the Savonlinna region in the province of South Savo, Eastern Finland (Figure 11.1). The study region was chosen due to popularity of the region among Russian second home buyers. Almost every tenth Russian property purchase is made in the Savonlinna urban area, which makes it the second home area most in demand among Russians (own calculations).

Method

Twenty-five thematic in-depth interviews were undertaken with Russian second home owners in the Savonlinna region during the summer of 2010. The information on foreign property purchases in the Savonlinna region was bought from the National Land Survey of Finland. Russian second home owners were distinguished from other foreigners solely by name, since nationality or home addresses of foreigners were not provided. In order to gain information on the local population in the region, a survey study was conducted with Finnish second home owners and Finnish local inhabitants from the Savonlinna region during the same time period as the interviews of Russian second home owners. Questionnaires were distributed to both groups (750 questionnaires per group), out of which 494 questionnaires were returned (186 from locals and 308 from Finnish cottage owners), resulting in a response rate of 33 per cent. Questionnaires were analysed with the SPSS software.

The thematic semi-structured interview guide contained five main sections: purchasing the second home, life at the second home, service use in the region, integration in the local community and background information on the second home and its owners. Questions on service use contained a separate section of the interview with a ready list of services and alternatives for answers: I do not use/have never used this service, sometimes, and every time I visit the second home. The list of services included 14 items: groceries, specialised stores, nature parks and sightseeing, road maintenance services, construction services, plumber and electrician services, medical treatment, theatre, concerts and movies, local events and celebrations, restaurants, well-being services, sport places (including beach, swimming pool, ski tracks, sports grounds), firewood supply and public transport. Questions on participation in local life were asked in the section on integration in the local community. These questions were open-ended and included such questions as: Do you or would you like to participate in any local associations, organisations or

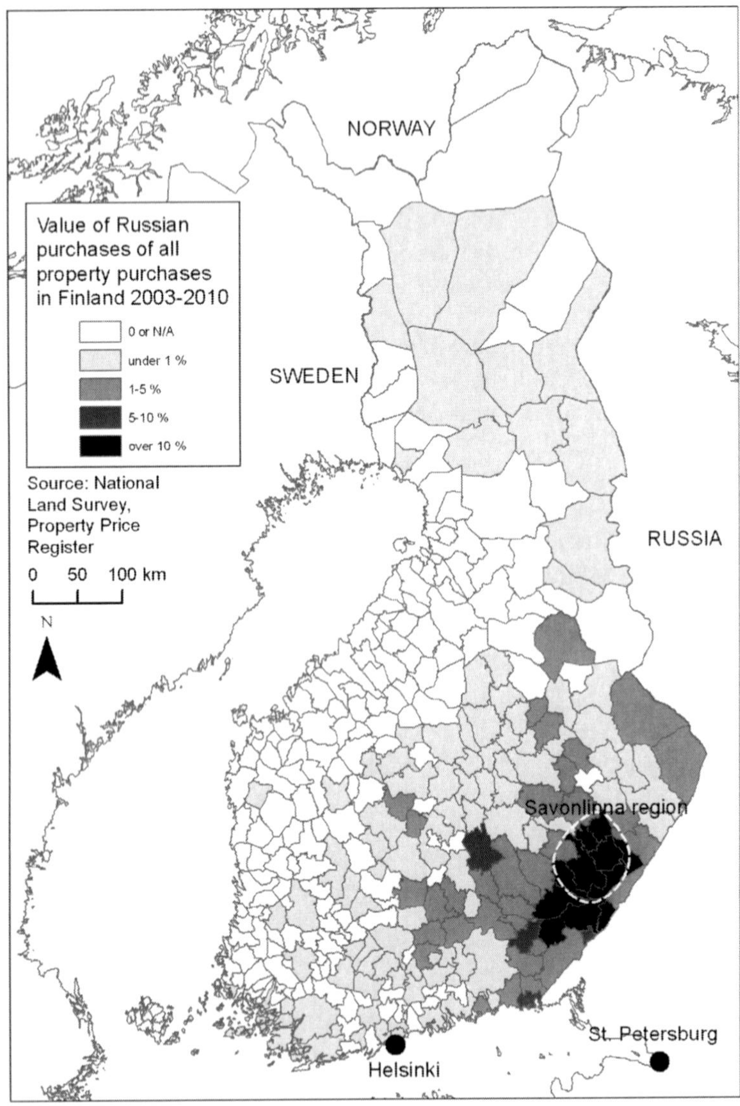

Figure 11.1 Share of Russians in the value of the Finnish property market (2003–2010)

committees? Do you know any of your neighbours or local residents? How often, on average, are you in contact with them? In what kind of circumstances/situations have you been in contact with them? Interviews were analysed by examining the answers of the specific section from the interview guide. Survey data were analysed using descriptive statistics, highlighting opinions and attitudes of local inhabitants and Finnish second home owners towards Russian second home owners in the area.

Results

Participation in the local community

Russian second home owners were asked to what extent they used local services at the second home site. Due to the alternatives provided, the usage of services was counted. According to the results Russian second home owners use groceries and specialised stores, visit restaurants and places for sport every time or almost every time they visit their second home. Russians also go sightseeing often, with approximately one-third of respondents going on a sightseeing trip every time they visit their second home. Some local services have never been used by Russian owners or have been used once. Many services, such as plumbing, road clearing and construction help, are provided by the second home seller, housebuilder or neighbour. Language barriers and the lack of experience in the area by the Russians have led to the creation of some personal networks for service supply, which are usually informal businesses. Language barriers also prevent Russian second home owners from visiting concerts, theatres and cinemas, and limits participation in local events. Questions on participation in local associations and organisations received mainly negative answers. Some of the owners do not see such a possibility due to language barriers; others would actually like to reduce social activities due to a busy life back in the home country. Moreover, Russians do not know of local associations in the area. Regarding membership of local organisations, the only one mentioned was a road cooperative, which is compulsory to participate in if the second home is located by a private road since fees for road maintenance are obligatory. However, Russians cannot understand the letters they receive and, thus, stay outside of any activity related to the cooperative.

Many owners have also pointed out the lack of any kind of information about the region and basic rules in Finland in general. Russian second home owners are ready to pay to get services in Russian or receive a local newspaper or brochures with some information about events and services. Lack of information and cultural ignorance are therefore further obstacles for participation in community life. Relations with the local inhabitants or Finnish cottage owners are considered as neutral or positive. Russian second home owners know their neighbours (in cases where they have neighbours), but contact is very limited due to the language barrier. Most contact is occasional greetings and waving to each other in passing and, rarely, short conversations in English. Some of the Russian second home owners maintained good relations with the previous home owner or with the Finnish housebuilder, with whom they sometimes socialise during their visits. Only one family from the respondents had a closer relationship with their Finnish neighbour, involving common saunas, barbecues and evening get-togethers. On the other hand, Russians do not want to disturb their neighbours and are afraid of intruding in their personal space, since frequent neighbourly visits and common activities are not a part of Finnish culture. However, Russian owners have a strong desire to overcome existing poor contacts and the informational vacuum. They have plans to learn Finnish, with a third of respondents having already started or intending to start learning the language. Russians have plans to integrate more in the new society, and to get to know their neighbours and the cultural particularities of Finland.

Finnish second home owners from the area and local citizens show less interest in Russian owners in the area. Fifty-six per cent of locals and 52 per cent of Finnish cottage owners have Russian second home owners in the same neighbourhood or village. However, 65 per cent of locals and 77 per cent of cottage owners say they have never been in contact with a Russian second home owner. Moreover, more than half of the respondents want to have very little or no contact with Russians (51 per cent of locals and 61 per cent of cottage owners). Despite such personal opinions and attitudes towards Russian second home owners, almost half of the respondents (49 per cent of locals and 47 per cent of cottage owners) think that it is fairly or very important to have good relations with the Russians.

The results indicate that these three groups in the Savonlinna region have different attitudes and expectations towards each other. A lack of understanding and absence of communication prevents Russian owners from participation in local life and utilising local services. On the other hand, Finns are not eager to communicate and have common activities with the Russian newcomers.

Economic impact or inaction?

Second homes in Finland make an important contribution to the rural economy. Because of the decline of rural populations in Finland, the relative number of persons occupying second homes is growing: about 70 per cent of unoccupied houses in rural areas are used as second homes (Pitkänen, Sikiö and Rehunen 2012). As in other Nordic countries, second home owners are becoming a new source of life in rural Finland, as they use the existing infrastructure and support local services, and thus contribute to the local economy (Hall, Müller and Saarinen 2009). Russians are a new group of second home owners in Finland. However, their share in the real estate economy has already become very significant in some municipalities (Figure 11.1). Russians accounted for 0.56 per cent of activity in the Finnish property market in 2003–10. In the study region of Savonlinna, the economic impact accounts for 15 per cent for the same period (own calculations). This percentage indicates only the investments in second homes in Finland. Other economic impact, such as use of services has mostly been seasonal in character and primarily supports local businesses: restaurants and shops, and leisure activities (sport equipment, fishing licence and others). In addition to these services, economic impacts include monthly contributions to the local economy such as payments for water, electricity, municipal rates and refuse removal. Other services, such as public transport, medical treatment, construction or electrician services are not yet used by Russian second home owners but may be so over time. Those Russians who use these services, in most cases, received them from the housebuilder or the closest Finnish neighbour. This indicates the absence of knowledge about the community and strong interpersonal network which prevents the local economy from receiving higher levels of benefit from Russian second home owners in the area.

Finnish local inhabitants and second home owners from the Savonlinna region are not very positive about the economic contribution of Russian second home owners to the area. Only half of the locals (48 per cent) and 35 per cent of cottagers consider that Russians bring new jobs and business opportunities to the area. Russians are not fully recognised as a source of the rural revival either. About 34 per cent of the local inhabitants agreed that Russians bring life to the region, while only 21 per cent of cottage owners agreed with this statement. Locals and cottage owners are even more sceptical about the idea that Russian presence in the area helps maintain property values (20 and 7.5 per cent respectively). Finns almost unanimously consider that second homes in the area are sold exclusively to Russians in order to get a better price: 87 per cent of local inhabitants and 80 per cent of Finnish cottage owners think this way. Thus, Russians have raised property prices in the area, according to 81 per cent of locals and 68 per cent of cottage owners. As a result, the majority of locals (61 per cent) and second home owners (61 per cent) from the Savonlinna region think that Russian opportunities to buy properties in Finland should be restricted. The highest resistance to Russian second home owners and desire to restrict property ownership is expressed by Finnish second home owners and local inhabitants over 50 years old: 50 per cent out of 61 per cent of cottagers, and 46 per cent out of 61 per cent of locals.

The economic impact of Russian second home owners is most significant with respect to second home investments. Other services in the area are not widely used, which is partly a result of the unofficial supply of services Russians receive from locals. From the Finnish point of view, Russians are not perceived as a necessity for regional development, and their presence in the area is not desired by the majority of the respondents.

Discussion

This chapter has explored the involvement of Russian second home owners in the local community through service use, contacts with locals and participation in local events and associations. The opinions of local inhabitants and Finnish second home owners in the Savonlinna region are also presented. The study used mixed methods of data collection: interviews and surveys. According to the results, the social and economic role of Russian second home owners is still marginal. This could be explained by several factors. First, recent second home ownership has not yet resulted in active community participation. New places require familiarisation in order to encourage community participation (Manzo and Perkins 2006) that has not yet developed among Russian second home owners. Second, cultural differences and language, which are usually major obstacles in community involvement (Umemoto 2001; Casado-Díaz 2009), are the biggest barriers to participation by Russians in local life. The absence of a common language prevents the understanding of norms and rules, as well as the culture and values of the host society. In the end, these can lead to alienation of foreigners since they cannot participate in local activities due to language barriers (Umemoto 2001). To make the situation worse, Russian second home owners are afraid to be proactive and they are not aware of rules and cultural particularities. Not all the Russians are eager to participate in local life, but a basic knowledge of rules and knowledge about the Savonlinna region is what everybody wishes for. Third, planning strategies which could enhance community dialogue (Flora and Flora 1996; Umemoto 2001) are not applicable for second home owners in Finland, as they stand back from participation in decision-making at the community level (Nylander and Leppänen 2006; Hall 2008).

One of the possible ways to support community participation is through informal personal networking with inhabitants (Flora and Flora 1996). The unofficial supply of services by local inhabitants to Russian second home owners could be viewed as a possible way to get Russians more involved in the community. However, these types of contacts have a purely economic base, and currently do not often lead to deeper relationships between Finns and Russians. Other contacts occur mostly through occasional greetings. Moreover, rare contacts are partially a result of the spatial distribution of second homes in Finland, where distance between second homes can vary from a hundred metres to several kilometres. As a result, despite an intention to study Finnish and integrate more, Russian second home owners are still quite alienated from the local community. Other studies show that foreign second home owners engage in activities with their own nationals in the area and get some knowledge about the area through these social contacts (British in Spain, Americans in Mexico to name a few) (Casado-Díaz, Kaiser and Warnes 2004; Casado-Díaz 2009; Haas 2012). However, in the case of Russian second home ownership, social ties with their own nationals also remain undeveloped. There are no organisations for integration into a new society as in mature destinations such as Spain (see Haas 2012). Most of the Russians do not know other Russian second home owners in the area, and those who do happen to have a Russian neighbour do not actively socialise with them.

Russian second home owners in Finland account for about 1 per cent of the Finnish property market, and Russians have a share in the value of Finnish property purchases up to 0.56 per cent (see Figure 11.1), and 15 per cent in the study region of Savonlinna. Thus, the economic impact is unevenly distributed and is only significant in specific areas. At the moment the Russian owners' economic impact is distinguishable only in second home investment (including any construction activities) and compulsory monthly payments to the local economy (municipal tax, water, electricity and garbage removal). Other impacts are concentrated on expenditures to local businesses through restaurant visits, shopping and expenses related to leisure activities. The use of services related to the maintenance of a second home is still an undeveloped practice due to recent property ownership, language barriers and maintaining personal contact with the construction company. The unofficial services provided by Finns to Russian second home owners are an additional source of informal income for housebuilders, neighbours and sellers, but as yet not for the Finnish economy.

Locals in the Savonlinna area and Finnish second home owners do not consider Russian owners as a source of economic support for rural areas, even though Russian investments are a significant share at the national level. Although about half of the Finnish respondents consider that Russians help bring life to the region, only a third consider that they contribute to its development. Russian second home owners are accused of raising property prices and displacing local people who cannot afford to buy expensive second homes. If true, this would be a negative economic and social impact of foreign second home development (Müller *et al.* 2004; Hoogendoorn and Visser 2010, 2011; Hall 2011; Paris 2011). However, the displacement effects of second homes are often exaggerated (Marjavaara 2007), and the wider housing supply issues often need to be considered (Müller 2006; Hall 2011). Nevertheless, more than half of the Finnish respondents would like to restrict Russian opportunities to purchase properties in the Savonlinna region and have limited contact with Russian second home owners. The majority of those who wish to restrict Russian second home ownership are over 50 years old. This can be explained by the influence of historical memory and the effect of the period of the Soviet Union's 'otherness' and overall negativeness towards Russians (Paasi 1999) which they have experienced in the past.

Conclusion

The analysis of Russians' participation in the local community has shown an outsider's perspective of the second home situation. A permanent connection with the region through a second home did not make them more involved in local life. Russian second home owners are more alienated from the destination than attached to it. This is primarily due to cultural and linguistic barriers, which prevent Russian owners from deeper involvement and communication. Simultaneously, local citizens and Finnish second home owners do not see Russians as a source of rural development and economic inflow to the local economy. Finnish negative attitudes 'due to the fear of price hike' (Flora and Flora 1996: 218) and historical memories have led to a failure in the establishment of any kind of dialogue with Russians in the area and to integrate them into the permanent and second home communities. These positions only maintain the contested spatialities of leisure in the region.

The Russian view of the destination and the absence of local support hinder Russians' possibilities for community participation. Language barriers have led to an informational gap, which blocks wider service use and investments in leisure activities and other needs. Russian second home owners show weak participation and very limited selection of services that they use. Despite a common border, cultural and linguistic differences remain a major obstacle to reducing the knowledge gap between Finns and Russians (Paasi 1999; Pitkänen 2011). As this chapter illustrates, despite intense cross-border interactions the permanent presence of Russian second home owners in the Savonlinna area, and the occupation of a common leisure space, Finns and Russians do not know much about each other.

Acknowledgements

The authors want to thank Kati Pitkänen for providing the map and for her assistance in searching for Finnish language sources. The chapter was made possible with the financial support of the Academy of Finland (project SA 255424) and the North Karelia Regional Fund of the Finnish Cultural Foundation.

References

Åkerlund, U. (2011) 'Abstract: Routes to Malta – processes of property acquisition', in *Geographical Knowledge, Nature and Practice, Nordic Geographers Meeting 24th-27th May 2011 – Roskilde, Denmark*, Roskilde: University of Roskilde.

Benson, M. (2009) 'A desire for difference: British lifestyle migration to Southwest France', in M. Benson and K. O'Reilly (eds) *Lifestyle Migration: Expectations, Aspirations and Experiences*, Farnham: Ashgate.

Brax, T. (8 November 2010) 'Kiinteistöjen myynnin rajoittaminen EU:n ulkopuolisten maiden kansalaisille'. Eduskunnan puhemiehelle. www.eduskunta.fi/faktatmp/utatmp/akxtmp/kk_859_2010_p.shtml (accessed 11 June 2012).

Breuer, T. (2005) 'Retirement migration or rather second home tourism? German senior citizens on the Canary Islands', *Die Erde*, 136(3): 313–33.

Casado-Díaz, M. (2009) 'Social capital in the sun: Bonding and bridging social capital among British retirees', in M. Benson and K. O'Reilly (eds) *Lifestyle Migration: Expectations, Aspirations and Experience*, Farnham: Ashgate.

Casado-Díaz, M., Kaiser, C. and Warnes, A. (2004) 'Northern European retired residents in nine southern European areas: characteristics motivations and adjustment', *Ageing and Society*, 24(3): 353–81.

Flora, C.B. and Flora, J.L. (1996) 'Creating social capital', in W. Vitek and W. Jackson (eds) *Rooted in the Land: Essays on Community and Place*, New Haven, CT: Yale University Press.

Fountain, J. and Hall, C.M. (2002) 'The impact of lifestyle migration on rural communities: A case study of Akaroa, New Zealand', in C.M. Hall and A.M. Williams (eds) *Tourism and Migration: New Relationships Between Production and Consumption*, Dordrecht: Kluwer.

Gallent, N., Mace, A. and Tewdwr-Jones, M. (eds) (2005) *Second Homes: European Perspectives and UK Policies*, Aldershot: Ashgate.

Haas, H. (2012) 'Volunteering in retirement migration: Meanings and functions of charitable activities for older British residents in Spain', *Ageing and Society*, doi.org/10.1017/S0144686X12000669.

Hall, C.M. (2006) 'Amenity migration in the South Island of New Zealand: Contestation for land and landscape in Central Otago', in L. Moss (ed.) *Amenity Migrants: Seeking and Sustaining Mountains and their Cultures*, Wallingford: CABI.

——(2008) *Tourism Planning*, 2nd edn, Harlow: Pearson.

——(2011) 'Housing tourists: Accommodating short-term visitors', in D. Marcoullier, M. Lapping and O. Furuseth (eds) *Rural Housing, Exurbanization and Amenity Driven Development: Contrasting the Haves and the Have Nots*, Farnham: Ashgate.

Hall, C.M. and Müller, D.K. (eds) (2004) *Tourism, Mobility and Second Homes: Between Elite Landscape and Common Ground*, Clevedon: Channel View Publications.

Hall, C.M., Müller, D. and Saarinen, J. (2009) *Nordic Tourism*, Clevedon: Channel View Publications.

Hedström, M. (2011) 'Foreign second-homes in Norden'. Stockholm: NORDREGIO Nordic Centre for Spatial Development. www.nordregio.se/en/Metameny/About-Nordregio/Journal-of-Nordregio/Journal-of-Nordregio-2010/Journal-of-Nordregio-no-2-2010/Foreign-second-homes-in-Norden/ (accessed 24 April 2012).

Hiltunen, M.J., Pitkänen, K., Vepsäläinen, M. and Hall, C.M. (2013) 'Second home tourism in Finland – current trends and ecosocial impacts', in Z. Roca, M. Nazaré Roca and J. Oliveira (eds) *Second Homes in Europe: Lifestyle Issues and Policy Responses*, Aldershot: Ashgate.

Hoggart, K. and Buller, H. (1995) 'Geographical differences in British property acquisitions in rural France', *The Geographical Journal*, 161(1): 69–78.

Hoogendoorn, G. and Visser, G. (2010) 'The role of second homes in local economic development in five small South African towns', *Development Southern Africa*, 27 (4): 547–62.

——(2011) 'Economic development through second home development: evidence from South Africa', *Tijdschrift voor Economische en Sociale Geografie*, 102(3): 275–89.

Hui, E. and Yu, K. (2009) 'Second homes in the Chinese mainland under "one country, two systems": A cross-border perspective', *Habitat International*, 33: 106–13.

Jaakson, R. (1986) 'Second-home domestic tourism', *Annals of Tourism Research*, 13: 367–91.

Janoschka, M. (2009) 'The contested spaces of lifestyle mobilities: Regime analysis as a tool to study political claims in Latin American retirement destinations', *Die Erde*, 140(3): 1–20.

——(2010) 'Between mobility and mobilization – lifestyle migration and the practice of European identity in political struggles', *Sociological Review*, 58: 270–90.

Jell, G. and Jell-Bahlsen, S. (2003) 'Losing ground: Place-making, alienation, and (sub-)urbanization in rural Bavaria', *Dialectical Anthropology*, 27(1): 69–87.

Kaltenborn, B.P. (1998) 'The alternate home – motives for recreation home use', *Norsk Geografisk Tidsskrift*, 52: 121–34.

Kotilainen, J., Piipponen, M. and Pitkänen, K. (2010) 'Valtakunnanrajan vaikutus Itä-Suomen uusiutumiseen', in *Reports and Studies in Social Sciences and Business Studies* No. 2, Joensuu: Publications of the University of Eastern Finland.

Lampič, B. and Mrak, I. (2012) 'Globalization and foreign amenity migrants: The case of foreign home owners in the Pomurska region of Slovenia', *European Countryside*, 4(1): 45–56.

Lipkina, O. and Pitkänen, K. (2010) 'Abstract: Dacha perspectives: a study of Russian second home ownership in Eastern Finland', *Dialogues in Geography. Vuoropuhelu maantieteessä. XLIII Maantieteen päivät 29.–30.10.2010, Joensuu*, Joensuu: Kopijyvä.

Lipkina, O. (2011) 'Abstract: Dacha perspectives: reasons to have a second home in Finland', *Geographical Knowledge, Nature and Practice, Nordic Geographers Meeting 24–27 May 2011 – Roskilde, Denmark*, Roskilde: University of Roskilde.

——(in press) 'Motives for Russian second home ownership in Finland' *Scandinavian Journal for Hospitality and Tourism*, (Special issue on new perspectives on second home tourism).

Maanmittauslaitos (10 March 2008) 'Suomea myydään venäläisille: Venäläisten kiinteistökaupat kovassa kasvussa'. www.maanmittauslaitos.fi/tiedotteet/2008/03/suomea-myydaan-venalaisille-venalaisten-kiinteistokaupat-kovassa-kasvussa (accessed 11 June 2012).

Manzo, L.C. and Perkins, D.D. (2006). 'Finding common ground: The importance of place attachment to community participation and planning', *Journal of Planning Literature*, 20(4): 335–50.

Marjavaara, R. (2007) 'The displacement myth: Second home tourism in the Stockholm Archipelago', *Tourism Geographies*, 9: 296–317.

McIntyre, N., Williams, D.R. and McHugh, K.E. (eds) (2006) *Multiple Dwelling and Tourism: Negotiating Place, Home and Identity*, Wallingford: CABI.

Müller, D.K. (1999) *German Second Home Owners in the Sweedish Countryside: On the Internationalization of the Leisure Space*, Umeå and Östersund: Department of Social and Economic Geography.

——(2002) 'German second homeowners in Sweden: Some remarks on the tourism – migration – nexus', *Revue Européenne des Migrations Internationales*, 18(1): 67–86.

——(2006) 'The attractiveness of second home areas in Sweden: A quantitative analysis', *Current Issues in Tourism*, 9: 335–50.

——(2011) 'The internationalization of rural municipalities: Norwegian second home owners in Northern Bohuslän, Sweden', *Tourism Planning & Development*, 8(4): 433–45.

Müller, D. and Hall, C.M. (2003) 'Second homes and regional population distribution: On administrative practices and failures in Sweden', *Espace Population Societes*, 2003–2: 251–61.

——(2004) 'The future of second homes', in C.M. Hall and D.K. Müller (eds) *Tourism, Mobility and Second Homes: Between Elite Landscape and Common Grand*, Clevedon: Channel View Publications.

Müller, D.K., Hall, C.M. and Keen, D. (2004) 'Second home tourism impact, planning and management', in C.M. Hall and D.K. Müller (eds) *Tourism, Mobility and Second Homes: Between Elite Landscape and Common Grand*, Clevedon: Channel View Publications.

Nylander, M. and Leppänen, J. (2006) *Vapaa-ajan asukkaiden osallistuminen kuntien päätoksentekoon*. Raportti. Saaritoasiain neuvottelukunta, Sunnittelukeskus Oy. Sisäasianministeriön julkaisu 14/2006.

O'Reilly, K. (2000) *The British on the Costa del Sol: Transnational Identities and Local Communities*, London: Routledge.

——(2007) 'Intra-European migration and the mobility–enclosure dialectic', *Sociology*, 41(2): 277–93.

Paasi, A. (1999) 'Boundaries as social practice and discourse: The Finnish-Russian border', *Regional Studies*, 33: 669–80.

Paris, C. (2011) *Affluence, Mobility and Second Home Ownership*, London: Routledge.

Pitkänen, K. (2011) 'Contested cottage landscapes. Media representation of foreign inbound second home tourism in Finland 1990–2008', *Fennia*, 189(1): 43–59.

Pitkänen, K., Sikiö, M. and Rehunen, A. (2012) 'Abstract: Hidden life of rural North: A study on empty dwellings in rural Finland', *Rural at the Edge, The 2nd Nordic Conference for Rural Research 21–23 of May 2012, Joensuu, Finland*, Joensuu: Maaseudun uusi aika ry.

Puzzo, C. (2007) 'British migration to the Midi-Pyrenees', in C. Geoffroy and R. Sibley (eds) *Going Abroad: Travel, Tourism, and Migration. Cross-cultural Perspectives on Mobility*, Newcastle-upon-Tyne: Cambridge Scholars.

Sievänen, T., Puota, E. and Neuvonen, M. (2007) 'Recreational home users: Potential clients for countryside tourism?' *Scandinavian Journal of Hospitality and Tourism*, 7 (3): 224–43.

Tilastokeskus (2011) 'Saapuneet vieraat ja yöpymiset kaikissa majoitusliikkeissä muuttujina'. stat.fi (accessed 8 June 2012).

Torres, R. and Momsen, J. (2005a) 'Gringolandia: The construction of a new tourist space in Mexico', *Annals of the Association of American Geographers*, 95: 314–35.

——(2005b) 'Planned tourism development in Quintana Roo, Mexico: Engine for regional development or prescription for inequitable growth?' *Current Issues in Tourism*, 8: 259–85.

Truly, D. (2002) 'International retirement migration and tourism along the Lake Chapala Riviera: Developing a matrix of retirement migration behaviour', *Tourism Geographies*, 4: 261–81.

Umemoto, K. (2001) 'Walking in another's shoes: Epistemological challenges in participatory planning', *Journal of Planning Education and Research*, 21(1): 17–31.

Van Patten, S.R. and Williams, D.R. (2008) 'Problems in place: Using discursive social psychology to investigate the meanings of seasonal homes', *Leisure Series*, 30: 448–64.

Williams, A.M. and Hall, C.M. (2002) 'Tourism, migration, circulation and mobility: The contingencies of time and place', in C.M. Hall and A.M. Williams (eds) *Tourism and Migration: New Relationships Between Consumption and Production*, Dortrecht: Kluwer.

12 Lifestyle migrants in Central Portugal

Strategies of settlement and socialisation

João Sardinha

Introduction

For the last half-a-century, Portugal has been a destination for lifestyle and sun-searching migrants originating from Northern and Central Europe (Great Britain, Germany, Holland and Sweden above all), and North America (United States and Canada), the great majority of whom have settled in very specific Portuguese coastal regions where sun and leisured lifestyle options are considered abundant, and where the cost of living, in comparison to the countries these lifestyle migrants come from, is lower. These regions include, above all, the Algarve in southern Portugal and, to a lesser extent, the Costa do Sol (Estoril/Cascais) region on the western outskirts of Lisbon. In more recent years, however, an increase in lifestyle migration to non-coastal Portuguese regions has equally been witnessed, with many of these migrants searching out isolated/unpopulated areas, inexpensive real estate opportunities and ecological lifestyle environments to settle down in. Such has been the case in a number of Portuguese interior regions.

Known for their rural, less developed life and disparities since the 1960s, many of the regions that constitute the Portuguese interior have been unable to secure a sustainable economic upkeep for many of its peoples. In consequence, this has led to the depopulation of these areas, with outward flows having two primary destinations: first, the more prosperous Portuguese regions located along the Portuguese coastal belt (and above all to the two primary cities of Lisbon and Porto), and second emigration to other countries (namely France, Luxembourg, Germany, Switzerland, United States, Canada and Brazil). As a result of this outward mobility, the abandonment of the Portuguese interior has been quite noticeable, both visually and demographically (Hespanha 1996, 2004). Perhaps most evident is the ageing population in these regions. While younger generations have departed in search of work and a better living elsewhere, it is the elderly people who have stayed behind. The Portuguese interior is today marked and characterised by their faces, many of whom equally feel neglected by a highly centralised Portuguese welfare state that ignores these regions.

Still, abandonment is not unique to the people; there are other signs of abandonment, including homes that sit vacant with no one living in them, badly maintained roads, for seldom does anyone travel on them, schools left in ruins with no children to attend them, churches that sit empty as the local diocese no longer provides a priest for the dwindling population, and so on and so forth. Equally, the natural world is not immune to such neglect, as once cultivated agricultural lands now sit deserted, replaced, instead, with brambles, weeds and bushes; property-dividing stone walls, once a territorial marker of ownership, are now falling down and in ruins; not to mention farm animals, once a key fixture of sound and scenery of the landscape, today play a diminishing role in these settings. We thus lay witness to an interactive process – just as the rural exodus brings degradation to the landscape, this abandonment equally triggers apathy towards these regions, now considered insignificant territories possessing little value, where nothing happens and very little exists.

Of course, what many of the native peoples perceive of the Portuguese central interior – as a geographical area where opportunities to achieve a better livelihood are non-existent – many from outside these regions see opportunities for a less expensive, more tranquil lifestyle away from the mad rush of urban living. Moreover, as a consequence of outward migration and the subsequent abandonment of lands and properties – sometimes even entire villages – property price devaluation in the local real estate markets has become common, a factor that has equally become a primary point of attraction for many newcomers originating from countries considered economically more prosperous than Portugal (e.g. Great Britain, the Netherlands, the United States, just to name a few). As a result, replacing outward migration has, on one hand, been associated with expatriates searching out a less-expensive, more tranquil living further away from the beaches and closer to the countryside, and on the other hand, third-country counter-culture dropouts and ecologists who have come looking to escape certain societal norms in search of a more sustainable lifestyle.

I define these incoming migrants as lifestyle migrants, individuals who often possess sufficient economic security to allow them to move to a country which, although often not as developed as their country of origin, can provide them with the better quality of life they seek (Benson and O'Reilly 2009a).[1] Seen as an escapist form of mobility, lifestyle migration often makes up a self-realisation project that leads participants to search for the intangible 'good life' abroad. That said, it is important to also consider that the process of migration seldom ends after the course of mobility has been carried out, as also key is life *in* the post-migration period – the very existence of the migrant in the destination location and how life transformations are negotiated once settled. To understand the driving motive behind the migration processes it is key, however, to analyse the impact of mobility on the lives and identities of the migrants equally reveals a wider rhetoric of self-realisation.

It is exactly these points that frame the objectives of this chapter. I here set out to look at the migration trends, settlement patterns and socialisation strategies adopted by incoming lifestyle migrants who have taken up residence in two particular sub-regions of the Portuguese Central Interior: Pinhal Interior Norte (Interior Woodlands North) and Médio Tejo (Medium Tagus).[2] Through in-depth interviews, participant observation and internet blogs and cyber forum debate analysis, I look at the reasons why these migrants have opted to settle in Central Portugal, how they perceive their fitting in and acceptance, and formulate relations with local populations (inter-community connectedness) and how they construct and maintain intra-community relation and support patterns, including social, cultural and information network building.

Within the scope of this work, I consider that migration to rural spaces may accomplish the revitalised and dreamed- of self-fulfilment. Once in the 'new' space, however, also key is the negotiation of the lifestyle migrants' 'new' lives (Benson and O'Reilly 2009b). Within the context of the quest for a better way of life, these transformations are presented as challenges to be conquered through the migrant's individual and group agency. Such choices, however, enter another realm when the rural locality under study is taken into consideration. Thus, I set out to examine not only whether the migrants succeed in localising themselves, but also how and with whom they relate in the local. My interviewees reveal pros and cons of becoming part of the local community, drawing attention to their relationship with local social and administrative actors, and place themselves in stark contrast to their lifestyle migrant compatriots living in more traditional lifestyle migrant settlement areas in Portugal (the Algarve) when it comes to their settlement choice and everyday lives. Settling in these interior regions, many seek distance from their homelands, homeland culture and tourist areas, wanting instead to be a part of something new and different and, at times, exotic, this in the desired new and improved life. As Benson (2010) highlights, the desire for local belonging emerges as a driving force behind migration, a continued aspiration for post-migration lives, intrinsically linked to the migrants' definition of sense of self in the new setting. My study resonates with this argument, hypothesising that although initial mobility and settlement intentions constructed in the pre-mobility stage are often pre-studies and often even pre-prepared, any claims of belonging or rejection to a locality (home/host) only become clear when examined within the context of the complex social relations that characterise the lives of those experiencing the mobility. Within this line of analysis, this chapter sets out to analyse not only the 'why's behind lifestyle migrant settlement in Central Portugal but also the perceptions of integration and acceptance on the part of the Portuguese seen through the eyes of lifestyle migrants, as well as strategies of network building and support patterns constructed among these migrants.[3]

Methodological considerations and interviewee typologies

The results presented in this study draw on ongoing fieldwork with lifestyle migrants who have settled in the two Portuguese interior regions of Pinhal Interior Norte and Médio Tejo. In order to permit an analysis of similarities, patterns and differences, this study relies on the data triangulation technique (multi-method data collection) (Arksey and Knight 1999) as a means to deepening and validating understanding. The presented findings are the result of in-depth interviews, participant observation and monitoring of specific internet blogs and cyber forums. In relation to carrying out interviews, before entering the field, one primary source was utilised as an intermediary between the researcher and the subjects to be interviewed, namely the socialisation network group 'Portugal Friends'. Led by a husband and wife team, Portugal Friends organises social functions in the Pinhal Interior Norte and Médio Tejo communities in the towns of Tomar, Torres Novas, Alvaiázere, Ansião and Lousã. The primary form of interviewee recruitment was done at the social events organised by this informal network. Further recruitment was also carried out at the Mirando do Corvo car boot sale, a monthly event in the town of Miranda do Corvo (Pinhal Interior Norte) organised by northern European expatriates residing in the area that brings together large concentrations of lifestyle migrants. Interviews were guided by a semi-structured interview schedule containing the principal lines of questioning clearly directed at answering the hypotheses to be investigated. Beyond face-to-face conversations, some interviewees supplied further information, thoughts and reflections via an online questionnaire, a technique chosen to give interviewees time to reflect on their answers. In addition, as well as events fit for recruiting and carrying out interviews, it should be noted that the Portugal Friends social gatherings and the Miranda do Corvo car boot sale have equally provided privileged occasions to carry out participant observation and carry out casual conversations. Lastly, hand-in-hand with the *in loco* fieldwork, screening internet blogs and debates on community pages and expatriate cyber forums, on one hand, provided secondary views on specific issues; on the other, in the case of lifestyle migrant bloggers, provided an avenue to follow specific migrant life paths, experiences and opinions.[4] That said, the findings to be debated in this chapter are based on 40 interviews collected from January to March of 2011 and on entries observed in the blogs, community pages and cyber forums followed.

The vast majority of the interviewees originated from the United Kingdom (28), with the remainder being from the Netherland (5), the United States (2), Ireland (2), Germany (1), Canada (1) and South Africa (1). The mean age of the interviewees was 57 years with the youngest being 27 and the oldest 77. Of the 40 interviewees, 15 were retired while the other 25 were active individuals.[5] When it comes to characterising economic upkeep or professions of the lifestyle migrants interviewed, age 50 serves best to define those who take up full-time employment (under 50), and those who live off savings and hobby activities (over 50). There are a number of individuals in their 50s who, although not of retirement age, have taken up a semi-retired lifestyle in Portugal, living off their savings or investments. These individuals tend to be highly qualified who have retired from their often well-paid jobs in their countries of origin and have invested locally in Portugal in profitable hobby activities or in local tourism and/or development activities. Young lifestyle migrants, on the other hand, often depend on their qualifications to earn a living. A command of the English language, for example, is a resource many use to their advantage when it comes to finding employment in the local job markets (e.g. language teaching). This issue will be further discussed later. Lastly, it is also worth mentioning that due to the current economic crisis, some of the young migrants spoken to have recently taken up a pendulum lifestyle because of work opportunities. Although not abandoning Central Portugal outright, some still maintain jobs in their country of origin that they return to seasonally.

Central Portugal: Who moves here and why?

In Portugal's more traditional lifestyle migrant destination, the Algarve,[6] Torkington (2010) points out that many lifestyle migrants do not speak the local language, they often live in the same areas, in the same types of accommodation (apartments, townhouses or villas in integrated resorts), that they look physically similar, behave in a similar fashion and go to places (bars, restaurants, sports and fitness clubs) where they meet up with their compatriots. Lacking a command of the Portuguese language (at least in the first stages of arrival) is very applicable to lifestyle migrants in Central Portugal; however, this is where the comparisons stop. The defining contrasts of the lifestyle migrants in Central Portugal are more varied. Their territorial dispersion, in fact, does not favour the clustering described by Torkington, as many opt for the solitude of the countryside. This dispersion, as well as the fact that the presence of these individuals in Central Portugal is numerically much lower than in the Algarve, also implies that amenities specific to this population are uncommon; thus routine meeting points (bars, restaurants, clubs, etc.) are pretty much non-existent.

In attempting to personify the lifestyle migrants in Central Portugal, however, two distinct characterisations can be made (although there are crossover points as well). On the one hand, there are those individuals who come searching for a quiet, leisured and inexpensive lifestyle, but who equally give importance to amenities and culture. These are older migrants who, at the tail-end of their careers, opt for a tranquil lifestyle in a warmer climate; there are also younger individuals or families unhappy with specific situations in their countries of origin and, as a result, choose a 'new start' in a new part of the world that is seen as being able to provide them with a reliable foundation on which they can build meaningful lives (O'Reilly 2000; Sunil *et al.* 2007; Hoey 2009). On the other hand, there are those best described as counter-culture dropouts or neo-ruralists who move to Central Portugal to escape the hustle and bustle of big city living (Benson 2009), many of whom covet the idea of community living, an idyll often impossible to accomplish in urban centres (Halfacree 1997). Central Portugal has, in fact, come to attract groups of ecologists looking to escape certain societal norms and in search of a more sustainable lifestyle. Foreign permaculturists, especially, see these rural areas as ideal locations to carry out their chosen lifestyles.

Ultimately, whatever the mobility circumstance may be, the search for the good life as a comparative project is a consistent theme in the decision-making process (Benson and O'Reilly 2009a,b). Be that person a 'rural idyllist' looking to an environment fit for a sustainable lifestyle, a 'bourgeois bohemian' searching to find him or herself in the confines of rural Portugal or a 'counter-urbanist' trading in the big city lifestyle for a less hurried lifestyle in the country, the often ultimate aim is that of providing meaning to life in an environment that possesses the personal components that will permit doing so (van Dam *et al.* 2002). That said, given the motives and desires of these migrants to relocate, a pertinent question worth asking is: How did the decision to move to the location where these individuals have taken up residency come about? In an attempt to shed light on this question, I revert to two narrative accounts:

> We lived in the Algarve for five years and realized it wasn't 'real' Portugal. When we arrived in Portugal in 2001 life was similar (in the Algarve) to what it's like here now. But the Algarve keeps growing and there's been all kinds of construction going on there. Also crime started to grow there and that, of course, is a problem. In fact it was when we installed security cameras in our house that we knew this was not the way we wanted to live. So from there we started looking elsewhere in Portugal. That's how we ended up here (in Central Portugal), where life is quiet and where people are gentle and friendly. … It was a pleasant surprise to us though, as we didn't know the area before coming up to have a look.
>
> (English, female, born 1953)

> We drove around the country and explored everything. We got to know it very well but we fell in love with this area. It's all in the authenticity here. Real, simple people; real authentic culture, traditions, festivities and landscape – that's what I love here and that's why I'm here. You don't get this in the cities, you can't find it in the Algarve. Why would I move to the Algarve, so I can run into English people every day? Isn't that the reason why we want out of England? I didn't move to Portugal because of the fancy parties and the golf. I moved here to be free, way from the mad rush, to learn and to take in the local life, to eat and drink, and learn how to make wine, olive oil and other goods. … Here in this part of the country you can do all that and you can do it the real way, the way it's been done for ages, where consumerism isn't as evident and where you can still live cheaply. You can buy land with ruins on it very cheaply as there's so much available. Have a look around and you'll see. Everything's for sale.
>
> (English, male, born 1949)

The above citations tell us a series of things: first, and as expressed by many of the interviewees, Central Portugal was discovered in an unexpected fashion, either during a travel period in Portugal or after taking up residency elsewhere. Moreover, we also witness two primary reasons for opting to take up residency in Central Portugal: (1) that of lower property and living costs than other Portuguese regions, and (2) that of a more genuine, simplistic and safe Portuguese way of life. Concerning the first point, being acquainted with southern European ways of living and with the characteristics offered up by southern European countries and regions, the object of 'moving south' is a combination of 'escaping the north' and all that is associated with it (cold climate, expensive lifestyle, urbanisation, undesirable jobs, etc.) and 'finding refuge in the south'. Keeping this primary objective in mind, the process of 'shopping' for a location, beyond the importance of finding a place where one can 'accomplish the escape', is also that of affordability. Central Portugal may, therefore, be seen as a substitute for other southern European locations that may be out of the price range of those whose ultimate goal was a move south. Here in these regions they find the location that best fits their budget.

Furthermore, after a well-contemplated and studied search, many also 'handpick' Central Portugal because of what it is – remote, secluded and away from the beaten track of tourists and urbanisation. In defence of this argument, and as was pointed out in the second quotation above, it is felt that moving to Portugal's traditional lifestyle migration destination – that of the Algarve – is not completely moving away from one's native land, but simply replacing it with another geographical location where there's more sun and recreation, given the heavy concentration of northern Europeans found here. Some, therefore, explain avoiding the Algarve for this very reason: to steer clear of heavy concentrations of expatriates and tourists.[7]

Now for younger lifestyle migrant families, an attractive reason for taking up residency in Central Portugal is also that of a safe environment, something many claim this part of the country offers their family and, above all, their children. Many describe the polar opposite between what some referred to as the deterioration of societal values in their countries of origin in comparison to the non-violent environment they claim to find in Central Portugal, a place where family values are described as being important to the people. Thus, beyond the 'back to nature' philosophy, many consider 'back to values' to be equally important.

It, therefore, becomes a matter of choice, as those who settle in these interior regions are not looking to coastal 'fun in the sun' as much as they are attracted to an antiquated, traditional lifestyle where there is greater security in a non-urbanised environment, along with the fact that what is desired is the getting up close with the local culture, landscape and people (Geoffrey 2007; Benson 2009; Benson and O'Reilly 2009b). In the words of Hoey (2009: 34): 'Lifestyle migrants recognize the essential role of place in creating a lasting sense of self. They self-consciously engage in this process, choosing particular places as personal therapeutic landscapes.' For those who have settled in Central Portugal, attraction to the landscape, culture and sense of well-being is undoubtedly a major draw, one that outweighs any sort of proximity to large urban areas or large concentrations of fellow nationals. The 'personal therapeutic landscapes', for these migrants, are, thus, their own unique findings in Central Portugal that serve to complete their search for the sought-after utopian ideal.

Inter-community connectedness: insertion and acceptance

For lifestyle migrant individuals, mobility is presented as a way of overcoming dissatisfaction, be it with work, society, climate, lifestyle, etc., in their homeland. As elucidated by Benson and O'Reilly (2009a: 610), for these migrants, the act of taking up a new life elsewhere is 'the act of taking control of their lives, or as releasing them from ties and enabling them to live lives more "true" to themselves.' Resulting from this mobility, however, Benson and O'Reilly (2009a: 610) further explain that, under these circumstances, the pre- and post-migration life, 'may not reflect objective reality; the presented advantages of life in the destination are often romanticized accounts'. Concerning the lifestyle migrants found in Central Portugal, although many articulated being content with their 'new' lives and personal projects, not all aspects of settlement and insertion were rendered in a positive light.

As articulated in the previous section, lifestyle migrants have opted for Central Portugal because this region provides them with the opportunity to fulfil life projects in an idyllic place. However, in conjunction with achieving their own goals, many also feel that they are playing a part in giving something back to the land and to the communities. What has been abandoned and often considered useless by the local population, these migrants consider of great value. Thus, they invest in large tracts of land and start to recultivate them, they buy old stone homes that are in ruins and rebuild them, and, in settling in these rural communities, they contribute to adding numbers to the dwindling population. Moreover, these individuals not only become consumers, they also contribute to local economies via the setting up of businesses and through the promotion of the regions. Many active lifestyle migrants, for example, become 'self-employed expatriates' in their new surroundings (Stone and Stubbs 2007). As other studies have pointed out (Befus *et al.* 1988; Madden 1999; Stone and Stubbs 2007; Benson and O'Reilly 2009b) it is common for lifestyle migrants to use their business ventures as a means to an end, using them to finance their new lifestyles. In the case of the migrants under study, while enterprise choices vary, many establish businesses aimed at providing services for other migrants or tourists, such as establishing homeland product sales businesses, real estate ventures, media (e.g. newspapers), guest accommodations (e.g. bed and breakfast), online businesses, among others; others invest in traditional endeavours, namely in arts and crafts, agriculture, traditional home restoration, etc.[8]

Aside from those who venture out with their own businesses, also worth scrutinising are the economic undertakings carried out by the ecologist/permaculturist lifestyle migrants. In the case of these individuals, although life principles are more often than not based on self-sustainability principles, although not exclusively, many partake in the local economies, primarily through local market sales of home grown agricultural products and other food products (e.g. canned food goods, jams, etc.), homemade clothing, arts and crafts, eco-home construction (e.g. yurts), and spiritual and health practices (e.g. yoga and meditation classes).

Now the sentiment expressed by the entrepreneurial lifestyle migrants of Central Portugal is that achieving economic objectives brings feelings of 'mission accomplished' as both lifestyle and economic idealisms are achieved. The desire of wanting to be their own boss is explained by the fact that self-employment is often seen as a more fulfilling alternative, allowing these individuals greater control over their life (Hoey 2005). This further serves to explain the size and financial terms of the entrepreneurial endeavour, as self-sufficiency and auto-sustainability are principal valued aims. Moreover, having visions of entrepreneurial grandeur would imply a greater amount of time spent dealing with the Portuguese business world many consider hard to deal with and manoeuvre within, for, as expressed by many of these migrants, seldom is the accomplishment of certain goals (economic and otherwise) easy to carry out in Portugal due to practical obstacles. Building on this issue, asked to reflect upon their insertion into Portuguese society, as well as their relations and dealings with members and institutions of the host society, one respondent summed up a transversal sentiment shared by many: 'We feel welcomed by the people, but not the bureaucracies' (English, female, born 1953).

A general opinion is that the Portuguese of Central Portugal have welcomed newcomers with open arms. Many of the interviewees spoke of the generosity and friendliness on the part of their neighbours and local community, for example:

> Our neighbours often share their vegetables and fruits that they grow. They welcome us and invite us to go with them to meetings and festivals. The people are always so welcoming of us. They want you to be a part of the community.
>
> (American, male, born 1949)

> We were building our house and living in it without any water and heating, but our closest neighbours were great. They said we could use their water, they provided us with firewood … That's the community spirit you have here.
>
> (Irish, female, born 1979)

> They [the Portuguese] are very family based. The family we rent our house from invites us to help pick grapes and olives and pine cones, and we join them for celebration lunches. We were asked to join their family for New Year celebrations, which we were very happy to do. They are helping us integrate into Portuguese society, which is really good.
>
> (English, female, born 1952)

This welcoming reception has equally led many lifestyle migrants to become more community minded, with many expressing partaking in such community activities as fund raising for local charities, supporting the local firefighters, helping the local folklore dance groups, volunteering at community festivals, among others. For lifestyle migrants, volunteering is at times seen as a performative expression of transmigrants' cultural bifocality, reflecting both a high level of commitment to the country/region of settlement as well as being a feature of community spirit and traditionalism often associated with life in the country of origin (see Haas 2012).

Now such community involvement, be it via entrepreneurial endeavours, volunteering activities or neighbourly contact, according to many of the interviewees, holds one drawback: communication. Paradoxically, although many interviewees point out the difficulties they have in learning Portuguese, they also point out that these difficulties are 'part of the adventure', with many equally pointing out that many Portuguese, even in non-tourist regions such as Central Portugal, go out of their way to speak English, often making the comparison to Spain where, in the words of a number of respondents, 'there isn't as much an effort on the part of the Spaniards to speak in English'. As a result, in this case, although lack of the Portuguese language is described as a personal shortcoming for many, it is made up for by the willingness of the Portuguese to not let communication be a stumbling block. On the flipside of this micro-level sense of welcomeness, many expressed the frequent impossibility of becoming entirely integrated in the host society when bureaucratic obstacles get in the way of doing so (mind you they are also aware that these obstacles are not unique to them, as they are common to society at large). Also talked about were government restrictions on private businesses; overbearing regulations on car import; paperwork and confusion involving the hooking-up of electricity, water, telephone and internet; as well as the bureaucracies encountered in the public and service sectors (banks, health centres, etc.). Many also referred to corruption and loopholes often needed to be traversed in order to resolve issues, the lack of customer service, the 'cutting of corners', the 'it's who you know factor' in getting things done, etc. Still, when the lifestyle migrants weigh up the pros and cons, the result can perhaps be best summed up via the fact that if they keep on building their lives in Portugal and showing no intention of returning to their origins, this equally implies that the positives outweigh the negatives. In the words of one respondent:

> I don't mind putting up with the occasional snobby shopkeeper, or a day or two without water in the summer if, in return, I get peace of mind, tranquillity, sunshine, great wine and an all around better quality of life.
>
> (English, female, born 1967)

Intra-community connectedness: network building and support patterns

As we have seen, lifestyle migrants in Central Portugal have opted for this part of the country for a variety of reasons, one of which is the lack of routine contact with expatriates and tourists. This, however, does not imply that most will 'turn the other cheek' when encountering such individuals, quite the contrary in fact. If, on one hand, constructing bridging capital with members of the host society is easy (given that such capital is readily offered up by members of the host society), constructing bonding capital, on the other hand, will often depend on one's need for contact with those who find themselves in the same predicament (other lifestyle migrants) in the new environment (Casado-Díaz 2009).[9]

As previously mentioned, one of the primary sources for this work has been the social network group Portugal Friends. In analysing the 'meso-level' of socio-cultural information and support networks (e.g. clubs and associations), Portugal Friends is the only physical network of its kind in Central Portugal. The introductory page of this social group's website, describes the network's objectives as follows:

> In a foreign country where the local language is not native to you, the difficulty in social interaction becomes even more obvious, and finding new friends or a social circle can present a challenge. Portugal Friends was developed from a need for people, … mostly foreigners or Portuguese people who speak English or have lived in other … countries, to share their common ideas and interests and enjoy good company.
>
> (www.portugalfriends.com, accessed 1 March 2011)

Portugal Friends thus provides a social element to the lives of lifestyle migrants living in Central Portugal through regular weekly gatherings and events such as: coffee mornings, group walks, fund-raising events, seasonal dinners, among others. The social network provides the opportunity to meet with others who share a similar cultural background, perhaps the same language (mostly English) as well as interests, offering a socialisation space for lifestyle migrants who may perhaps be feeling isolated.[10] Asked to comment on their interactions with other lifestyle migrants outside this organised network, the interviewees referred to physical distance as a factor that often reduces interaction. Drawing on the words of one interviewee:

> Not everyone has found their dream place to live in a village where other expats live as well. So, for some people, it's either you learn Portuguese or you have nobody to communicate with on a regular basis outside of your spouse, your children or our family back home. … A lot of people here either knew someone living here from 'back home' before moving here or discovered others living here when they were looking around. Often

> people have studied the area before moving and end up knowing other expats in the area.
>
> (Dutch, male, born 1951)

The gravitation towards others who reside in the same location is in fact described by many as a natural process due to the one commonality of being a lifestyle migrant and all that it entails. Given the reduced population number and dispersion, sub-group formation based on nationality equally 'takes a back seat' when it comes to forming relations between the migrants. Even when there are physical distances involved, the majority claim to possess closer ties with other lifestyle migrants, for with the Portuguese – although 'welcoming' and 'friendly' as many define them to be – there are barriers such as language and lifestyle differences, among others.[11]

In the migration setting, leisure and social events created by lifestyle migrants provide opportunities for camaraderie among the migrants (O'Reilly 2000; Casado-Díaz 2009), a facilitator when physical proximity among migrants is not so common. Thus, in accumulating social capital, by embedding themselves in the lifestyle migrant social structure locally, they are contributing to reducing isolation and reducing distance to the homeland via the degree of connection with other lifestyle migrants. Although space and distance does not always permit regular contact, the migrants rely on organised networks as a prime mechanism that facilitates creating intra-community ties and creating bonding capital.

Conclusion

This chapter has looked at lifestyle mobility in two Portuguese regions located in Central Portugal (Pinhal Interior Norte and Médio Tejo) not historically known for attracting these types of migrants. That said, it set out to ask why lifestyle migrants have taken up residency in Central Portugal, how they perceive their own integration and acceptance on the part of the Portuguese, and what strategies of network building and support they possess. As Benson and O'Reilly (2009a) point out, the representations of the destinations chosen by such migrants can be categorised under three main headings: the rural idyll, the coastal retreat and the cultural/spiritual attraction. The lifestyle migrant opting for Central Portugal as the preferred geographical location to achieve his or her dream of a better lifestyle fits perfectly into the first and third options, giving lesser importance to the second. These are individuals who value rural comfort, living in an environment where solitude and tranquillity are particularly valued. For these migrants, 'the rural' offers them not only the possibility of belonging, but also for self-transformation and personal renewal, not to mention the possibility of being close to an authentic side of Portugal via its historic rural past and traditionality. Thus, for many of these migrants, by presenting themselves as adhering to the moral principles of rural and traditional living, they distinguish themselves from other lifestyle migrants in other settings in Portugal (namely the Algarve) where beach-going and sun-worshipping are the primary variables pursued.

Many lifestyle-seeking migrants show their interest in wanting to contribute to the regional socio-cultural preservation, often doing so via their entrepreneurial endeavours as well as hobby activities. Dealing with the local culture and its people becomes an obvious part of the everyday lives of these lifestyle migrants in the new destination. Lifestyles following migration involve the (re)negotiation of habits and behaviour, often influenced and altered according to local practices and population. Lifestyle migration is thus a project that often continues after the initial act of migration. Of course the support system one may require in that search is equally important, a system that may be pre-defined before migration and found to be different in the post migration. The inter- and intra-community connectedness (or lack thereof) is very much key to this support system as the lifestyle migrant will equally measure the extent to which his/her lifestyle is truly the one sought – after agreeing with the availability and personal desire to integrate and relate to others – by Portuguese and other lifestyle migrants.

As witnessed, a number of mismatches at different levels exist when it comes to reasons for picking these regions to live in and when it comes to inter/intra-relationship strategies. When it comes to pitting the escape intentions of many (search for solitude, away from tourists and other lifestyle migrants) Central Portugal is pin-pointed as idyllic given its off-the-beaten path location on the Portuguese tourism map. This, however, does not fully imply that intra-relations with other lifestyle migrants are not welcomed and searched for. In addition to that, we see that many carve out entrepreneurial endeavours aimed at other similar migrants. Still, many present themselves as benign lifestyle migrants who embrace and feel embraced by their local communities, a pattern not common to the traditional lifestyle migration destination of the Algarve (Torkington 2010), where larger concentrations and access to lifestyle migrant amenities curb lifestyle migrant–local population contact. In the case of the two central Portuguese regions studied, however, achieving a better way of life rests on integration into local life. Many feel this is accomplished not only through the 'warmth of the welcome' on the part of the locals, but also via their own offerings to the local communities, accomplished through developing contributions and participating in social-cultural activities.

Notes

1 Previous research has attempted to link these mobility forms to wider phenomena using umbrella concepts such as retirement migration, leisure migration, (international) counter-urbanisation, second home ownership, amenity-seeking and seasonal migration (King *et al.* 2000; Casado-Díaz 2006).

2 Pinhal Interior Norte and Médio Tejo are two of the 28 Nut III statistical sub-regions of Portugal. According to Portuguese 2011 Census, the two regions had a combined population of 352,031 (Pinhal Interior Norte with 131,371 and Médio

Tejo with 220,660) accounting for 3.33 per cent of Portugal's total population. Since 1960 the two regions combined have lost nearly 20 per cent of their population, with Pinhal Interior Norte being the hardest hit region the two, having lost nearly 30 per cent of its residents.

3 In this study a 'privileged' voice is given to lifestyle migrants. In doing this, it is also worth noting that I here run the risk of presenting a one-dimensional argument. Although questions of objectivity can arise in relation to inquiries pertaining to integration, the aim of this chapter is to examine the perspectives of these individuals. Nonetheless, it is important to remember that other arguments may exist from members of the host society.

4 The personal blogs consulted include www.portugalpermaculture.blogspot.com, www.livingthedreamportugal.blogspot.com, www.ribeiravelha.com, www.emmashouseinportugal.com, www.permaculturinginportugal.net, www.atomicdogma.com and www.globalwanderings.co.uk. Community blogs and forums followed were: www.portugalfriends.com, www.expatsportugal.com, www.gekkoportugal.com; and www.he-he-portugal.com/.

5 It should be noted that some of the retirees have taken early retirement; in all cases self-imposed for those under the age of 60.

6 Previous research on lifestyle migration to Portugal has focused mainly on the Algarve region. See, for example: Williams and Patterson 1998; King *et al.* 2000; Williams *et al.* 2000.

7 O'Reilly (2003) points out that in terms of sought-after lifestyle and chosen destination, the boundaries of what is lifestyle migration and what is tourism are often blurred. Torkington (2009) equally states that British lifestyle migrants in the Algarve have the somewhat ambivalent status of being considered as much tourists as residents, even if Portugal is their principal (or indeed only) home. Lifestyle migrants of Central Portugal, on the other hand, wish to make these boundaries quite clear.

8 Entrepreneurial activities undertaken by these migrants are often a departure from the careers they had before migration. In fact, it is often the case that many lifestyle migrants have little to no previous experience in establishing and running businesses, thus often the opportunity of migrating is equally the opportunity to follow their professional dreams (Hoey 2005; Benson and O'Reilly 2009b).

9 Following Putnam (2000), bonding capital – the formation of strong ties among individuals within a group – and bridging capital – the formation of cross-cutting ties between people from different groups – are two kinds of social capital.

10 Beyond the socialising element, Portugal Friends often also provides an opportunity for participants to publicise their entrepreneurial and artistic endeavours, as many see in these gatherings the opportunity to distribute business cards, etc.

11 Although not given specific attention to in this article, there are also lifestyle migrant 'counterculture/hippie communities' found in these regions of Central Portugal. Given the communal state of inhabitance and lifestyle practice carried out by these individuals, contact is above all in-group.

Bibliography

Arksey, H. and Knight, P. (1999) *Interviewing for Social Scientists: An Introductory Resource with Examples*, London: Sage.

Befus, D., Mescon, T., Vozikis, G. and Mescon, D. (1988) 'The characteristics of expatriate entrepreneurs', *International Small Business Journal*, 6: 33–44.

Benson M. (2010) '"We are not expats; we are not migrants; we are Sauliacoise": Laying claim to belonging in rural France', in B. Bönisch-Brednich and C. Trundle (eds) *Local Lives: Migration and the Politics of Place*, Aldershot: Ashgate, 67–84.

Benson, M. (2009) 'A desire for difference: British lifestyle migration to Southwest France', in M. Benson and K. O'Reilly (eds) *Lifestyle Migration: Expectations, Aspirations and Experiences*, Aldershot: Ashgate, 121–36.

Benson, M. and O'Reilly, K. (2009a) 'Migration and the search for a better way of life: a critical exploration of lifestyle migration', *The Sociological Review* 57 (4): 608–25.

——(2009b) 'Lifestyle migration: Escaping to the good life?', in M. Benson and K. O'Reilly (eds) *Lifestyle Migration: Expectations, Aspirations and Experiences*, Aldershot: Ashgate, 1–14.

Casado-Díaz, M. (2009) 'Social capital in the sun: Bonding and bridging social capital among British retirees', in M. Benson and K. O'Reilly (eds) *Lifestyle Migration: Expectations, Aspirations and Experiences*, Aldershot: Ashgate, 87–102.

——(2006) 'Retiring to Spain: An analysis of difference among North European Nationals', *Journal of Ethnic and Migration Studies* 32(8): 1321–39.

Geoffrey, C. (2007) 'From "Chamouni" to Chamonix: The British in the Alps', in C. Geoffrey and R. Sibley (eds) *Going Abroad: Travel, Tourism and Migration. Cross-Cultural Perspectives on Mobility*, Cambridge: Cambridge Scholars Publishing, 93–109.

Haas, H. (2012) 'Volunteering in retirement migration: meanings and functions of charitable activities for older British residents in Spain', *Ageing and Society*, 1–27, doi:10.1017/S0144686X12000669.

Halfacree, K. (1997) 'Contrasting roles for the post-productivist countryside. A post-modern perspective on counterurbanisations', in P. Cloke and J. Little (eds) *Contested Countryside Cultures: Otherness, Marginalisation and Rurality*. London: Routledge, 70–93.

Hespanha, P. (2004) 'O Abandono Rural e a Desertificação', in R. Jacinto and V. Bento (eds) *Fronteira, Emigração, Memória*. Guarda: Centro de Estudos Ibéricos. https://woc.uc.pt/feuc/getFile.do?tipo=2&id=6085 (accessed 22 October).

——(1996) *Sociologia Rural e Urbana. Temas e Problemas*. Coimbra: Faculdade de Economia da Universidade de Coimbra.

Hoey, B. A. (2009) 'Pursuing the good life: American narratives of travel and a search for refuge' in M. Benson and K. O'Reilly (eds) *Lifestyle Migration: Expectations, Aspirations and Experiences*, Aldershot: Ashgate, 31–50.

——(2005) 'From Pi to Pie: Moral narratives of noneconomic migration and starting over in the postindustrial Midwest', *Journal of Contemporary Ethnography* 34(5): 586–624.

King, R., Warnes, A. and Williams A. (2000) *Sunset Lives: British Retirement to Southern Europe*, Oxford: Berg.

Madden, L. (1999) *Making Money in the Sun: The Development of British- and Irish-owned Businesses in the Costa del Sol*. Research Papers in Geography 36, Brighton: University of Sussex.

O'Reilly, K. (2000) *The British on the Costa del Sol*, London: Routledge.

——(2003) 'When is a tourist? The articulation of tourism and migration in Spain's Costa del Sol', *Tourist Studies* 3(3): 301–17.

——(2000) *The British on the Costa del Sol*, London: Routledge.

Putnam, R. (2000) *Bowling Alone. The Collapse and Revival of American Community*, Princeton, NJ: Princeton University Press.

Stone, I. and Stubbs, C. (2007) 'Enterprising expatriates: lifestyle migration and entrepreneurship in rural southern Europe', *Entrepreneurship and Regional Development*, 19(5): 433–50.

Sunil, T., Rojas, V. and Bradley, D. (2007) 'United States international retirement migration: the reasons for retiring to the environs of Lake Chapala, Mexico', *Ageing and Society* 27: 489–510.

Torkington, K. (2010) 'Defining lifestyle migration', *Dos Algarves*, 19: 99–111.

van Dam, F., Heins, S. and Elbersen, B. (2002) 'Lay discourses of the rural and stated and revealed preferences for rural living: Some evidence of the existence of a rural idyll in the Netherlands', *Journal of Rural Studies*, 18: 461–76.

Williams, A., King, R., Warnes, A. and Patterson, G. (2000) 'Tourism and international retirement migration: new forms of an old relationship in southern Europe', *Tourism Geographies*, 2(1): 28–49.

Williams, A. and Patterson, G. (1998) '"An empire lost but a province gained": a cohort analysis of British international retirement in the Algarve', *Population Geography*, 4 (2): 135–155.

13 'Living apart together' in Franschhoek, South Africa

The implications of second home development for equitable and sustainable development

Sanne van Laar, Ine Cottyn, Ronnie Donaldson, Annelies Zoomers and Sanette Ferreira

Introduction

This chapter aims to examine the reality of second home development and ownership in a small town in South Africa and provide an analysis on the implications for equitable and sustainable development. The aim is to reveal the economic and socio-spatial impacts induced by second home development on the local level with a particular focus on the property market dynamics in Franschhoek. Next to the economic implications for this town, we will also concentrate on a more controversial issue related to second home development: the relation with gentrification and the displacement of permanent residents. After a contextual introduction we will elaborate more on the methodology of our research on which this chapter is based. The results will be presented next, starting with an outline of our study area and the circumstances of second home ownership, followed by our analysis of the empirical data collected.

Second home development in South Africa: an introduction

Prior to 1994 when South Africa became a democratic state after decades of apartheid rule, second home investment in the country was mainly restricted to South African ownership. With the 'opening-up' of the country in the early 1990s through the lifting of sanctions, South Africa experienced a dramatic increase in international tourism. The country was then viewed as a value-for-money destination, and the region which benefited most from this expansion was the Western Cape Province – which in turn has become known as an area in which to invest in a second home (Visser and Van Huyssteen 1999). However, even today South Africa ranks as one of the most unequal societies in the world, where differences of race and class generally coincide, producing a wealthy white minority and poor black majority. The burden of poverty is exacerbated by limited access to basic services, poor housing, limited employment opportunities and inadequate infrastructure, all consequences of apartheid. The potential for viewing second home owners (especially foreigners) as perpetuators of socio-economic segregation was eventually put on the national policy agenda. In 2006 the *Progress Report of the Panel of Experts on the Development of Policy on the Regulation of Ownership of Land in South Africa by Foreigners [Non-Citizens]* (Gutto *et al.* 2006) recommended that the South African government place a moratorium on the sale of property to foreign buyers; however, to date the policy formulation has not yet been finalised, as the issue would have major political and economic ramifications. A scheme for such a policy is, however, not far-fetched; it would stem the tide of this perpetuation, or slow the creation of a polarised spatial landscape in South Africa – to which the second home development scenario is directly relevant.

According to Gallent and Tewdwr-Jones (2001) regions with affluent permanent residents and leisure-time budgets generate the potential demand for second homes. Conversely, in other regions lesser relative affluence and economic stagnation fuels depopulation, increasing the availability of surplus housing stock which often becomes the focus of second home demand (see Sardinha in this volume). In this context gentrification is a powerful process which plays an important role in remodelling the physical, economic and social characteristics of specific areas (Paris 2009). As Visser and Kotze (2008: 2567) note, gentrification, being urban or rural, refers to the class dimensions of neighbourhood change. In short, there are not only changes in housing stock, but also changes in housing class, where the local residents of an area are replaced by a more affluent segment of society. There is a clear, proven causal relationship between the growth of second home ownership and problems of affordability for lower-income households and first-time buyers (Paris 2009). The socio-economic advantage of second home owners causes a situation where this demand generates a rocketing 'price rally' on all properties and, when property prices rise, so too do property tax burdens for permanent residents (Shucksmith 1983). Local residents can therefore be outpriced from the local land and housing market. The present understanding of gentrification-induced displacement now also includes processes by which exclusion is pre-emptive; no one but a range of the wealthy middle class can find some sort of literal and figurative space in those areas of investment. Next to this real gentrification, second home development can also give rise to the symbolic gentrification of the public space, grounded in retail and consumption (Janoschka, Sequera and Salinas in preparation). Symbolic dimensions such as the shifts towards a service economy, new commercial activities, and new types and organisation of labour play a significant role in this concept, previously referred to as 'tourism gentrification' or 'commercial gentrification'. The public space is 'prepared' for the tourist via cultural production or 'artistification', the establishment of institutionalised cultural production facilities constructing an artificially new and somehow pretentious identity (Delgado 2008). There also exists a sense of elitism in second home nodes (Jaakson 1986; Marjavaara 2008) which often creates a distance between the tourists and the locals. The cost of those spaces created through second home development results in the maintenance or creation of residential class segregation (Visser and Kotze 2008).

Methodology

Quantifying second home ownership in South Africa is impossible owing to the shortcomings of the current census data. The extent of such ownership across the country can therefore only be determined on a case-study by case-study basis. Fortunately there has been a great interest in second home research since the mid-2000s (Rogerson 2012; Hoogendoorn and Visser 2011a,b, 2010a,b; Hoogendoorn, Visser and Marais 2009; Visser 2004a,b, 2003). Some of the trends in the impact of foreign second home ownership in South Africa have been similar to research carried out on this phenomenon in different geographical contexts. Hoogendoorn and Visser (2010a) noted that there are two main discourses concerning these various impacts. The first is the neo-liberal approach, focusing on the nexus between tourism and urban development and the potentially desirable aspects of second home development; this looks mainly at the economic advantage and its role in a post-productive countryside. Positive impacts of second home development are to be found in employment creation and taxes for the local authority. The focus of the second approach is on the undesirable consequences: second home development is seen as the expression of capital accumulation, uneven development, displacement of the local community, escalating property prices and housing shortages, and the foreignisation of space (Zoomers 2010). Although second home owners sometimes represent only a small percentage of the total population of a destination, the socio-cultural, spatial and economic impacts of their presence can often change the total fabric of a locality (McWatters 2009). These processes have not developed evenly, and the impacts differ from location to location (Visser 2004a,b; Marjavaara 2008). Motivations for obtaining a second home and the factor of distance from the permanent residence have been investigated extensively (Jaakson 1986; Katelborn 1997, 1998; Müller 1999; Müller, Hall and Keen 2004). Other much-debated topics involve the impacts second homes have on an economic, spatial and socio-cultural level (Gallent *et al.* 2005; Gallent 2007; Hall and Müller 2004; Flognfeldt 2004; Atkinson *et al.* 2007; Hui and Yu 2009; Hoogendoorn *et al.* 2009).

Buying your own 'second home in paradise' happens typically in countries with lower economic development, where the standard of living is low and the acquisition of property and land is affordable (Zoomers 2008), making it very much a controversial and debated topic around the world as well as in South Africa. This chapter aims to examine the reality of second home ownership in a small town in South Africa. Field research was conducted in Franschhoek over a three-month period in 2011. Two questionnaire surveys were conducted, one among 61 second home owners and the other among 86 of the permanently resident local population. Given the relative low number of cases in the quantitative study, results cannot be considered significant in statistical terms. The quantitative data are used in support of the stated arguments throughout the research based on an additional 32 in-depth interviews that were held with different stakeholders including villagers, local business people, real estate agents and civil servants.

Study area

Franschhoek – meaning 'French corner', named after the settlement of the first group of 180 French Huguenot immigrants in April 1688 – is located 70 kilometres from Cape Town. It developed over the centuries as a service centre for the agricultural community living in the Franschhoek valley, where mainly wine grapes and fruit were grown, and continue to be grown to the present day. Connected to the wine industry is the tourism sector – Franschhoek has become known for its award-winning restaurants and is claimed to be the 'culinary capital' of South Africa. Tourism has of late overtaken agriculture as the main economic base; it is even claimed that the town is considered one of the top five destinations in South Africa for both domestic and foreign tourists (CNdV Africa Planning and Design 2010). In addition, the social geography of the town has also changed since the mid-1990s when Franschhoek was transformed from an Afrikaans-speaking rural agricultural town into an English-speaking tourist destination (Willemse 2008). As Torkington already argued in Chapter 6, language choice within the linguistic landscape of a place is never arbitrary and can be linked to social positioning and new power relationships within the community. At present there are an estimated 15,500 residents in the town, distributed as follows: 887 households in Franschhoek South, 1,944 in Groendal and 1,700 informal dwellings in Langrug, in Franschhoek North. The duality of space in South Africa is represented perfectly in the urban landscape of Franschhoek and, as a model apartheid town, the legacy of apartheid planning is vivid in the artificial and visual separation of white and black: Franschhoek South was for the whites, and Franschhoek North or Groendal for those then classified as non-white. To undo this spatial legacy and transform the community a new model for land reform, housing and empowerment was developed in the 1998 'Social Accord' (Franschhoek Municipality 1998). The Social Accord focuses on creating an integrated and non-segregated town which will be able to cope with the housing shortage for unskilled and unemployed migrants to Franschhoek North. The basic principles of the agreement were spatial effectiveness, the provision of appropriate housing for all income groups with the acquisition of individual title and ownership, the prevention of urban sprawl, the preservation of land values, and the integration of Franschhoek into a single village (Franschhoek Municipality 1998).

The circumstances of second home ownership in Franschhoek is in line with international conceptualisation: a residence is considered a second home when the primary residence is somewhere else, and is where the owner spends the majority of their time (Koch-Schulte 2008). In the popular media, Franschhoek has been depicted as a town experiencing a second wave of colonialism from a perceived influx of non-South Africans, especially since 1994. For the purposes of this study, the only available method to determine the extent of this second home ownership was to make use of the municipal rates-based address listing – the assumption was that second home owners will have their accounts mailed to their primary place of residence. A total of 883 residential properties were identified from this source for Franschhoek South, of which 319 were assumed to be second homes. A significant percentage of these were foreign owners (33 per cent) with the bulk made up by South Africa owners (67 per cent). The research furthermore showed that there is no specific spatial clustering of foreign and local second home owners. Other second home studies in small towns in South Africa have not witnessed such a dramatic increase in second homes under foreign ownership (Cottyn and van Laar 2011).

In order to get a better understanding of who would buy a second home in Franschhoek and why, a questionnaire survey was conducted in 2011. All potential second home owner sites were visited, and a total of 61 willing owners, representing 19 per cent of second home owners, participated in the survey, most (42) of them foreign, the remaining 19 South Africans (referred to as domestic second home owners). The majority of foreign owners are from Europe (90 per cent), of whom most are British (79 per cent), followed by Dutch and Americans. In the case of the domestic second home owners, the majority of the respondents have their primary residence in the provinces of the Western Cape (53 per cent) and Gauteng (27 per cent). A summary of the demographic analysis from the survey is shown in Table 13.1, differentiating between domestic and international profiles.

The majority of foreign respondents can be categorised as empty-nesters, falling into the segment of international retirement migration. On the other hand, the domestic second home owners are middle-aged, predominantly in a two-person household, with a significant percentage (27 per cent) being full-nesters. In addition, as can be expected, both domestic and foreign owners are economically active, classified as upper-level income earners.

Müller (1999) emphasises that 'rural idyll' is a motivational factor of second home owners, in pursuit of a more 'natural' rural lifestyle of laid back living. Lifestyle choices for a great part determine the purchase of second home properties in Franschhoek. The opportunity to wine and dine in the tranquil ambience of beautiful surroundings was identified as the second- and third-most important motivation for both groups, and can be associated with their perceptions of a more rural lifestyle. The domestic second home owners indicated that escaping busy city life was by far the main motivation for obtaining a second home in Franschhoek. This has also been revealed by

Table 13.1 Demographic, economic and residential characteristics of second home owners in Franschhoek (domestic n=19, International n=42)

Demographic characteristics			*Economic characteristics*			*Residential characteristics*		
	Domestic	*Foreign*		*Domestic*	*Foreign*		*Domestic*	*Foreign*
Age			*Current occupational status*			*Status of property before converting to second home*		
31–50	32%	7%	Retired	16%	44%	Newly constructed	21%	29%
51–60	42%	29%	Own business	48%	23%	Primary residence	11%	31%
61–80	26%	64%	Employed	31%	33%	Second home	32%	21%
			Other	5%	0%	Vacant plot of land	36%	19%
Household composition			*Main source of income*			*Obtained through whom*		
1 person	5%	7%	Pension	5%	30%	Local real estate	79%	76%
2 persons	68%	74%	Salary	32%	23%	International real estate	0%	0%
3+ persons	27%	17%	Own business	37%	20%	Project developer	16%	21%
Not answered	0%	2%	Other	21%	22%	Individually	0%	2%
			Not answered	5%	5%	Inherited	5%	0%
Highest educational qualification			*Annual Income*			*Year of purchase*		
< Bachelor	16%	31%	<€50,000	26%	30%	1990–2000	11%	12%
Bachelor	42%	36%	€50,000–100,000	11%	23%	2001–2003	16%	21%
Honours	10%	7%	€100,001–500,001	42%	20%	2004–2006	32%	31%
Masters >	32%	24%	€500,000	21%	22%	2007–2008	10%	17%
Not answered	0%	12%	Not answered	0%	5%	2009–2011	31%	19%

Source: van Laar 2011

Visser (2006: 358), who argued that 'the last decade has seen an increase in the development of second homes purposed for weekend getaways in regions located near to prominent economic and urban hubs'. When asking respondents about the main function of their property, lifestyle choice was quoted once again as a key factor. For the foreign second home owners, the main function of their property is that of a vacation home (82 per cent); however, this differed for the domestic second home owners: although they indicated that lifestyle choices were the main motivation for obtaining a property in Franschhoek, they stated that the main function of their property was that of investment (61 per cent) – showing that second homes are not purely for recreational and leisure purposes. An additional source of income and a return on the investment was to be achieved by renting out the property. A striking 48 per cent of domestic second home owners rented out their property, or parts of it, whereas only 21 per cent of foreign second home owners did likewise.

A summary of the second home owners' visitation, mobility and locational characteristics in Franschhoek is provided in Table 13.2. Interpenetration is the level to which cultures and communities which seem distant come face to face at a local level, and as such stresses diversity (Shaw and Williams 2002: 26). The tourist–host interaction is usually brief and temporary as usually the tourist stays in the destination for a short time; mostly there is little

Table 13.2 Summary second home owners' visitation, mobility and locational characteristics

	Second home function	*Frequency of visit*	*Length of stay*	*Form of mobility*	*Location relative to primary residence*
Domestic	Main function being investment, followed by vacation home. Respondents falling in the weekend zone, no distinction between holiday and vacation home.	For those who use the second home for leisure purposes the frequency is quite high. For those owning a second home for investment purposes, frequency of visit is low.	For those who own a second home for leisure purposes, functions mainly as vacation home. They stay longer than 3 days or for a weekend. Compared to foreign respondents the length of stay is much shorter.	Significant percentage of domestic respondents the form of mobility is circular. Nevertheless this is not exclusively as also seasonal patterns became visible.	On average the location relative to primary residence is independent. Also for respondents falling in the weekend zone, a significant percentage uses their second home as a holiday home.

opportunity to develop a meaningful relationship between tourists and hosts (Reisinger and Dimanche 2009). Due to their length of stay and possible attachment to and involvement in the region or place where they own their second home, in this type of tourism the distinction between the two categories of host and guest becomes blurred (Sherlock 2001). In a second home context, as Marjavaara (2008) noted, second home tourists are neither tourists nor permanent residents, but rather a category in between. Sherlock (2001) labelled this group as 'new residents'. Permanent residents may perceive this group to be tourists, but often second home owners consider themselves part of the host community (Strapp 1988; Sherlock 2001). For Müller (2000: 38) mobility can be characterised as circulation when the second home function is a weekend home, and seasonal when the second home functions as a vacation home. Weather is by far the most important motivation for foreign retirement migrants (Gustafson 2001), and along with seasonality considered the main motivation for foreigners to buy in Franschhoek. The survey found that they would typically visit their second homes between November and March, the main summer season in this area, providing a Mediterranean climate. During the months between May and September there is virtually a total absence of the foreign second home owners (van Laar 2011).

In the survey among permanent residents, the so-called 'swallows' (the name frequently used for both foreign and South African second home owners in Franschhoek) are not regarded any more as tourists, but rather seen as part of the community. As one of the respondents remarked: 'They are not tourists, but also not part of the community. I see them rather as visitors.' Eighty per cent considered the swallows as part of Franschhoek's community and only 20 per cent still considered them tourists. Following the words of the respondents, the categories of host and guest are fluid and contested, yet this same polarised opposition is continuously used to express their experiences. Being a local is still connected to a certain commitment to the place or community. For the domestic second home owners the mobility pattern is not as straightforward. Almost half of the respondents visit their property at least once a month and almost a quarter of them even on a bi-weekly basis. However, there are also some domestic respondents whose mobility pattern is more seasonal instead of cyclical.

A great percentage of owners purchased their properties from other second home owners, implying that the second home owners' market is rising: research revealed that for both foreign and domestic second home owners the market value of the properties increased significantly. Real estate agents are the most favoured resources for purchasing property; as most second home owners made use of an estate agent (see Table 13.1) the initial acquisition of second homes has injected investment capital into the local economy by generating work for local agents and related services. No international agency has yet 'discovered' Franschhoek as a potential sales market. Furthermore, a significant number of both respondent groups indicated that they renovated or made alterations to the property after purchase.

The economic impacts of second home development have been a matter for ongoing research (Hoogendoorn and Visser 2010a,b). Second home owners are considered to be returning guests, implying more security and therefore a more sustainable base for economic development. As argued by Hoogendoorn and Visser (2010a) the economic impact of second homes depends for a great part on property type, usage and locality. These in turn are determined by capital injections, by means of expenditure on daily necessities, the hiring of domestic employees, paying municipal taxes or the creation of tourism-related products by second home owners and/or their tenants. Spending behaviour is an important feature for examining the economic implications of second home development (Müller 1999; Hall and Müller 2004; Atkinson *et al.* 2007). Spending behaviour entails different types of cash expenditure: day-to-day spending (on tangible commodities on a daily basis); investment spending (which adds to the physical stock and is durable) and services spending (on intangible commodities, e.g. employees). Franschhoek second home owners make a substantial contribution to employment generation, as 53 of the 61 respondents make use of support services such as domestic workers, gardeners, gardening services, pool maintenance and security services. In addition second home owners spend a significant amount of money in the local economy, making use of commercial businesses and local amenities. The domestic second home owner on the other hand makes more frequent use of gardening services and gardeners per month. This indicates different capital flows to various segments of the local service industry. On average a foreign second home owner pays €210.5 (R2358) per month on rates and taxes whereas the domestic second home owner pays only €152 (R1704); this difference in price is, in essence, a reflection of the relative value of each group's properties (van Laar 2011).

Property market dynamics in Franschhoek

Through purposive sampling a survey was conducted among local residents who were interviewed on their awareness of second home development and its scale in the area. In the local survey, 86 respondents filled out the questionnaire. More than three-quarters (78 per cent) agreed with the statement that Franschhoek has become an exclusive location where only a certain class of people can afford to live, and that this is directly attributed to an increase in foreign property ownership. According to real estate agents based in Franschhoek (various interviews) the average entry-level property at the time of the survey was around €223,202 (R2.5 million) for a family house, and that prices ranged between €133,921.4 (R1.5 million) and €892,809.3 (R10 million).

One particularly popular type of development has been the gated estate, some of which have been constructed along the Main Road in the infill areas of the town. Only the relatively wealthy middle class (Table 13.1) can afford to own property here. This brings us to one of the most controversial issues related to second home development: the displacement of permanent residents through this process of exclusion. Due to the in-movement of more wealthy second home buyers who can outbid local permanent residents, housing prices rise, as do the market values of the houses surrounding them. A shop-owner in Franschhoek tells this story in a personal interview held in 2011:

> In 2000 there was a house for sale in Franschhoek, asking price €44,640 (R500.000). I put in my offer, but a foreign couple did a counter offer and bought the place for €89,281 (R1 million). In 2007 they sold it again for €223,202 (R2.5 million) without any upgrading or change. I got pushed out of the market by foreigners, me as a South African owning a business in town. They can pay prices no South African can afford.

It is on this inflated market value, which is fixed for four years in the municipal property evaluation, that the tax rates for the ownership of property are based. With taxes rising to an amount people living in Franschhoek cannot afford any longer, they are forced to leave. As one respondent indicated, in three years' time the rates she had to pay increased from €1,250 (R14,000) to €3,392 (R38,000) annually. A large number of locals are selling their property. As respondents indicated, the trend is mainly pensioners, the most vulnerable among the middle- and high-income group (local resident Franschhoek, personal communication 2011). As a 72-year-old inhabitant tells:

> They are forcing people out with the evaluation of the houses. It has become unaffordable, certainly for pensioners. Before, I knew all people in Franschhoek, now I am a stranger in my own town. But if they give me €450,000, I move out … I don't have a choice.

This group is replaced by an influx of people from a younger age category with higher incomes. The town, once a solid and stable community (Franschhoek South) has now become a transient community with a continuously changing composition. The continuous process of displacement explains the few born-and-raised 'Franschhoekers' found today: only 9 per cent of the respondents indicate that they have been living in Franschhoek all their lives. The majority of the respondents in the resident survey moved only recently (less than 5 years previously) into Franschhoek (45 per cent). Next to that, as many as 21 per cent of the local respondents appeared to be foreign, and live permanently in Franschhoek, some of them converted from second home owners to first home owners (Cottyn 2011).

What the research revealed was that, while indeed the perceptions and aspirations of the locals and the second home owners who share this same space differed in some way, there were some common concerns as well. An important finding is that next to the differences in experience and opinion between the two major groups (local residents and second home owners) conflicts are also found within the two groups. The paradox in this finding is that they all seem to share common concerns about the increasing exclusivity of the housing market and its implications for local residents. In general the local residents consider their personal interaction with 'swallows' or second home owners to be positive; they are accepted as a part of life in Franschhoek. With respect to the rising property prices, a striking majority sees foreign ownership as the chief culprit. Most of the respondents agreed with the statement that the increase in prices and property values in the town makes it unaffordable for most people to live in the area. Many of the second home owners themselves consider the rising property rates and taxes to be no longer reasonable. Paradoxically, many among them do recognise that the property values which determine these taxes are driven higher by foreign buyers entering the local property market. Rising prices together with the displacement of local residents are often quoted by respondents as the major negative effects of foreign second home ownership. Although Franschhoek has gone through all of these major changes over the last years due to both tourism and second home development which have not always been positive, there is remarkably still no hostility between second home owners and permanent residents. One explanation might be the blurred distinction between host and guest in an almost newly composed community. It is important to note that when respondents make reference to people instead of processes, they tend to be less negative; although many recognise the negative impacts discussed above, only a few tend to blame second home owners personally (Cottyn 2011).

Conclusion

Even though second home ownership can be considered an intriguing economic sector with the potential to generate employment, there is an increasing debate about its negative implications: areas of the rural landscape being converted to urban building land, the concentration of this land in the hands of well-to-do minorities, the foreignisation of space, the processes of gentrification, and rapid price increases forcing 'permanent' local residents to move in the direction of less attractive marginal areas. There is a dilemma, namely, that second home ownership has on the one hand the potential to contribute to economic growth (and is itself a consequence of economic growth) and on the other hand is increasingly a hindrance to government policies, by creating new social 'gaps' and elements of a 'new apartheid'.

Where once it was mainly a domestic phenomenon, since the demise of apartheid in South Africa second home development has become very much a matter influenced by foreign buyers; low property prices and a stabilising political climate prompted foreigners to buy second homes in South Africa. According to the neoliberal approach, the main advantage of second home development is its economic value to the destination and its community. It is evident from the study that positive economic implications can be associated with the second home owners presently in Franschhoek. Nevertheless, it is argued that second home development in Franschhoek can be seen as a force for gentrification, causing the displacement of local residents, changing the fabric of the local community and its sense of place. It is contended here that second home owners should essentially be viewed as 'gentrifiers'. When looking at the prices paid for second homes and the effect it has on the property market together with the advantageous socio-economic status of the second home owners, second home development in Franschhoek can be seen as one of the forces that have been underpinning the gentrification of the town. Due to their influx the property taxes of local residents rose to the sky and for many this became unaffordable. The transformation into a tourist destination with the creation of a somehow 'artificial' identity and atmosphere also shows the symbolical gentrification of the town. Despite this, however, according to local residents there is no enmity between hosts and guests. The spatial duality of host and guest become contested and due to this blurred distinction between insider and outsider in this second home context, paradoxical findings have been revealed, about their ability to live apart together.

In Franschhoek, due to the rapid foreignisation and gentrification processes, it is increasingly difficult for the South African government to undo the spatial legacy of apartheid. Rather than achieving their policy goal of 'creating an integrated and non-segregated town which will be able to cope with the housing shortage for unskilled and unemployed migrants in Groendal and Langrug', the integration of Franschhoek into a single village with appropriate housing for all income groups is less and less feasible. To the extent that groups are living apart *together*, this is mainly happening between groups within Franschhoek South, while keeping neighbours in Groendal and Langrug at a distance. While inequality between racial groups remains high, second homes are resulting in the deepening of residential class segregation. For the moment, in Franschoek, people are increasingly living *apart* together.

References

Atkinson, R., Picken, F. and Tranter, B. (2007) *Second Homes in Australia: Charting Growth of Holiday Home Ownership and its Community Impact*. Paper No.10, Housing and community research Unit, Hobart: University of Tasmania, 1–27.

CNdV Africa Planning and Design (2010) *Stellenbosch Municipal Spatial Development Framework Draft Status Quo Report*, Stellenbosch: Stellenbosch Municipality.

Cottyn, I. (2011) *The Spatial and Socio Cultural Impacts of Second Home Development: A Case Study on Franschhoek South Africa*, unpublished Master thesis, University of Utrecht.

Cottyn, I. and van Laar, S. (2011) 'The socio-cultural and economic implications of second home development in Franschhoek, Western Cape, South Africa' in *Development Around the World*, Department of International Development Studies, Utrecht: Universiteit Utrecht.

Delgado, M. (2008) 'La artistizacion de las politicas urbanas: El lugar de la cultura en las dinamicas de reapropiacion capitalista de la ciudad', *Scripta Nova, Special Issue: X. Coloquio Internacional de Geocrítica*. www.ub.edu/geocrit/-xcol/393.htm (accessed 8 August 2012).

Flognfeldt, T. (2004). 'Second homes as a part of a new rural lifestyle in Norway', in M. Hall, and D. Müller (2004) (eds) *Tourism, Mobility and second homes: Between Elite Landscape and Common Ground*, Clevedon: Channel View, 233–43.

Franschhoek Municipality (1998) *Land and Housing Development Policy Framework. Agreement 16 February 1998*, Stellenbosch: Stellenbosch Municipality.

Gallent, N. (2007). 'Second homes, community and a hierarchy of dwelling', *Area* 39: 97–106.

Gallent, N. and Tewdwr-Jones, M. (2001) 'Second homes and the UK planning system', *Planning Practice and Research*, 16(1): 59–69.

Gustafson, P. (2001) 'Tourism and seasonal retirement migration', *Annals of Tourism Research* 29 (4): 899–918.

Gutto, S. *et al.* (2006) *'Progress Report of the Panel of Experts on the Development of Policy on the Regulation of Ownership of Land in South Africa by Foreigners [Non-Citizens]'*, Report and recommendations by the panel of experts on the development of policy regarding land ownership by foreigners in South Africa, Pretoria. www.pmg.org.za/files/gazettes/070914land-panelreport.pdf (accessed 22 March 2011).

Hall, M. and Müller, D. (eds) (2004) *Tourism, Mobility and Second Homes: Between Elite Landscape and Common Ground.* Clevedon: Channel View Publications.

Hoogendoorn, G. and Visser, G. (2011a) 'Tourism, second homes and an emerging South African post-productivist countryside', *Tourism Review International*, 15: 183–97.

——(2011b) 'Second homes and economic development issues in small town South Africa', *Tijdschrift voor Economische en Sosiale Geografie*, 102(3): 275–89.

——(2010a) 'Second home-led local economic development in small town South Africa', *Development Southern Africa,* 27(4): 547–62.

——(2010b) 'Second homes and small town development in South Africa', *Tourism Recreation Research*, 35(1): 53–64.

Hoogendoorn, G., Visser, G. and Marais, L., (2009) 'Changing countryside's, changing villages: reflections on second homes in Rhodes, South Africa', *South African Geographical Journal*, 91(2): 75–83.

Hui, E.C.M. and Yu, K.H. (2009) 'Second homes in Chinese Mainland under "one country, two systems": A cross border perspective', *Habitat International*, 33: 106–13.

Jaakson, R. (1986) 'Second-home domestic tourism', *Annals of Tourism Research* 13: 367–91.

Katelborn, B.P. (1998) 'The alternative: Motives of recreation home use', *Norsk Geografisk Tidsskrift* 52 (3), 121–34.

——(1997) 'Nature of place attachment: A study among recreation homeowners in Southern Norway', *Leisure Studies*, 19: 175–89.

Koch-Schulte, J. (2008) 'Planning for international retirement migration and expats: A case study of Udon Thani, Thailand', unpublished Master thesis, The University of Manitoba.

Marjavaara, R. (2008) 'Second home tourism. The root to displacement in Sweden?' Umea University: Gerum, 1–67.

McWatters, M.R. (2009) *Residential Tourism: (De)constructing Paradise*, Clevedon: Channel View Publications Ltd.

Müller, D.K.(2000). *Second Home Tourism and Sustainable Development in North European Peripheries.* Umea: Department of Social and Economic Geography, Umea University.

Müller, D.K., Hall, C.M. and Keen, D. (2004) 'Second home tourism impact, planning and management', in C.M. Hall, and D.K. Müller (eds) *Tourism, Mobility and Second Homes: Between Elite Landscape and Common Ground*, Clevedon: Channel View.

Müller, D.K. (2002) 'German second home development in Sweden', in Hall, C.M. and Williams, A.M. (eds) *Tourism and Migration: New Relationships Between Production and Consumption*, Dordrecht: Kluwer, 169–86.

——(1999) *German Second Homes in the Swedish Countryside*, Umea: Vetenskapliga Bokserien.

Paris, C. (2009) 'Re-positioning second homes within housing studies: Household investment, gentrification, multiple residence, mobility and hyperconsumption', *Housing, Theory and Society* 26(4): 292–310.

Reisinger, Y. and Dimanche, F. (2009) *International Tourism: Cultures and Behavior*. Burlington, VT: Elsevier.

Rogerson, C. (2012) 'Rethinking South African urban tourism research', *Tourism Review International,* 15: 77–90.

Shaw, G. and Williams, A.M. (2002) *Critical Issues in Tourism: A Geographical Perspective*, 2nd edn. Oxford: Blackwell Publishers.

Sherlock, K. (2001) 'Revisiting the concept of hosts and guests', *Tourist Studies*, 1(3): 271–95.

Shucksmith, D.M (1983) 'Second homes', *Town Planning Review*, 54: 174–93.

Strapp, J.D. (1988) 'The resort cycle and second homes', *Annals of Tourism Research* 15, 504–16.

Van Laar, S (2011) *Economic Implications of Second Home Development in South Africa: Case Study on Franschhoek*, unpublished Master thesis, University of Utrecht.

Visser, G. (2006) 'South Africa has second homes too! An exploration of the unexplored', *Current Issues in Tourism* 9 (4 and 5): 351–83.

——(2004a) 'Second homes and local development: Issues arising from Cape Town's De Waterkant', *GeoJournal* 60: 259–71.

——(2004b) 'Second homes: reflections on an unexplored phenomenon in South Africa', in C.M. Hall and D.K. Müller (eds) *Tourism, Mobility and Second Homes*. Toronto: Channel View, 169–214.

——(2003) 'Visible, yet unknown: Reflections on second-home development in South Africa', *Urban Forum* 14(4): 379–407.

Visser, G. and Kotze, N. (2008) 'The state and new-build gentrification in central Cape Town, South Africa', *Urban Studies* 45(12): 2565–93.

Visser, G. and Van Huysteen, K. (1999) 'Guest houses: The emergence of a new tourist accommodation type in the South African industry', *Tourism and Hospitality Research* 1(2): 155–75.

Willemse, L. (2008) *The Extent and Impacts of Land Cover Change in the Franschhoek Valley*, unpublished honours project, Department of Geography and Environmental Studies, University of Stellenbosch.

Zoomers, A. (2010) 'Globalization and the foreignization of space: The seven processes driving the current global land grab', *Journal of Peasant Studies*. 37(2): 429–47.

——(2008) *Buy your Own Paradise: Over Land, Mobiliteit en Ontwikkelingsbeleid*. Faculteit Geowetenschappen, inaugural lecture, Universiteit of Utrecht.

Part IV

Epilogue

14 Final reflections and future research agendas

Heiko Haas, Michael Janoschka and Vicente Rodríguez

Looking back at the contributions provided in this volume one is astounded by the multifaceted nature of lifestyle migrations to be encountered at the beginning of the twenty-first century. The phenomenon has experienced a constant diversification and internationalisation within the last decades and it appears that, at least from the perspective of qualitative observation and research, that there has also been a significant growth in terms of people involved in leisure- and lifestyle-oriented mobilities. Moreover, we can also testify that this growth is taking place in particular geographical settings at different rates. The diversification is most clearly detectable in the accruement of new destinations on the research map, and the continuously widening panorama of potential lifestyles and individual aspirations to be realised in these destinations, epitomised in terminologies like 'quest migrants' and 'utopian lifestyle migrants' or the more traditional 'retirement migrants' and 'second home owners', only to mention a few examples from this book. Along with the general proliferation of lifestyle migration and residential tourism, new problems, questions and research areas have appeared on the agenda. The broad range of empirical and theoretical approaches in this volume not only reflects these changes, but also a steadily growing research interest of various academic disciplines in the topic. In this respect, the epilogue will give some ideas and suggestions for possible future research and outline some of the major research strands that could be of interest and importance.

First of all, aspects that could help us to broaden our understanding in general refer to theoretical considerations as well as practical questions of application such as research techniques and methodological issues. The vast majority of research on lifestyle migration is conducted qualitatively or ethnographically. It is beyond doubt that this has resulted in various revealing and highly informative accounts, and the qualitative approach allows for deep and detailed insights into the realm of lifestyle migration. However, in many cases a better understanding of the quantitative side of the phenomenon would be tremendously interesting. Although we would estimate that probably millions of people worldwide are involved in mobilities related to lifestyle and leisure, no actual figures can be given since access to reliable statistical data is often difficult and comparisons are rarely possible. Although complex and cost intensive, more in-depth statistical research in particular national areas could help us to clarify, for example, to what extent lifestyle migration is solely a small elite phenomenon of an adventurous minority, or if it is indeed taking place on a much larger basis. Here, more quantitative information is yet to be obtained.

Another less explored aspect refers to the general meaning of mobility and the often multi-local character of many lifestyle migration settings, where transnational connections between places of origin and destination areas are maintained by regular visits, the keeping of multiple households, or even virtually via internet and telephone communication (Gustafson 2008; Urry 2007; McIntyre, Williams and McHugh 2006). Here the borders between permanent migration and mobility are constantly blurred and individual strategies of movement and settlement show a great variation depending structurally, for example, on the accessibility due to airports and low cost airlines. Research on mobility patterns, transnational life worlds and everyday realities is therefore of high importance in order to gain a better understanding of the dynamic and fluid nature of lifestyle migration and its spatial characteristics. Methodologically, the application of equally mobile and multi-sited research strategies (Falzon 2009; Coleman and von Hellerman 2011) in countries of origin and destinations could help to elucidate the varying residential strategies and their impacts on family relations and personal social networks, for example. The role of the new media and communication technologies like voice over IP services (e.g. Skype) in such pluri-local living arrangements is also an important factor to be researched in order to broaden our knowledge of how social relations are lived and maintained across distances today (Eliot and Urry 2010). These aspects could also be connected to more general theoretical reflections about the role of individualisation, consumption, mobility, communication and strategies of self-realisation within lifestyle migration, particularly before the backdrop of social distinction and the commodification of lifestyle choices within neoliberal capitalism. In many narratives lifestyle migration often represents a growing desire for an alternative way of life and self-actualisation in a post-materialistic context, combined with the search for a less anomic and more authentic life (Benson and O'Reilly 2009). However, and ironically, lifestyle migration is simultaneously the unmistakable expression of the exact conditions which many lifestyle migrants wish to escape: neoliberal consumerism, globalisation and privileged hypermobility.

Additionally, there is a general historical dimension to lifestyle migration and residential tourism which has not attracted much attention so far. As in the case of Europe, it was in the nineteenth century when parts of the bourgeoisie and the aristocracy could afford to escape from the cold middle European winters to selected seaside resorts with more pleasant and temperate Mediterranean climates, while another domestic and less travel-extensive strategy in many European and other places consisted in spending the summer in a second residence in the countryside outside the cities (Williams, King and

Warnes 1997; Rolshoven 2002). The internationalisation of such leisure-oriented mobilities was increasingly made possible by the establishment of railroads providing accessibility to these destinations, primarily located in southern France, Italy and northern Spain (Garay and Cànoves 2011). Later, and parallel to the expansion of mass tourism beginning in the middle of the twentieth century, forms of temporary or permanent relocations such as retirement migration and residential tourism gained wider popularisation and democratisation in the sense that some parts of the growing European middle classes could now also afford such a luxury. The historical development of the precursors of lifestyle migration, such as thermal tourism or the literary depictions of the journeys of bohemians writers and painters have left profound traces in the cultural representations of these places. This socio-cultural legacy of lifestyle-oriented migrations and their specific historical development in the receiving destinations, as well as the development of multi-local living arrangements and habitation practices of social elites, for example, represent a fascinating yet largely unexplored research field for social historians (see Müller and Hall 2004: 7–11 for a review on the historical dimensions of second home research).

Another crucial factor is the importance of economic components in lifestyle migration and residential tourism since the phenomenon is inextricably linked to the prosperity and affluence of larger social groups. Many contributions in this book have revealed how differences in wealth are an important stimulus for lifestyle migration, a project where quality of life is a consumable and intangible good that is more affordable in another country than in one's country of origin. However, although not all lifestyle migrants may be considered 'rich' by the economic standards of their societies of origin – the example provided by Paul Green in this volume is quite illustrative in this respect – they are nevertheless socially 'privileged' in as far as they can choose where to live and they have usually attained the assets to plan accordingly (Croucher 2012). Such personal economic and social circumstances are quite important to keep in mind, particularly considering that 'budget' is a huge factor in the migration decision which is often based on considerations of where to get more quality of life from one's money, consequently leading to economic gaps between lifestyle migrants and local populations. However, most research on lifestyle migration focuses primarily on the migrants themselves, for example on aspects like their motivations, decision-making, chosen lifestyles and questions of identity. Far less explored are the structural conditions and their responsibility in forming and establishing destinations for lifestyle migration and residential tourism, particularly in regard to economic aspects (see Gosnell and Abrams 2011). For example, the role of national and international real estate promoters and financial investors in the lifestyle migration scenario to date is largely unexplored, although their potential power in changing destinations from small-scale insider locales to excessively urbanised and commodified lifestyle migration areas is beyond doubt. Plenty of places have followed the typical route from the inconspicuous and proverbial fishing village, once explored by adventurous domestic and international travellers and backpackers alike, to large-scale mass destinations for tourists and lifestyle migrants. Examples from Spain, Portugal and Latin America can verify this evolution showing how international marketing and branding of real estate promoters – often combined with favourable governmental regulations for such developments – are pivotal aspects in the consolidation of such destinations. Here, a clear distinction between tourism and lifestyle migration destinations in most cases cannot be drawn, since both factors usually coincide and boundaries between tourism and lifestyle migration are often fluid and blurred. However, research into the planning practices and development strategies of finance investors and political decision-makers could help to shed a light on such structural parameters and conditions which may finally determine the route of development in many upcoming lifestyle migration destinations. This, again, emphasises the general importance of economic aspects when considering lifestyle migration and particularly its impact on destinations, most importantly in times of economic crisis. Spain can serve as a prime example in which a heavy economic crisis mainly based on a real estate speculation bubble is largely affecting a national economy; a process where second homes for residential tourism have played an important part. The particular case of Spain has shown how the development model built on the construction of holiday homes was led *ad absurdum.* Nevertheless, residential tourism in many destinations is a means of economic growth, since it may provide employment in various sectors, the service and construction sector in particular, but also tax revenues, improvements in infrastructure and chances for innovation (Eaton 2010). Here, economic models of development and strategies for the sustainable implementation of residential tourism are a promising and much needed research topic for economists and social scientists.

These aspects give rise to another important and largely neglected aspect in lifestyle migration research, its impact on destinations and local populations. As already mentioned above, most research on lifestyle migration focuses on the migrants but barely on the local populations and their perception of the scenario (Schriewer 2008; Huete and Mantecón 2011). The examples given in this volume from Bastos, Lipkina and Hall, and van Laar *et al.* have shown how fruitful research among local people living in lifestyle migration destinations can be, particularly in settings where social inequalities between local residents and newcomers are prevalent. Apart from the migrant's subjectivities, in future research a much stronger voice should be given to those affected by residential tourism and the social effects it has on a local scale, particularly in regard to the real estate market and processes of gentrification, power relations and possible structures of exploitation and socio-cultural domination (see Escher and Petermann; van Laar *et al.* this volume).

Other possible structural impacts of lifestyle migration refer to national health care systems and services, for example, particularly in the case of retirement migration (Legido-Quigley *et al.* 2012). As most of the studies in this volume and in general have evidenced, lifestyle migration in many instances takes place after retirement, a biographic circumstance that provides the social actors involved with the necessary leisure time and also the general pecuniary requirements for such moves. As the case of Spain, again, has shown, the massive influx of older migrants may not only aggravate the already existing demographic imbalance and population ageing, but may also causes problems in regard to health care entitlements and demands for related services (Haas 2012). According to this, one particularly important aspect in the future will be linked to the affordability of medical and care services. The increase in costs and the lack of services of long-term care and retirement homes in many developed countries may be an important factor for the future growth of retirement migration based on health care considerations. Since many countries of the 'Global North' are facing dramatic demographic changes, on the one hand, combined with a lack of resources to maintain welfare states at their current level and standards, on the other hand, already existing forms of medical tourism and health care-related mobilities are sure to increase. Considerations regarding the affordability of health and medical care are an important factor for many higher-aged lifestyle migrants and an important stimulus for migratory moves. Retirement homes in Thailand and Eastern Europe, for example, are a growing market targeting Northern Europeans, and the affordability of health care is an important factor stimulating the moves of lifestyle migrants worldwide. Therefore, lifestyle migration as a research subject is closely linked to aspects of global ageing and national health care policies as well as varying individual strategies and mobility patterns in relation to medical services between countries origin of lifestyle destinations. Examples of remigration in the case of health problems and the realisation of internments and repatriations can also be observed in this context (Rosenmöller, McKee and Baeten 2006; Oliver 2008) It is this intersection of individual aspirations and health care entitlements within a globalising market of medical and health care tourism which provides fertile ground for future research.

Another aspect concerns the political and legal side of lifestyle migration and residential tourism. In strong contrast with asylum seekers and other forms of forced migration, lifestyle migration usually takes place on the basis of a privileged citizen status guaranteeing free and voluntary movement or – financial resources provided – specific visa schemes for this particular group (see Green this volume, for example). The differences in formal and legal rights of older migrants, as researched by Ackers and Dwyer (2002, 2004) in the case of Europe, for example, as well as the various visa schemes provided by nation-states seeking this particular group of immigrants, and their differing legal entitlements are important issues to be considered in upcoming research. Also, processes of political participation and contest in lifestyle destination areas could be addressed more vigorously. As pioneered by Janoschka and Durán (this volume), research on the political involvement of lifestyle migrants and civic engagement (Haas 2012) combines a productive perspective not only on local conflicts, problems and inequalities but also on different cultures of participation and concepts of citizenship practices.

But it is not only the social impact which lifestyle migration has on particular destinations and which may lead to contested spatialities of lifestyle migration, but there are also the ecological and environmental aspects which have not been given full attention so far. This is even of greater importance since lifestyle migration and residential tourism often take place in destinations with high natural amenities such as mountains, seaside, lakeshores or rural areas (Cadieux and Hurley 2011). For example, as studies from Spain have evidenced, although the residential tourism model at first sight is perceived as a way of establishing a form of quality tourism generally considered less severe and ecologically less harmful than mass tourism, the real ecological impact of second home tourism is actually much higher, particularly in regard to water consumption, an issue of outstanding importance in the arid south of Spain (Hof and Schmitt 2011; Zasada *et al.* 2010). Urbanisations for lifestyle migrants located in low-density tourist areas with their lush gardens, private pools and golf courses pose a massive threat to sustainable water management, and their ecological impact is far higher in comparison to areas with a high density of mass tourism (Hof and Schmitt 2011). Other important aspects in this respect are excessive urbanisation and land use in ecologically sensitive areas such as sea and lake shores (Yepes and Medina 2005), issues of sewage and clarification plants, degradation of landscapes (Zasada *et al.* 2010) and sustainability (Gordon *et al.* 2010), as well as the increase in pollution due to growing amounts of air and ground traffic. These ecological consequences of lifestyle migration and residential tourism – phenomena with a large carbon footprint – should be given much closer attention in upcoming research.

As these suggestions and thought-provoking impulses illustrate, the research fields lying ahead are of a wide range which calls for greater interdisciplinary exchange and cooperation in future investigations. Additionally, the internationalisation and spreading of the phenomenon, as demonstrated in this volume and others (e.g. Benson and O'Reilly 2009; Mazón, Huete and Mantecón 2009) will continue and give rise to new destinations each with their particular history, trajectory and involvement of specific actors. Herein exists the exciting and promising potential for future research into the contested spatialities of lifestyle migration and residential tourism.

References

Ackers, L. and Dwyer, P. (2002) *Senior Citizenship? Retirement, Migration and Welfare in the European Union*. Bristol: Policy Press.

Ackers, L. and Dwyer, P. (2004) 'Fixed laws, fluid lives: the citizenship status of post-retirement migrants in the European Union', *Ageing and Society* 24(3): 451–75.

Benson, M. and O'Reilly, K. (eds) (2009) *Lifestyle Migration: Expectations, Aspirations and Experiences*. Farnham: Ashgate.

Cadieux, K.V. and Hurley, P.T. (2011) 'Amenity migration, exurbia, and emerging rural landscapes: global natural amenity as place and as process', *GeoJournal* 76: 297–302.

Coleman, S. and von Hellermann, P. (eds) (2011) *Mulit-Sited Ethnography: Problems and Possibilities in the Translocation of Research Methods.* London: Roultedge.

Croucher, S. (2012) 'Pivileged mobility in an age of globality' societies (2): 1–13; doi:10.3390/soc2010001.

Eaton, M. (2010) 'Foreign expatriate service provision in Portugal's Algarve', *Tourist Studies* 10(1): 75–92.

Eliot, A. and Urry, J. (2010) *Mobile Lives*, London: Routledge.

Falzon, M. A. (ed.) (2009) *Multi-sited Ethnography. Theory, Praxis and Locality in Contemporary Research*, Farnham: Ashgate.

Garay, L. and Cànoves, G. (2011) 'Life cycles, stages and tourism history. The Catalonia (Spain) experience, *Annals of Tourism Research* 38(2): 651–71.

Gordon, B., Sarmiento, F., Russo, R. and Jones, J. (2010) 'Sutsainability education in practice: Appropriation of rurality by the globalized migrants of Costa Rica', *Journal of Sustainability Education*, 1: 1–20.

Gosnell, H. and Abrams, J. (2011) 'Amenity migration: diverse conceptualizations of drivers, socioeconomic dimensions, and emerging challenges', *GeoJournal* 76: 303–22.

Gustafson, P. (2008) 'Transnationalism in retirement migration: the case of North-European retirees in Spain', *Ethnic and Racial Studies* 31(3): 451–75.

Haas, H. (2012) 'Volunteering in retirement migration: meanings and functions of charitable activities for older British residents in Spain', *Ageing and Society*, doi:10.1017/S0144686X12000669.

Huete, R. and Mantecón A. (2011) 'Sociological insights on residential tourism: host society attitudes in a mature destination', *European Journal of Tourism Research*, 4(2): 109–22.

Hof, A. and Schmitt, T. (2011) 'Urban and touristic land use patterns and water consumption: evidence from Mallorca, Balearic Islands', *Land Use Policy* 28: 792–804.

Legido-Quigley, H., Nolte, E., Green, J., La Parra, D. and McKee, M. (2012) 'The health care experiences of British pensioners migrating to Spain', *Health Policy* 105: 46–54.

Mazón, T., Huete, R. and Mantecón, A. (eds) (2009) *Turismo, urbanización y estilos de vida. Las nuevas formas de movilidad residencial.* Barcelona: Icaria.

McIntyre, N., Williams, D. and McHugh, K. (eds) (2006) *Multiple Dwelling and Tourism: Negotiating Place, Home, and Identity.* Wallingford: CABI.

Müller, D.K. and Hall, M.C. (eds) (2004) *Tourism, Mobility and Second Homes: Between Elite Landscape and Common Ground*, Clevedon: Channel View.

Oliver, C. (2008) *Retirement Migration: Paradoxes of Ageing.* London: Routledge.

Rolshoven, J. (2002) 'Südliche Zweitwohnsitze. Ein Beitrag zur kulturwissenschaftlichen Mobilitätsforschung', *Schweizerisches Archiv für Volkskunde* 98(1): 345–56.

Rosenmöller, M., McKee, M. and Baeten, R. (eds) (2006) *Patient Mobility in the European Union: Learning from Experience.* Copenhagen: World Health Organization.

Schriewer, K. (2008) 'Los norteuropeos residentes en España vistos por los españoles', K. Schriewer and M. García (eds) *Ni turistas ni migrantes. Movilidad residencial europea en España,* Murcia: Ediciones Isabor, 77–81.

Urry, J. (2007) *Mobilities*, Cambridge and Malden, MA: Polity Press.

Williams, A.M., King, R. and Warnes, T. (1997) 'A Place in the Sun: International Retirement Migration from Northern to Southern Europe,' *European Urban and Regional Studies* 4: 115–34.

Yepes, V. and Medina, J.R. (2005) 'Land use models in Spanish coastal areas. A case study of the Valencia Region', *Journal of Coastal Research* 49: 83–88.

Zasada, I., Alves, S., Müller, F.C., Piorr A., Berges, R. and Bell, S. (2010) 'International retirement migration in the Alicante region, Spain: Process, spatial pattern and environmental impacts', *Journal of Environmental Planning and Management*, 53(1): 125–41.

Index